Women Writers of the Southwest

WALKING
THE
TWILIGHT II

edited by

KATHRYN WILDER

Northland Publishing

For the Earth Mother,

that we may learn to listen,

and to speak.

FIRST IMPRESSION

ISBN 0-87358-648-4

The text type was set in Weiss.
The display type was set in Weiss Italic and Castellar.
Cover illustration © 1996 by Barbara Lambase.
Designed by Trina Stahl and Mary Wages.
Production by Mary Wages.
Edited by Jill Mason, Kathleen M. Bryant, and Erin Murphy.
Production supervised by Lisa Brownfield.

Manufactured in the United States of America

Library of Congress Catalog Card Number 94-28280
Library of Congress Cataloging-in-Publication Data

Walking the twilight II : women writers of the Southwest / edited by
Kathryn Wilder
p.   cm.
ISBN 0-87358-648-4
1. American literature—Southwestern States. 2. Women—Southwestern States—Literary collections.
3. Southwestern States—Literary collections. 4. American literature—Women authors.
I. Wilder, Kathryn, 1954-   .
PS566.W35 1996

0570/5M/3-96

Contents

ERUPTION

RETURN

Acknowledgments

My eternal gratitude goes out to the following:

to my parents, Helen and Ed Bigelow and Robert B. Green, for placing stepping stones of support and encouragement along my path;

to my sons, Kenney and Tyler, for giving me reason;

to my dear friends Liz Besmehn, Mark Gant, and Lynda German for giving me—and my work—guidance and definition, and for believing in me even when I didn't;

to Rebecca Lancaster, my best friend of thirty years, for being that;

to Andrea Scharf and Michael Evans-Smith for their wonderful connections and generosity, and to all the others who helped me along the way;

to Trudell VanBurkleo, whose gifts transcend lifetimes;

and, especially and again, to Mark, who continues to walk beside me through the raw stories and rugged lands of the country we call home.

Introduction

Stones and Jawbones

Here are the long heavy winds and breathless calms on the tilted mesas where dust devils
dance, whirling up into a wide, pale sky. Here you have no rain when all the earth cries for
it, or quick downpours called cloud-bursts for violence. A land of lost rivers, with little in it
to love; yet a land that once visited must be come back to inevitably. If it were not so there
would be little told of it.

—MARY AUSTIN, *The Land of Little Rain*

I'M TIPTOEING THROUGH CRYPTOGAMIC crust, ever so careful not to damage the velvet-like, moss-covered soil with heel or toe. I step from rock to stone, to cowpie to bare spot to stick, heading toward a curve of redrock that swells into a higher rock and then another, ocean waves caught in their surging rhythm and cast to sandstone. At times I feel frustrated, wanting simply to stride freely down a path, cryptogam be damned, but there are no paths here and I'm not willing to make one.

I'm forty years old, and have lived four times longer than some of the fungus at my feet, and not nearly as long as others. In these four decades I have been well weathered: dried by sun and wind and pain, moistened by tears and rivers and rain, polished smooth, roughened up, worn, discarded, pieced back together, and now my buckskin dress is just that in which nature has clothed me—brown white skin textured with scars and wrinkles and stretchmarks: the stories of my life.

Reaching the slab of red stone that tilts sideways toward the sky, I climb it on all fours. Through the pads of my feet and my fingers, desert warmth spreads upward, meeting the sun's rays on my back and the blood pounding in my veins and I want to revel in it, to curve my body to the earth's, let the sun in, and become prayer. But I must get to the top first.

Maintaining cat-like posture as I scramble, I am closer to the earth than usual. My eyes dart back and forth across the rockface, scanning for special objects as if I were a pack rat or a raven. I stop to touch a small stone, to pull it in for closer examination, to redeposit it in its place like a puzzle piece. I pause for glitter, for anything shiny that resembles quartz or aluminum, as in the innards of geodes or scraps of foil or poptops. White stops me in my tracks—which, with relief, I am not making on this solid rock— and bleached bone compels my fingers earthward.

Straightening up, I fondle the lower jawbone of a desert snake (the teeth lining the inside of the jaw offer me only this general identification). I have found many jawbones in my wanderings—of mule deer, wild burro, beaver, skunk, coyote, cat—and pondered at the meaning. Leaving this snake jaw in a shelter of sage, I continue my ascent toward the perch I decided upon from our campsite downstream. The rock is steep and rough, and I feel both pain and exhilaration as my toes and fingers grip the sharp etchings of wind and propel me upward.

Perhaps cat-like in posture and destination, I am not so cat-like in fearlessness, and I am grateful when the rock rounds out in front of me and I can sit safely on the edge of the world. As my panting ceases, my gaze spreads like cloud shadow over a desert aglow with slanted sunlight. Desert details, from the tiniest filaments of cryptogamic soil to the vast expanses of red rock and blue sky, stretch before me. The Canyon is out there somewhere, and through it threads the mighty Colorado, while here within my reach is a half-foot-square plot of land encrusted with a soil so delicate I could wipe out years of growth with a mere thumbprint. One huge rock over, a lone juniper clings for its life to more such soil, a testimony to implantation by wind or wing, to the workings of the system.

I, too, am testimony, as is the dirt road carved between rock wall and streamside, the contrail bisecting bright blue overhead sky, the orange flash of a tent downcanyon. I wince, and for a moment curl in on myself in despair—there is no true wilderness left here, there, anywhere—but then I feel the sun nudging my shoulder. Like the touch of my purest love, who has disappeared into redrock crevices far upstream, sun is irresistible to me. I unfold, lie back, feel rock pockmarking my body from beneath, sun penetrating my skin from above, breasts rising in velvet air with each deep breath I take; I spread my limbs and hair across time, close my eyes, and feel the earth carrying me. . . .

Drifting, I see raven feathers and fossilized shells, twisted sticks and obsidian chunks, sprigs of sage, owl down, rocks rough as canyon walls, stones polished river-smooth, sun-whitened femurs and jawbones and pelvises lined up like stairways to the sky.

Drifting, I think how the totems I see in my wanderings I also find in the dwellings of those I recognize as clan, how I am far from alone in this activity of constant scrutiny and sometimes collection of the organic gifts that lie upon the land.

Drifting, I wonder just what it is that speaks to us as we stoop to pluck these treasures from sand and stone, from redrock and riverbed. And what is it that propels us to leave this one in its place, to borrow that one from the earth to be returned later, at some right time?

What voices do we hear, truly? Is it the Earth Mother, saying *Come, lean close. Listen and you will hear me breathe. See the glitter in this stone? Move closer now to touch it; pluck it from my skin and hold it to your cheek, your heart. Like the shell taken from the shore in which you can hear the ocean, through feather, stick, and stone you can hear me. And—if you listen close enough—I will tell you stories. Stories old as me, wise as women, tales you need to know to do your work, to pay attention, to pass on.*

Lying on slickrock, cradled by Earth, caressed by Sky, I know no greater contentment. A soft breeze wanders over my skin, gentle fingers. Drifting, I turn my head so my ear touches stone. I listen.

Like scars, stretchmarks, and wrinkles, the landmarks of the earth's surface are altars upon which tradition, ceremony, memory, and story are placed. And in this land where the earth's covering is so sheer, so simple, the stories read close to my soul. As I listen, it comes to me that the talismans I find in the form of rock are reminders to stay grounded; feathers teach me to feel the stirrings of spirit air; porous lava and solid obsidian tell me of the power of fire; common driftwood takes me to the river, Earth blood.

The sum of all the parts says again: *Listen. Earth and her creatures have much to tell.* And then, with the clarity of the fine white line on the horizon before me where desert earth meets desert sky, I know that the jawbones carry another message. *Speak,* they say.

As I have been writing this, some strange things have happened. Here's the first: I take a draft to the writing workshop I'm teaching and share it with the women there. I do this partly because I want feedback and partly because I want to show them writing process (some of it comes from a free-write I did alongside them one orange September evening). The following Tuesday, I get a copy of a friend's new book in the mail. It's lovely, yet as I begin reading I recoil in a twisted sort of panic. We are writing about the same thing, this friend and I. I don't mean generally, either, but in detail; while she walks up slickrock on all fours, "animal-like," I'm traversing the same terrain, also on all fours, "cat-like."

I take this writer's dilemma to my class. "You are witnesses," I say. "You know I wrote this before I read that." They nod solemnly. I read the piece from the lovely book aloud. They respond with oohs and ahs, guttural exclamation points, meditative silence at the end. And then, dutifully, they discuss how my writing and message differ from the other writer's. I agree half-heartedly.

A week later, the book's author calls me. In the midst of a passionate discussion about words, I tell her the similarity in ours. She is not surprised; after all, we are women, desert wanderers, writers—we're bound to have words in common. "Don't change a thing," she says. "But," I start to whine, "*they* [readers, critics, reviewers] will think I copied you." "*You* know the truth," she says. And I do.

The second strange thing: Another week passes. Another friend calls. Her story has just been workshopped by her writers' group. In the process, people referred, with some degree of scorn, to this "new generation of women nature writers." They said they didn't want to hear any more "desert stories." It was even implied that those of us who write about the Southwest, about redrock and slickrock country specifically, are look-alikes, our uniqueness disappearing under the hot desert sun like water. I find these accusations as disturbing as number twelve boot tracks in cryptogamic soil. And I take this opportunity to address those who, for some mysterious reason, are ruffled so by those of us who "love the land" in all its erotic and primitive rawness, who find the deepest of sensual pleasures in the contact of skin on sandstone.

Many of us used to love the land from afar and were content with the awe we felt over Monument Valley postcards, Ansel Adams's black-and-whites of the Mojave Desert, Mary Austin's words honoring the same, Georgia O'Keeffe's canvas encapsulations of bare-boned southwestern wildness. Edward Abbey mixed sex, booze, and rebellion into a less-than-subversive statement to get closer, to take action, and empty-beer-can-lined dirt roads and rivers survive as monuments to his fame.

Some of us, whether despite or because of this indoctrination I don't know, have ventured closer, and as we move in toward the womb of the Earth Mother what we find is a stirring deep within us, within our own wombs. That stirring could be a brush on canvas or a pen scratching across paper—its vibrations are that subtle, its meaning that strong. And what happens is: We open up from the inside out. As with the most powerful release, something stirs in our centers, grows stronger as its circles broaden, climaxes in huge waves of pure Earth energy, and we lie open to the Universe, open to the power of sun on slickrock, of slanted light on redrock, of the movement of water. And what we find is: We are also open to the power *of our own words*.

Like some sort of genetic code, our words are who we are, and when we find ourselves in alignment with Earth and Universe, the words flow. *We* flow. And, like the rivers of the Colorado Plateau whose ultimate end is drainage into the Colorado River, our words end up in story.

Of course, not all writers, be they men or women, share the same connection with the land; not all writers who share that connection need it to write, or write of it when they feel it. As similar as we may be, we are also unique, like each stone I pick up as I pass through the landscape of this lifetime. So, as some of us may choose to honor Earth with the words She has given us, others may choose not to—there is no right or wrong way.

As editor of *Walking the Twilight* and this, its sequel, I have spent two concentrated years reading, relishing, and reviewing words written by women about this southwestern country. What I have found is this: There *is* similarity in story, style, voice, and passion; after all, like siblings, these stories all come from the same union of Earth and Sky. And yet, like siblings, and stones, there are also differences. I would not condescend to say that all women who write of the Southwest are "women nature writers," nor all their stories "desert stories." But if there is a new generation of writers, and if the common ground upon which we stand is Earth, and if our words are about Her, and for Her, and if that makes our writings appear to be a new literary genre, then what I have to say is this: It's about time!

I am honored to have been asked, by feather, stick, stone, and jawbone, to pick up stories, return some like puzzle pieces to their sources, borrow others for a time, and make a twilight collage of women's words. Through these words—of our emergence, our presence, and our eruptions—we shall return, again and again, to this land of creation, of re-creation, in an attempt to prevent its destruction.

EMERGENCE

Making Sacred, Making True

PAULA GUNN ALLEN

PAULA GUNN ALLEN, 56, says her life, like her work, "is a journey-in-between, a road that leads to the place where the four rivers meet, where I am going, where I am from." A lesbian feminist of Laguna Pueblo, Lakota Sioux, and Lebanese-American blood, she was born in Cubero, New Mexico, and raised with the Pueblo traditions of her mother's people. She holds a BA, an MFA, and a Ph.D., and has written A Cannon Between My Knees *and* Skins and Bones *(poetry);* Spider Woman's Granddaughter *(anthology);* The Woman Who Owned the Shadows *(novel);* The Sacred Hoop *(essays); and* Grandmothers of the Light: A Medicine Woman's Sourcebook *(traditional stories). Paula teaches in the Native American Studies program at the University of California, Berkeley.*

WHEN CHANGING WOMAN WAS born, she was found among flashing lightning so bright it was blinding, a rainbow was showering the peak of the spruce-covered mountain with brilliant colors. First Man of the Emergence People heard her crying, though he was blinded by the light of rainbows. Just as he first heard her crying, the light vanished and dark rain began to fall. He couldn't see, but he went toward the sound of an infant's cry.

First Man, maker of much of the earth, had gone up to the top of Giant Spruce Mountain to find out what caused the strange phenomena he and his family could see from below. For four days a cloud had covered the peaks, first only the top, then a greater portion each day until on the fourth the entire mountain was cloaked in a dark, heavy shroud. He, First Woman, and their only surviving son and daughter were in the vicinity because they had been forced to flee the alien monsters who sought to destroy the people. These four were the only survivors, and they were

3

desolate. They believed they could not continue to live. They had no heart left to go on. He determined to climb the mountain in pursuit of good fortune, following the rainbow, the trail of the cloud, the scent of the falling rain, the lightning tracking down from the sky, all pointing to the source of the mystery he sought to explore.

Perhaps he hoped to discover some reason to continue with their struggle. I suppose he didn't know what else to do. So he went in pursuit of long life and happiness for his people. Even on the edge of darkest despair, he sought for a reason to hope, to go on.

The day Changing Woman came to earth, she was found in the midst of the dark cloud that had shrouded the peak—amid the rainbow, amid the lightning, amid the rain. Her coming was mysterious. She signaled her presence with a thin wailing cry so that First Man could find her despite shattering brightness, suffocating darkness. But what he saw as he reached the place of the crying—when the lightning stopped flashing, the rainbow muted to a familiar, soft hue, the rain lightened into a fine mist, and the dark cloud thinned and evaporated into a serene sky—was not the tiny infant he expected, but a small turquoise figure. It was the size of a newborn but proportioned as a full-grown woman.

Who could it be? What sort of mystery did he behold, lying quiet and still at his feet?

Mystified, resourceful, First Man picked up the figure and carefully carried it back to First Woman and the rest. "Take it and care for it like one of our own," he said.

When Changing Woman was born, alien monsters bent on annihilating the people controlled the land. Talking God and Growling God and the other holy people who had helped create the Emergence People also helped them now. Two days after First Man took Changing Woman home to his wife and daughter to care for, Talking God came and signaled them to meet with him at the top of the mountain in twelve days.

When they arrived there, they met Talking God and Growling God, Blue Body and the Wind, along with Wind's brother Darkness and the brothers of the Woman Who Becomes a Bear. Also at the gathering the Emergence People saw the Image-Bringing People, the Daylight People, the Blue Sky People, the Yellow Light People, and the Darkness People.

Standing among the Daylight People, Talking God stood holding another small female image made of white shell. The Emergence People saw that this figure was identical to the turquoise figure they had. In a ritual manner, Talking God and Growling God laid out the two figures and two ears of corn, placing them between two soft skin blankets. They made a circle with an opening to the east so that Talking God and Growling God could enter and leave freely.

When all was in readiness all the people chanted and sang until the two gods who had been hiding in their house in the east came around the circle and entered, parting the two buckskin blankets. They asked Wind to breathe life between the soft skins. Three times the chanting and singing, the entry and parting, the request and leaving occurred, and yet a fourth time the sequence was repeated. On the fourth round, the gods did not ask Wind to breathe between the blankets, but instead they thanked him for already having done so. And the turquoise figure was the Air Spirit Person Changing Woman; the shell figure was now White Shell Woman; the white ear of corn became White Corn Boy and the yellow ear of corn had become Yellow Corn Girl.

After this, the two gods sent White Corn Boy and Yellow Corn Girl to live among the holy people, and everyone returned to their homes, leaving Changing Woman and White Shell Woman alone on the mountaintop. They were newly made Air Spirit People, left with no instruction about where to go or how to proceed.

After eight days of waiting to see what their life would be, four days where they had been given life and four days farther up the peak where they could see all the earth spread out below them, the Air Spirit Women were feeling lonely. Changing Woman spoke to her sister, saying she had been wondering if the sun was also an Air Spirit Person. Eagerly, White Shell Woman admitted she'd also been lonely. She said she had wondered if the water in a lively brook that flowed clean and sweet from the mountainside was an Air Spirit Person.

Boldly, Changing Woman suggested that they should each pursue their thought. She, she said, intended to watch Sun carefully every day to see if she could discover the exact nature of the being who sailed so serenely overhead.

True to her word, the next morning Changing Woman went to a sunny spot at sunrise and lay upon a flat rock where she could watch Sun make his way over her throughout the day. She wore no clothing, for they had not been given any other than the buckskin blankets that they used against the chilly nights, and as she reclined she spread her legs comfortably, making it possible that Sun's rays could fully warm her.

Following a like inclination, White Shell Woman that same morning went to a waterfall along the brook's path. She found a shallow place where she could lie comfortably and, like her sister, let her legs fall open so that the spray washed gently over her.

For four days the sisters spent many hours contemplating the beings they hoped to contact, hoping thereby to gain a mate and to assuage their loneliness. Then for four days they stayed near their camp at the top of the high peaks of Giant Spruce Mountain. All but consumed with longing and loneliness and that odd feeling that Diné say girls on the threshold of womanhood feel, on the fourth day White Shell Woman felt a movement low in her belly. She let out a small cry and told Changing Woman what had happened. Changing Woman assured her that it was good. The feeling was that of life moving within her, she said, and added that she herself had felt a movement within herself earlier. She was triumphant. Hadn't they spoken in the long days just past about the possibility of making beings like themselves, just as they had been made? It seems they had succeeded in doing so.

In another four days they felt their labor begin, and soon each gave birth to a son. The son of Changing Woman was Monster Slayer and his brother was Child of Water. Together they would slay all the alien monsters but four and make the earth a place where the human beings, the five-fingered beings as the Diné call them, could live and flourish.

The four monsters they didn't slay were Old Age Woman, Cold Woman, the Poverty Creatures, and Hunger Man. Monster Slayer wanted to destroy them, because he had promised Sun, his father, that he would eradicate all the monsters. But his mother, Changing Woman, had told him that he had been successful against all the monsters she wanted destroyed. "Some things are better left as they are," she told him, as Indian mothers have been telling their children since that time.

Of course, he didn't listen. But when Wind whispered to him where he could find each of these monsters, he sought them and discovered the wisdom of his mother's words. As Old Age Woman pointed out, killing her would mean that the five-fingered beings would have no reason to have children. And when a boy reached his sexual peak, or a girl reached her womanhood, they would not engage in sex and much of the joy and depth of their lives would be lost. Nor, she added, would they grow and thrive if she wasn't there to quietly and slowly sap their energies so they would age. Youth would lose its meaning, and wisdom would be unattainable. That's what she said.

Cold Woman didn't mind dying, as she made clear to Monster Slayer. She was wretched as she was, she said, and dying would be very welcome. But the problem with her disappearance was that the heat of the sun would wither all of life without cold to lessen its blast.

The same thing happened with the Poverty Creatures, who informed Monster Slayer that their job was to help people care about themselves, their families, and the earth. Without the threat and fact of poverty, they said, no one would have any reason to be inventive, no one would ever make anything new. Thus, the five-fingered beings would not use their creative natures and they would languish being less than their fullest selves.

Monster Slayer then sought and found Hunger Man, but Hunger Man explained that without him there would be no reason for people to cultivate plants. They would lose their taste for cooking and eating. Many of the pleasures of being together would be denied them. They would not learn to tend to livestock and would miss most of all their close relationship with the sheep.

In the end, Monster Slayer returned to his mother and agreed that her assessment of the situation was the right one. "Some things are indeed better left as they are," he said.

IN ORDER to get the weapons and skill to destroy the alien monsters, Monster Slayer and Child of Water had had to make a long, dangerous journey to Sun's house. It was with the help of Spider Woman that they were able to find their way to Sun's eastern home. They had inadvertently gained the interest of the alien monsters and fled their home in an attempt to protect their mothers from harm. In their confusion, they fled along the Path of the Rainbow blindly, not realizing that they had taken a forbidden way. In time they came to Spider Woman's house, which was beneath the ground. They climbed down into her house at her invitation, and at her urging told her their story. They said they did not know who their fathers were, but that their mothers were Changing Woman and White Shell Woman.

Spider Woman told them she recognized Monster Slayer as Sun's son, and that she would help them get to his home far above them in the sky. The way was perilous, she warned them, and they would face many alien monsters who lived between earth and sky.

"But I will give you this hoop," she said, showing them a hoop made of the feathers of Monster Eagle. "You must hold this before you and face your attacker boldly, without fear. Then sing the chant I will teach you, and you will be safe."

Not only did they face the peril of the alien monsters, she told them, but four great dangers stood along the way they must take: the great rocks that crush, the knife-edged reeds that rend, the needle-spiked cactuses that pierce and shred, and the boiling sands that sear all who pass.

"You must use the hoop to pass through these perils and persevere. If you fail, all will perish. Do not be alarmed that your father is not glad to see you. He will probably be almost as difficult as the alien monsters or the dangerous places. Be quiet and do as he says. I have helped you because this is your task to do, and now you have the power to get help for yourselves and your people."

As they left her place, she bid them good-bye. "Go on your journey, and walk in beauty," she said.

After many fearsome events, they finally came to the house of Sun. There they faced his suspicion and met the trials he had set for them, but when he finally accepted Monster Slayer as his son, he tried to set a condition on the youths' use of what he had taught and given them. His condition was that they make an agreement that Changing Woman would become Sun's wife.

Of course Monster Slayer knew his mother better than that. A woman of decision and ability, she would brook no agreements on her behalf. "She makes her own decisions," he told his father. "You'll have to ask her yourself."

When all but the last four alien monsters were finally destroyed, Sun came to check on the youths' progress. On receiving their report, he agreed that they had indeed done well. Then he asked the young men to pass a message from him to Changing Woman. He wanted her to meet him at the summit of Giant Spruce Mountain in the space of four days.

At that time, Changing Woman, seeing that her son was grown and the alien monsters defeated, felt the urgings of her inner self to leave there and find a place of peace for herself. She told her son and White Shell Woman what she intended.

White Shell Woman agreed with her decision to go, saying that she too was weary of mothering and warring and wished to live alone for a time.

On the day she and Sun were to meet, Changing Woman climbed to the summit and went to the place where she had sought him as a mate. As she sat remembering the one time Sun joined her, she recognized how much she had changed, how the tumultuous years of their wars with the alien monsters had firmed her nature. I am not the maiden I once was, she thought. I have become a woman, secure in my judgment and decision. What I once longed for seems not so attractive now. I was born amid the rainbow. Dark cloud and Male Rain attended my first cry. The turquoise mountain was my beginning, and the Air Spirit People are my home.

She remembered, not without bitterness, how warm and sweet Sun had felt inside of her the only time he'd come to her, and how she had longed over the years to feel him inside her again. She had told her son of her anger at him. "Once I longed for him and opened myself to him. It was a partnership I wanted. But he has not returned to see me even once, not once has he even spoken to me. Now he wants to see me, I wonder why. Maybe he wants to brag about his son," she had said.

Engrossed in her memories, Changing Woman did not at first see Sun as he approached her. He came toward her, deep bronze and radiant, smiling. And he attempted to embrace her, but she demurred. She longed for peace as she had once longed for companionship, having tasted motherhood, and having raised her son and endured dangers and heartache. She wasn't sure she believed in her maidenly dreams of crystal fastnesses and shining joining. She knew the beauty of winter and summer, of sky and earth, and within herself she was content.

Sun knew her thought, but he hoped to change her to his way of mind. "Our son agreed that you would become my wife," he said.

"What difference does it make to me what someone else agrees to?" she asked. "Unless I enter into an agreement myself, there is no agreement. No one else decides for me."

But Sun persisted. "I gave you a son and helped him defeat the alien monsters. For that, you owe me," he said.

"I did not seek your help, as you know," the lovely woman said. Her face was serene and clear in her certainty. "You gave what aid you chose, and then only because your trials committed you. You had no choice in that. Monster Slayer is as much your son as mine."

And Sun withdrew, moving away for several paces from the woman he wooed. He searched his thoughts carefully and found there the loneliness and dreariness of his splendid and inexorable life. He found there an exhaustion with sameness, with what he could not change. Determined to end his pain, he at last turned to Changing Woman. "I need you," he said simply, revealing his true mind. "Please come and live with me. You are alone and I am alone. What good is it, to be so lonely?"

Changing Woman heard the loneliness in his voice. She knew that it matched the loneliness of her own heart. But while she understood the rightness of his thought, she also knew there were certain matters he should understand. Quiet a while, she at last responded. "If I come to live with you, you must give me a fine hogan in the west, as fine as the one I have heard you have in the east.

"Build it on the water so I can be free of earth peoples' quarrels. I have been too much involved in war. Around my hogan you must plant white shell, blue shell, turquoise, haliotis, soapstone, agate, redstone, and jet because I wish them always near me in their beauty. And as I shall be lonely during your long days away, you must give me many elk, buffalo, deer, long-tails, mountain sheep, jackrabbits, prairie dogs, and muskrats for companionship.

"Should you make a house for me where I can live in peace and where I can walk in beauty, then I will consider becoming your wife," she said gravely.

Sun was offended at her demands. "Who are you that you should make these demands?" he blazed.

"I am the wife you long for," she replied softly. "Think about it. It is you who long for our match. I would be as content to remain alone. And you are bored and life to you is dreary, for you are of the sky, and always must be the same. I am of the earth, and I change with the seasons. You are always moving while I remain in place. In these ways, we complete each other, make the world of being whole.

"You and I are of the same spirit stuff, and so we are of equal worth. As unlike as we are, we are similar; and if there can be no harmony between us, then there can never be harmony anyplace in the universe.

"If such harmony is to occur, then you must take my needs seriously and treat them with respect. My requests must be important to you. Every exchange between us must be equal. What I take from you, I give in equal measure. That is how it must be."

Sun was silent for a time. Then slowly he went to her and his heart was clear. This time they embraced as equals, for Changing Woman could see that he understood.

Finally the day of Changing Woman's departure came. Two groups of holy people, the Mirage People and the Ground Mist People, came with her to herd the animals accompanying her. Before she left, she said good-bye to White Shell Woman, Monster Slayer, and Child of Water. She told the boys they were now men who could stand on their own.

During her journey, her body changed dramatically. Her breasts became full and heavy, her hips spread and rounded, her belly filled out, and the fullness of her womanly beauty shone. During the journey also, the herds swiftly became numerous, many breaking away and going to range all over the continent.

Four days after they left her home, they arrived at the mountain known as San Francisco Peak in the language of the whites, where Changing Woman and the holy people with her stopped to perform a certain ceremony. Laying her across the top of the mountain with her head to the west, the direction she was heading and where she would live with her husband, the holy people stretched out her arms and legs and massaged her body. Changing Woman told the people to do the same with all maidens who reached puberty, which the Diné do even now, attempting to mold the bodies of maidens into the lovely lineaments of Changing Woman.

So Changing Woman moved to her western home, to become the wife of Sun. It is said that when they are having difficulties in their relationship, the harmony of the whole world decreases and many suffer.

After Changing Woman went to the west, White Shell Woman, Child of Water, and Monster Slayer also moved away. They went toward the San Juan Mountains. In the San Juan valley, where two rivers join, the men stopped. There, they declared, they would make their home. They can still be seen in the shimmer of light when the water rises from pools formed by a summer rain. In the moist, bright air you can see their forms shimmering.

White Shell Woman continued alone to the mountain near the emergence place of her people long ago, before they fled the alien monsters. In her heart she longed for them, and for the earth-surface people who would come. For four days she wandered from peak to peak, sleeping in a different high fastness each night. As the days passed, she recognized her loneliness. I should have listened more carefully to my sister, she thought. She cautioned me against coming here alone, fearing I would be lonely.

On the fifth day, she heard the familiar sound of Talking God approaching her. Soon he was with her, and she told him all that had transpired and where she and Changing Woman had gone. "Now she has gone to the west, and I have returned here. I long for companionship," she confided.

Talking God told her he would return in four days' time, and he went away. While she awaited his return, White Shell Woman made a strong house, one with a door opening to the east and a window facing west.

When four days had passed, Talking God returned, and with him were a number of holy people, including Changing Woman, who carried two soft buckskins over her arm. The other holy people had brought two ears of corn, which they carried into the house on a turquoise dish.

Talking God arranged the corn within the buckskin, and through his powerful ceremonial force, they transformed the ears of corn into two people, one male, one female. They were brother and sister. When they were finished, White Shell Woman led them into her hogan. She was very happy.

Some time after the ceremony, Talking God returned and introduced these five-fingered beings to two other kinds of beings, one male and one female. They were Sky Mirage Boy and Ground Mist Girl. He gave White Shell Woman two ears of corn and told her, "Grind them, but only one grain at a time."

White Shell Woman told Sky Mirage Boy and Ground Mist Girl that the man and woman who lived with her were made out of corn, and that as they were brother and sister they could not marry. "But children must be born for the people to become stronger and prosper," she said. "Maybe you can each marry one of them, then all will be well."

Following her advice, they did, and so the earth-surface people came into being. Soon each couple had children, and their households were thriving.

White Shell Woman chose one of their daughters for her companion, and she loved the child dearly. The child lived with her and slept with her at night, keeping her from being lonely, filling her heart.

But twice Talking God came to talk to her out of the hearing of the people. The second time, she spoke to the child, saying, "Grandchild, I must leave you. The holy people have sent for me, and I must go. I won't forget you or your people, be sure of that," she said. Then she vanished into the shimmering mountain air.

Four nights after she vanished, the child had a dream of her, in which White Shell Woman said she was well and happy. "The holy people have built me a house of white shell that is beautiful," she said. "I will live in that house forever. I don't think I will be seeing you again, nor will you see me in this form. But I won't be far. Look for me when it rains. The soft falling Female Rain, the corn that grows because of that rain will encompass me. Look carefully with a good heart and you will see me in them sometimes."

And when she awoke, the child told her people what White Shell Woman had said. "'Look for me in the soft, gentle rain, and seek me in the growing corn.' That's what Grandmother told me," the child informed them. "That's what she said."

Spirit Babies

PHYLLIS BARBER

PHYLLIS BARBER, a rare native Nevadan, was born in Henderson (which was known as Basic Townsite in the 1940s) because there was no hospital in Boulder City at that time. She graduated from Las Vegas High School and has lived in the West ever since—California's Bay Area, Utah, and, currently, Colorado. Cofounder of the Park City, Utah, Writers at Work Conference, Phyllis is a faculty member of the Vermont College MFA in Writing Program who writes extensively about her heartland and the Mormon experience. Her novel And the Desert Shall Blossom *won the 1988 Utah Arts Council Literary Competition;* How I Got Cultured: A Nevada Memoir *won the 1991 Associated Writing Programs Series in Creative Nonfiction; and her short fiction has appeared in many literary magazines.*

Delta patted her lips with a paper napkin, crumpled it, and swished it into the basketball net clamped to the top of the wastebasket. She pulled her hefty arms off the counter, eased off her stool, and rinsed her bowl under the tap. "Give me your cup, J.L. I'll rinse it out."

He drained the bottom, handed her the mug, and then leaned against the kitchen counter, his arms folded. "Okay, tell me one more time. What happens when you see him?"

"Well, the first dream, he looks like he might be a gymnast when he comes down at least a thousand stairs, little old baby, half crawling, half rolling down those stairs. He's laughing all the way, though. In between the crawling and the rolling, he's reaching his arms up to me and saying, 'Mama, Mama.' He's wearing a little white robe, but it barely covers him. That's how I can tell it's a him, you know. Then, instead of finishing up with those thousand stairs, he starts to fly and roll like an airplane. He cruises over my head, close to my hair so I can feel some of it lifting up with the electricity, and says, 'I'm waiting, Mama.'

"I mean, what can I say? I can't sleep for all the things this child says to me in the night. Sometimes I think he might even be a prophet."

"Why doesn't he come see me?" J.L. pulled up his Levi's by the belt loops again and tucked his shirt in the back. "I've got something to do with this, I think. I'm the man of the house."

Delta turned her glowing face to her husband. "You sure are, honey." Her auburn hair was backlit by the square of morning light in the window, a pale fire smouldering on top of Mt. Delta.

Suddenly, he smiled like a sunning snake, happy with the first day after winter. "Delta," he said, looking at his wife with that bashful look he sometimes had. "You sure are pretty when God talks to you. Seven kids, and I still feel my blood rising in me. Even when you aren't all dressed up, just here in the kitchen in your sweats and high tops. I did a good thing when I chose you."

"You didn't choose me, Johnny Lester Bradford. We chose each other before we ever came to this earth. Don't you remember?"

"Well, sort of." J.L. squinched his left eye and puckered his lips in thought. His straw brown hair was tinted pure sunlight, his eyebrows too. "Tell you the truth, Delta, I don't remember seeing you before that night at the Milton Ward's potluck dinner, eighteen years ago. You were pouring water in glasses and wearing the brightest yellow like sunshine."

"Johnny Lester," Delta said, cozying her backside against his belt buckle and feeling the top of her seventy-two-inch body tucked under his chin. "Put your arms around me, honey. Just hold me and believe with me."

He wrapped her tightly against his body and rocked her with a little Motown. "My girl, talkin' 'bout my girl. . . ." He stroked the letters on her purple sweatshirt, most especially the "O" that covered her breast.

"You better get your body off to work, J.L. Night's a better time for taking care of dreams." Reaching over her shoulder, she flipped his ear, then turned and applied a half nelson, something he'd taught her once when she wanted to break into high school wrestling. She wanted to be called Delta Dawn, the Rumbler, or better yet, Thunder of the Morning.

J.L. jabbed a mild elbow into her ribs and bridged out of the hold. "I'll think about you on my long haul to Vegas today. I'll be back tomorrow night, then we'll talk about this baby in your dream." He popped the Zion National Park cap on his head and settled it just so, pulled on the rim, then curved it between two hands. "Why don't you dream a little dream of me?" he whispered, and winked as he pulled the door closed behind him.

Delta Ray Bradford untwisted the orange-covered wire on the bread bag. "Dream a little dream of me," she half-sang underneath her breath, lining up ten pieces of whole wheat bread on the counter, slathering each with canola margarine, light mayo, tunafish, and topping with pickles, sprouts, and Bibb lettuce. She counted out five brown paper bags, shook them open, then peeled ten carrots and sliced them into sticks. Fruit rolls. One banana each. Cranapple juice in a box with the straw attached to the side. A piece of homemade carrot cake made with whole wheat flour Delta had ground herself.

She sat at the kitchen counter and pulled a worn box of magic markers out of the cluttered drawer. In her best Palmer's penmanship, she wrote out five notes—one for each of her schoolchildren, each one slightly different from the next. "Keep a smile on your face," she wrote with a green felt tip pen. "Remember who loves you," she wrote on another piece of paper. "Love one another."

She lined the notes up side by side and, using the yellow marker, made her secret mother symbol on each one: the figure-eight sign for infinity. Then she plucked the red pen out of the dog-eared, gray-cornered box. Uncapping it with a flourish, she patiently drew the outline and filled in the contours of five pairs of generous lips, then sealed each note with a kiss of her own.

WHEN DELTA Ray arrived at Midtown Mart that afternoon, she told her three-year-old, Tara Sue, to sit quietly in the basket while she secured Jared in the seat of the grocery cart with the pink nylon strap provided by Midtown. He was a climber of the first order and she knew if he escaped the cart, there was no telling what he'd find on the floor. Squashed grapes. Ignored pennies. Dirt, plenty of it. His little old hands would reach up to the lip of the produce shelf and pull tomatoes and oranges in a shower upon himself. Then he'd squash those ripe tomatoes in his hands, red pulp dripping down his plump little arms, and laugh like he'd invented laughing.

Secretly, Delta Ray was proud of him and his ways, but she knew better than to show this joy in public. As she pulled the buckle tight around Jared's pudgy waist, she heard whispers behind her.

"Do you think Delta Ray's pregnant again?" she heard good old VerJean whispering to Sandy, one of the checkout girls. "She always looks as if she might be pregnant."

Delta Ray busied herself with pulling a coloring book and crayons out of her gigantic Mexican straw bag. "You color those animals any old color you want, Tara Sue," she said, handing her the book and the yellow box with green stripes, "but just stay put in that basket. No standing while we're in the store. Get the message?"

Tara Sue shook her head vigorously with a good-girl yes. But then Delta Ray heard busybody VerJean again. "Delta's got a lentil for a brain."

Usually, Delta tried not to use her strength in public, but today she almost shot a threatening look in VerJean's direction. Delta could be imposing, being exactly six feet tall. Her chest was, after all, except for her breasts, a close replica of her father's. He'd been a linebacker in the regional high school all-star game once upon a time. But Delta repressed the impulse, pretending to be more interested in the front page of the newsprint advertiser in her hands. It featured a picture of a swordfish with a broad-bladed pirate's sword drawn in place of its snout. Then she sucked in her stomach muscles and lifted her chin.

"I'm pregnant with the spirit," Delta Ray said slowly with emphasis as she glided the grocery cart toward Sandy's checkout stand and VerJean. "Blown up like a dirigible, flying for God." She stopped in front of the two women, smiled as if she were the Mother of Cosmic Content, and held Jared's chin in her hand. "My blessed ones," she said as she kissed his eyebrow and patted Tara Sue's blond curls. "Angel babies."

VerJean didn't look up. She scribbled a note on her shopping list, all the time acting as if she didn't have a mouth on her. Sandy acted busy as a bee. Dressed in a red-check Western Days shirt with a red-fringed yoke and wearing a cut-out cowboy hat badge with "Sandy-O" written across the hat band, she plumped open a paper bag and waved politely at Delta Ray pushing her cart into the pasta aisle.

Muzak was playing "Let It Be." Delta Ray hummed. She plucked a thin box of fettuccine from the shelf and tried to balance it on Jared's head. He laughed. "Speaking words of wisdom, let it be," she sang.

At that very moment, however, she happened to see one of the laws of the land being shattered like a stone tablet against rock. At the end of the aisle, right by the expensive nuts, she saw Jeff Jex's hand dart out of his pocket and grab three cellophane tubes of cashews. Like lightning, he hid them in a deep pocket of his baggy beige shorts, faster than Delta Ray could sing the last "let it be."

"Hey you," she shouted. "What do you think you're doing?"

Delta Ray's cart sang down the aisle, the lopsided wheel adding its own rhythm to the Muzak. She whizzed past long-grain rice, Chinese noodles, water chestnuts, and bamboo shoots. Ca-chunk, ca-chunk, the wheel, the spaces between the floor tiles. Ca-chunk. Let it be. God's own chariot winging out of the sky, landing on Aisle 6, catching young Jeff Jex in an unsavory act.

"Okay," Delta Ray said, her voice booming out of her expansive chest. "What's going on here?"

Young Jex gave Delta Ray the finger. "Fuck you," he said, his lips lingering over the f of the fuck, his delivery slow and impudent.

Delta Ray's eyes grew wider than a full moon on a clear night. "You don't say that to me, young man," she said, her fists on her generous hips. "Nobody speaks that way to me, especially not a thief."

"You cretin." Jeff Jex stood there with fists jammed into his thighs, his voluminous shorts low on his hips, his black hair jelled Elvis style.

"If I were you, young Jex, I'd be getting my running shoes on and fast."

"You're a joke, Mrs. Bradford, just like all your snot-nosed kids. Don't you care about pollution?"

Delta Ray hit faster than a jet. God's jet arrayed in purple sweat pants, a purple sweatshirt that said "Milton Boosters" across her broad chest. Kamikaze. Ke-yi. She tied up Jeff Jex with something close to a full nelson, though she kept it this side of legal. "I won't break your neck, you pompous little shit, but you better understand one thing."

Jeff Jex was white. Sweat poured down his temples and pooled underneath the lobe of his ear. His slick black hair fell like two commas over the sides of his face—two hanks of hair shaken out of place by Delta Ray Bradford, uncrowned Milton Wrestler of the Year. In one quick motion, he pulled the three packages of cashews out of his pocket, dropped them on the floor, and kicked them with the toe of his scuffed black cowboy boot. "Sexual harassment," Jeff screamed. "Get this nymphomaniac off me."

Jared was chanting "Mommy, Mommy, Mommy." Tara Sue was climbing up and over the edge of the basket to help her mother. Somehow, Delta Ray's maternal antennae could feel her daughter climbing, balancing, one leg on the outside of the cart, her chin scraping over the hard metal rods of the basket. Releasing the young man, she whirled around to see Tara Sue falling, falling, chin red. She whirled just in time to hear the crack of Tara Sue's head on the hard floor, the cherubic face still and doll-like and China-painted on the floor of the Midtown Market. Tara Sue: A picture of serenity framed with pieces of tile smudged with the dirt from people's shoes, their black heel marks, the crushed berries falling out of carts, falling to the floor, bruised beneath someone's careless heel.

"Tara Sue. My strawberry princess. My apple." Delta Ray kneeled over her daughter.

"Mommy, Mommy." Jared never stopped.

And Delta Ray rolled onto her hips and cupped Tara Sue's face in her hands. She closed her eyes and ears to all the sounds around her, and in her mind, watched her own body rise up out of the pasta aisle to the safe place where nobody could ever be hurt. She watched Tara Sue rise with her as she pushed aside the walls of the clouds. "You'll bless my baby, won't you?" she asked the first angel she saw, who happened to be carrying a trumpet. "You'll bless and protect my littlest angel girl and make her hair keep curling and her eyes keep shining like stars, won't you please?"

Sitting smack dab in the middle of Aisle 6 of Midtown Market, Delta rocked her baby love in her arms and finger-combed her fine-spun hair all the time she talked to the angel. "'Delta,' she used to call to me before she was born. 'Please let me come to your house, Delta Ray. Please.'" Delta looked up into the crystal-like eyes of the angel who lifted his trumpet to his lips and blew a long mournful sound that filled the heavens. It was one long, sad note. He blew and blew the same blue note as tears streamed out of Delta's eyes and someone handed her a linen handkerchief and told her to blow her nose.

And then the paramedics were there, the gray stretcher, the sound of Velcro ripping apart after the blood pressure check, dark blue shirts with gold patches on their sleeves, serious looks on their faces, Jeff Jex standing beside them, eyes blank like post holes, the commas of his hair still hanging forward over his ears. "She's got a weak pulse," one of the paramedics said. "Concussion, probably. Better get her over to General."

Delta Ray followed meekly, a lamb following dark blue shirts, a lamb only knowing one direction, only following one leader—the dark blue shirts into the red and white ambulance, into the wide-open back doors, gauges, timeless clocks, upside down bottles of clear fluid.

As the doors to the ambulance were closing, she saw Jeff Jex standing in the doorway of Midtown Market, surrounded by pots of pinkish coral geraniums, lobelia that was bluer than the angel's trumpet solo, and the gray leaves of dusty miller. She saw the dark blue and the gray more than anything at that moment, until they became ribbons of color draping across Tara Sue's white face. Tara Sue, the only thing her five senses could recognize. It wasn't until two blocks later, as the ambulance pulled underneath the awning of the hospital, that her brain finally registered the whole of the picture she'd seen. Jeff Jex had been holding Jared by the hand. Jared was crying. "Mommy, Mommy." Jeff Jex was reaching into his pocket, pulling out a dollar bill, handing it to Delta's two year old, kneeling down to beg Jared to stop crying. VerJean was watching through Midtown's glass door, leaning forward, her neck stretched, peering.

THE NIGHT was filled with crickets rubbing their legs—crickets and the smell of the stockyard and the irrigation water on the outlying pastures of hay tall enough to mow. The moon silvered the aluminum frame on the bedroom window and made the almost-asleep Delta Ray think of stripes. The flag at the post office. Beach towels through the wire fence of the town pool. The black and white of the neighborhood's picket fences as the ambulance sped by. The red stripe on the hospital floor, guiding her to the emergency room. A brown stripe on the wall. A green stripe above the brown stripe. Tara Sue. Her angel baby. Stripes of light through the venetian blinds across Tara Sue's face as she lay in the hospital room, barely breathing.

And she saw Bishop Sohm entering the room with his two counselors, his blue and white striped shirt, his farmer's tan face with the white stripe where his hat had been. The anointment. The rubbing of the oil in Tara's curls. The stripes of all the men's fingers gentle on Tara Sue's head. "By the power of the Holy Melchizedek priesthood," Bishop Sohm speaking, "I lay my hands upon your head for the purpose of giving you a blessing."

Little Tara. Life low in her. Poor in body. Bishop Sohm calling earnestly to God,

"Save this baby. Give her life." The men lifting their straw hats back on their heads, smiling contented smiles, shaking hands. "God bless you and Tara, Delta Ray," the bishop was saying. "The spirit tells me she's going to be fine. Say hi to J.L. when he gets back from his run to Vegas. We need him out on the welfare farm when things are right with Tara here." The men leaving. The door closing. Delta Ray staring down at Tara Sue, life still shallow in her. Delta Ray mumbling prayers, intoning her child's name, "Tara Sue, my baby," as if the sound, the calling, would bring Tara back. Tara Sue, still quiet, Delta Ray placing her own fingers on Tara's head, "By the power of Jesus, who I love, I bless you, Tara Sue Bradford. Blast out of this Chicken Wing the Reaper's got you locked in. Bridge out. Break free, my angel baby." Tara finally stirring, finally turning her head to the left side, finally holding Delta Ray's finger in her hand.

And now, her head crushed into a pillow, her eyes staring at the ceiling, Delta Ray listened to the crickets and smelled the irrigation water and waited for J.L.'s rig to pull into the yard. She held Tara Sue in her arms. Tara, still alive, still a three year old full of delicate life, still the same Tara Sue Bradford who tomorrow would be laughing and coloring butterflies on everyone's lunch sacks and watching her older sisters taking dancing lessons at Miss Jean's Studio for Acrobatics and Tap.

And as Delta Ray held Tara as closely as possible and felt her curls under her chin, the sound of the crickets hypnotized her. Their steady rhythm walked her into the world of dreams. She slipped through the dark tunnel of sleep and into a place with hundreds of children dressed in white, tons of children, seas of children. "Delta Ray," she heard them singing. "We're coming. We're coming. Won't you let us live with you, Delta Ray?" The children were dancing, shaking their hands in the air, some of them slapping the skins of ghost tambourines. "Give us bodies, Delta Ray. Let us be." Delta saw a familiar one doing a few flips and balancing on a beam of light. "My turn next, Delta Ray." And then J.L. danced into the dream. He arched his back, spread his arms, and grinned at her as Motown amped through the heavenly dance hall. "My girl. Talkin' 'bout my girl." Music filled every nook and cranny of her dream until she felt something on her shoulder.

"Delta," J.L. whispered, tapping her shoulder. "Delta. I'm home." He sat carefully on the bed, tossed his Zion National Park hat on one of the dresser mirror's spindles, lifted his wife's hair off her ear, and kissed her cheek.

"That you, J.L.?" she asked, groggy. "I just saw you dancing in my dream."

"Forget dancing. I'm ready to wrestle, Delta Ray, woman of my dreams." He smiled, his lips chalked white in a stripe of moonlight, and put his arm underneath her head. "If God says we should have more babies, then I'm willing to do my part. You're a good woman, Delta, and when I prayed last night, God told me He'd provide if we helped Him out. I even saw that gymnast baby in my dreams. He did a few flips and said, 'Hi, J.L. Sure hope to be seeing you soon.'" J.L. was smiling large and wide. "I felt real good about him talking to me. Came just before I went to sleep. Cute little tyke."

"There's so many," Delta Ray mumbled and rolled her head from side to side. "I saw hundreds and thousands of them."

"That's a lot of spirit babies, I'd say. But maybe we can assist one more of them, my honey love. Let me put Tara Sue to bed and then, maybe, we can come up with a new hold of some kind." He wiggled his eyebrows like Groucho.

Delta Ray tightened her hold on Tara. "I just want to hold Tara Sue for now, J.L. Feel her hair against my Adam's apple, glossy like it is. We almost lost her yesterday. Grocery cart. She fell. But, just as bad, I forgot all about Jared. Left him in the cart. We were lucky Jeff Jex was there to unbuckle him and VerJean was there to take him to her house. Even if he did call me a cretin and a nymphomaniac."

"A what? He always was a smart-assed little kid. A what?"

"Maybe he's right, J.L. Maybe I'm foolish about these spirit babies. Maybe I'm only a dumbcretinympho. . . ." She pulled the pillow out from under her head and pushed it into her face to drown her words.

"Is my Delta Ray losing heart?" J.L. lifted the corner of the pillow, then the pillow itself. "Come out of there. Escape time. Have I ever seen my Delta Ray back down under pressure? No sirree."

"I wish he would have called me something different," Delta said, curling fetal.

"But people don't understand the higher law like you do. They don't understand there's always room for one more. Let me take Tara to bed. Let me love you, Delta. Don't feel bad."

J.L. lifted Tara Sue into his arms, rocked her side to side as her chin rested on his shoulder, and kissed the tip of her ear. "People could be right about me," Delta said, staring up at the ceiling. "Let me hold her a little longer." Delta stretched long on her back and held out both arms like two stumps of trees in the dark shadows of the room. "Nobody can take away our Tara, can they J.L.?"

"No, honey." He eased Tara Sue back into her mother's arms, Tara limp with sleep. "I don't like seeing my warrior with the blues, though. Bridge out, like the wrestlers say. Nobody else but God knows anything worth remembering."

And J.L. climbed into bed, put his arms around both Tara Sue and Delta Ray, and the three of them fell asleep like that.

FROM *MotherTongue*

─────────

DEMETRIA MARTÍNEZ

DEMETRIA MARTÍNEZ, 35, was born and raised in Albuquerque, New Mexico. In 1987 she was indicted, and later acquitted, on charges related to smuggling Central American refugees into the United States. Her novel MotherTongue, winner of the 1994 Western States Book Award for Fiction, is set in Albuquerque and wraps itself around the lives of a young New Mexican woman and her Salvadoran political refugee lover. Demetria has been a columnist and editor for the National Catholic Reporter; *has authored a collection of poetry, "Turning," included in the book* Three Times a Woman; *has had work published in anthologies such as* Latina: Women's Voices from the Borderlands; *and lives in Tucson, Arizona.*

AFTER FINISHING HIS SHIFT at the cantina, José Luis sometimes crouched under the portal to look at silver and turquoise laid out on blankets in long furrows. He used to linger at the rug of a Navajo woman who sat on a precarious throne of milk crates as she awaited the day's harvest of tourist dollars. Now and again, groups of tourists engulfed her, cutting off my view of José Luis. This used to unnerve me. The Border Patrol had recently opened an office, declaring Albuquerque a border town—a city like El Paso or Brownsville, ordered to empty its pockets and produce its documents. I feared if I lost sight of José Luis, the Patrol might take him away in one of its avocado-colored vans. And they could have, easily; they were armed to the teeth. I believed that watching José Luis generated protective forces; I vaguely remember some Eastern texts I was reading about the power of mindful observation—ironic, given that sight was my least evolved sense. Where others saw indigo, I saw blue; where others saw teal, I saw green. It's the draining away of color that happens in a woman's life when she can't name her own reality. It is only now that I am able to go back and color in the pale places, creating a mural on the walls of the life I now inhabit.

To track José Luis, I developed a sixth sense. Scanning the sea of tourists, I managed to latch on to a white patch of fabric among earth-toned clothing the better-off tourists ordered that year from the Banana Republic catalogue. His swatch of T-shirt became a kind of hologram that revealed the whole of him to me in three dimensions. And I held to that vision until the tourists moved on, their purchases made, cameras banked with images of a "real" Indian. Looking back now, I wonder what troubled me more, the fear that the Border Patrol might see José Luis or that the tourists in his midst could not see him, at least not in three dimensions. No, he was very dark, a dishwasher, an illegal alien. Had he spoken English, it would not have mattered; he still would lack the credentials pinned on those with British or French accents. All over the city refugees were rendered invisible with each stroke of the sponge or rake they used to clean motel rooms and yards and porches. Unlike wealthy refugees who fled their pasts and bought homes in Santa Fe, people like José Luis lacked the money to reinvent themselves. So they became empty mirrors. A ghostly rustle of Spanish spoken in restaurants above the spit of grease on a grill.

I still have the ring, a simple silver band, that José Luis bought from the Navajo woman. He gave it to me, said it was just a small gift to thank me for being his friend. Years later, I gave it to a psychic who ran her fingers over it and said she saw a man with a scar on his forehead who was saying, I will return. Last night I took the ring from the shoe box and held it, my eyes closed, until I, too, saw José Luis: We were making love on a bed in a basement. I slipped the ring on, inhaled, and counted to seven. And I arrived at that stillness so absolute the chaotic fragments of one's life arrange themselves, if only for a moment, into a mandala of meaning. On the exhale I remembered that José Luis was the first man to touch me in a way that I could feel real pleasure, could feel my flesh yield up its own indivisible truth.

I was leaning against the white railing of the kiosk when José Luis came to me and said, This is for you. The ring fit only on my wedding finger; the fingers of my right hand have always been stronger and slightly larger around. I tried to say something, tried to crack the silence, but it was like taking aim at a piñata, blindfolded. I could not manage even a simple thank you. At last I said, We're married, no?, to la revolución. Yes, why not, he said as a smile swept across his face, dusting off the traces of fear that marked him. I knew at that moment that José Luis was seeing and wanting all that would come between us. I remember this now, as I stroke the ring, remember how he opened the door.

THE SANDIA Mountains, true to their name, ripened at daybreak, the color of watermelon. Here is a postcard of the Sandias, this is how they looked one early morning when José Luis and I were loading up Soledad's brown station wagon. Two friends of hers were borrowing it for a fishing trip. Roped to the top of the car, a canoe extended over the windshield like the beak of an eagle. Fishing rods poked out of windows like antennae. One of Soledad's friends—they did not tell us their names—adhered a Reagan-Bush sticker to the car's back bumper. In those days, the Border Patrol did not stop cars with Reagan-Bush or Right-to-Life stickers on them. Nor did the Patrol stop and question white men. In my memory, one of Soledad's friends that morning had blond hair and wore horn-rimmed glasses. Back then, when "fishing trip" meant transporting refugees north, a white man was an asset. Millions of years of genetic coding culminated in a kind of liturgy each time a Border Patrol agent waved him past the checkpoint outside El Paso.

I'm trying to remember how it is that, after Soledad's friends drove away, José Luis kissed me for the first time. It is like trying to take snapshots twenty years too late. At least I recall the smell—the sage we burned in a seashell for Soledad, who had called to say she had forgotten to bless the house before she left. If only I could follow the wisp of sage back in time to the moment. . . . The truth is, some of our tenderest moments are the ones I am least likely to remember. It has to do with what I said about sleep, how women like me sometimes flee, letting loving words or glances melt on the hot pavement of some nameless fear.

So forgive me if I embellish; even a conjured memory is better than no memory at all if you would dare to give your life what the world did not, a myth, a plot. Besides, I never intended to reconstruct him from memory, just from love, which may be the only way anyone can ever hope to get at the whole truth. So let me say what might-have-been and maybe the facts will break through.

We are sitting cross-legged on Soledad's paisley couch facing one another and drinking coffee out of the blue mugs. I see a man who is not the same one I met weeks earlier at the airport. He is talking about rumors he picked up from the other dish-washers, about how easy it is to cross into Canada and to ask for a lawyer, to apply for political asylum. He says several of his coworkers invited him to join their soccer team, the best in the city, made up of Guatemalans and Salvadorans. It was amazing to me, how José Luis had salvaged the makings of a life out of fate's refuge heap. Earning money, teaching me Spanish, helping Soledad's friends translate human rights alerts: His activities gave him the confidence of a man who pokes a bonfire with a stick, dignified by the skill of generating light and heat.

He asks, Have you ever kissed a man whose name you did not know?

I say, I knew the name but not the man.

I am trying to escape into abstractions, to speak with an authority all out of proportion to what I am actually saying. To dazzle him so he won't hear my heart galloping. I am about to get what I want and a rope of panic is stretched out before me as I run toward desire. I'm all stutters and sweat and clashing colors: purple pants, a green Lady of Guadalupe T-shirt. I'm afraid, after sitting cross-legged for so long, that my big toe will curl up in a cramp, my body an unruly cowlick. Then, he thanks me, yes, this really happened. He thanked me for sharing my sleeping pills with him, for making up a social security number based on numerology. Acts of solidarity, he said, his hazel eyes smiling. He touched my arm and I laughed, sipped from the chalice of happiness the universe set suddenly before me. He said, I love it when you laugh. Yes, it was real laughter, the kind that makes fences inside you fall. And seeing his opportunity, he crossed yet another border. Sweet collision of lips and tongues. I tasted Kahlua and chamomile and some other barely familiar herb, steeped and sipped in another lifetime.

Yes, I believe it happened that way; I feel joy *now* echoing in me, striking against the canyon walls of forgetting. Our faces floated above our bodies, helium balloons linked by static. Like a radio alarm clock, the cicadas started up. Time stopped. There began a never-ending August that, years later, I would remember every time I smelled the sea in a swamp cooler or tasted the sea in another man's mouth.

AUGUST 1982

He said he loves me. He said he *loves* me. (I used to plead with my first boyfriend to say it!) José Luis kissed me for the first time, but what he said means even more.

It's happening just as I knew it was meant to happen. Spanish lessons, a ring that fits on my wedding finger, our drives back and forth between Soledad's and Old Town. But most important of all, the word love. Without it my feelings spill all over the place—and it's always me (and my friends) who have to mop up afterwards.

Now I have reason to improve my Spanish. I have a word and a way of life to conjugate: Quiero, quieres, quiere, queremos. . . . To want and to love, the same thing! God, make this thing last. Make it last. I sound crazed, I know, but with good reason. My period's due any moment, and I have found true love. The kind that pulls all of life in one direction. It's too much. Already, his presence in my life is helping me forget all the sadness (what was it about?) that pulled me down for so long before he came to Albuquerque. And with the power of love I'm going to help him forget, too. Help him to forget the war that he fled from, that he says he still dreams about.

This morning I woke up to the sound of San Rafael's bells, and I remembered yesterday. I felt a grin spread through my whole body, pure bliss. The thought of being with him forever is intoxicating. But I've got to be careful. I've got to stay in the present. The minute I get hung up on the idea of *forever*, on what will happen tomorrow, I ruin everything. For all I know, the universe could get scratched like a record groove. We might do nothing but repeat yesterday morning over and over— couch to coffee maker, coffee maker to couch. (Yet what a gift this would be!)

From the Tao Te Ching: Heaven is lasting and Earth enduring. The reason for this is that they do not live for themselves alone; therefore they live long.

WE DID not make love, that is to say have intercourse, for weeks. Something per- versely Catholic kept our explorations above the waist, the old religion erotically charging the most humble expanses of skin. Inner elbow, collarbone, fingertips. We touched each other on Soledad's couch until 3 A.M., when the train's cry severed the night. It's late, we have to work tomorrow, he said. But I don't need sleep, I don't need food, just you, I answered. I unpeeled myself from him, removed myself like a ban- dage. The cruelty of limits stung: the need for sleep, food, a paycheck however small. If an hour were a house one could move into for good, I would have built a wall around the two o'clock hour, a brick wall arrayed against the disfiguring fury of the future.

He playfully yanked at my hair and patted my cheeks as if plumping up a pillow. He said he worried I might fall asleep while driving to Old Town. I assured him I would not; after being with him I always tuned in to a rock station, volume full throttle. He took my hand and walked me through the portal where red chile ristras were suspended like tongues of fire. We opened a rotting wood gate that led to the front yard. After I got into the pickup truck, he kissed me goodnight, lips and forehead, through the rolled-down window. If he asked me for a sleeping pill I gave him half of mine, snapping apart a chalky oval no bigger than an infant's thumbnail. I took a pill whenever emotions, good or bad, detonated, leaving a cloud of mental chatter I could not dissipate on my own. He said the pills helped him fall asleep after nightmares woke him up, causing his heart to race. It was as if our minds were satellite dishes, open to the murmurings of some dark universe. Signals bombarded us, signals we could not yet decode.

THEN ONE day it happened, it happened. I love you, José Luis. Te quiero, María. We opened each other up like sacred books, Spanish on one side, English on the other, truths simultaneously translated. I remember the scent of our sweat, sweet as basil as we pressed against one another on the basement bed. Lindita, mamacita, negrita: love words, the kind that defy translation. With his hands he searched my depths. When he found what he was looking for I moaned, felt a chill and then warmth as the seasons moved through me. Minutes later he came inside me, stiffened, sighed. Afterwards, he lit his cigarette on the flame of the Sacred Heart candle on the night table. He rubbed my feet with almond oil, talked in the dark about developments in El Salvador. We had both dreamed the night before about his country. I said, José Luis, last night I dreamed I was there, I smelled bougainvillea. He said, I dreamed I was there too, mi amor, but it was something about white phosphorus, napalm.

He stayed awake, talked to me; I didn't feel the doubts women sometimes feel when men fall asleep after making love, doubts delicate yet dangerous as asbestos fibers. Sometimes we held one another and listened to the shortwave radio that we had brought down from its place on the kitchen window sill. I remember a BBC commentator saying something about South Africa, and how his descriptions shattered like crystal wine glasses at the sound of a woman crying out in grief. But the sounds diminished as our bed bobbed away on the tide of sleep. Holding on to José Luis, my head pinned to his chest, I held on to the night, refused to let it slip through my hands. There were times I felt sad after making love. Intercourse often disappointed me. It could feel like a linear fitting of parts, a far cry from the creative pleasures of foreplay when we painted on the caves of one another's flesh. Perhaps it would have been different had I wanted a baby. Maybe then the act, with its audacious committing of present to future, would have touched the flaming core of my being. But I'm deceiving myself again. Lying. For a long time after José Luis left me I continued to believe a man could touch my essence, make me whole. All that time I could have been writing, touching the fires of my being and returning to the world, purified and strong.

You see, I was one of those women who is at her best when she wants something very badly. The mating dance, the yearning and flirting, surrenders and manipulations—I was good at that, so good at the pursuit that when I actually got what I wanted, terror appeared. Terror that wore the silly mask of disappointment.

Full Circle

MERION MORRIGAN SHARP

MERION MORRIGAN SHARP, 43, has been living in Arizona since 1970. After seventeen years of gypsy life in a military family, she was happy to stop moving, to feel the earth, to let her roots sink deep into the place she still calls home today. Also an artist, she says that her words and paintings carry her prayers and love for the land. Other than some short pieces she has contributed to the Flagstaff Women's Newsletter, *the following is Merion's first published work. She lives in Flagstaff with her son, Tanner.*

FROST CRYSTALS HISS AND curl from the edge of the ice scraper in Kallie's hand. Slowly, deliberately, she clears the windshield of her truck. Snowflakes dance and career about her head, dissolving in instant death as they touch the twin streams that course her cheeks. She brushes a snowy mitten across her face. There is nothing left for her to do. She has cried and cursed, laughed, pretended, watched, waited, and grieved; and still her heart has found no peace. It is time to go back to the beginning.

Waves of ice, fine cinders, and salt spray against the windshield as her truck bucks the drafts of a long line of semis. Heading west on the interstate, traffic moves fast despite the danger of black ice and perilous traction. Kallie white-knuckles the wheel. The vehicle lurches—each new blast of slush threatens to send her careening off into the trees. She is grateful for the need to concentrate on the driving. It keeps her present in her body, free from the bedlam of her mind.

At last she leaves the ponderosa forest. The San Francisco Peaks begin to dwindle in the east as she moves out into the patchwork of open grassland and pine that swells and sweeps west toward the Bill Williams Mountains. Snow clouds take on rain cloud personas, painting the sky from a palette of gray. Her hands relax. Again the tears come, and the turbulent thoughts she is trying to escape.

It's over . . . over . . . over, and she has to come to terms with that. It isn't what she wants, but she realizes it's not her choice. Evan has someone else now. He says he's happy. All she feels is slow death—poison spreading through every cell of her being. She needs to let go, make it final in her mind, her heart. She needs to make real the closing of this chapter of her life. Diamond Creek is calling.

Images of the past shine like refracted light through the crystal of her memory. A fiercely beautiful day in September—the Autumn Equinox—day before her twenty-sixth birthday. She was just a smooth-faced girl full of fantasies about life, still believing in true love, soul mates, and happily-ever-after. The sky was bluer than any bright bird's painted wing, cloudless as only an Arizona sky can be. The intense heat of summer radiated from the canyon walls of the creek drainage—a place wrought by cataclysmic forces, a place in constant flux, the creekbed always changing, bending to the will of water. There on a red island of rock, jutting from the canyon floor like a monument of stone, stood a gateway where energies converged and two souls were brought together.

She'd gone for adventure, taken money from her carefully hoarded savings to do something she'd never done before—a river trip. She couldn't foresee how it would change the course of her life. Couldn't see anything but what she had dreamed of—the beautiful man she had called to her from the heartwell of her deepest longing and loneliness.

When the three-day trip was over, Kallie knew enough about Evan to realize that he was not free to choose her. It should have ended as they drifted past the Grand Wash Cliffs. It should have ended as they de-rigged the boats on the stinking-hot shores of Lake Mead. It should have ended as she rode back to Kingman with the boat crew, perched on blackbags in the back of the truck with the sun going down on their shining faces. But it didn't. It was ending now, thirteen years later, with the weight and volume of all that time dragging heavily upon her spirit.

West she continues, dry-eyed now, past Williams. She feels a primal need to go back, to perform some sort of ritual that will ease the pain she feels like a great sucking wound in her heart. She can't bear it any longer. Her instinct for survival is leading her back to close the circle, to staunch the bleeding with the sacrifice of her dearest memories.

Somber clouds collide and spill across the sky in windy confusion, weeping the land into wetness. The miles rush by. Dropping in elevation, the landscape shifts through subtle changes, the way winter melts into spring without notice. Ponderosa gives way to piñon and juniper, cliffrose and prickly pear, their colors made rich by coats of rain.

When she reaches Ash Fork, she makes an instant decision to take the Crookton Road instead of staying on the freeway. More than often she and Evan had driven this abandoned stretch of Route 66. It was slower, and in the past had always prolonged the excitement and adventure of beginning another river trip. Now the old road, sadly dilapidated, carries her back in time. Bare brown stalks of sunflowers vie with golden grasses and dried coyote melons, crowding the pavement as yellowed weeds push through cracking asphalt toward the fading centerline. Again the tears come as ghostly reflections rush past like hitchhikers on the roadside.

"Oh Goddess, I hurt so much!" Kallie sobs aloud. She drives on, blind now to the vast, severe beauty of the passing scenery. Trapped in her thoughts of Evan with another woman, Evan spending his days with someone other than her. Trapped on the edge of a great emptiness that yawns unspanned between her and the man she vowed to love till the end of time.

Kallie knows this is crazy. It has been a long time since she and Evan were truly happy. Twelve years of marriage and a child didn't change anything. Their mutual pain and need brought them together and eventually destroyed the illusions she fought so hard to maintain. Illusions about who Evan was, who she was. She sees now how she gave up her own dreams to be with a man she thought would make her feel whole, would take away that awful longing inside.

Never before has loneliness seemed so near as in this place of distant boundaries. The land stretches out empty in all directions, featureless, the way her life feels right now. She pushes at the loneliness, testing the resilience of it, trying to will it away. With relief she spots the sign directing her to Seligman. Coming into town, she passes the turnoff to the local dump. More memories linger down that road, and she slows involuntarily, trying to recollect them. Laughter, crazy antics while dumping the trash they carried off the river, treasures found—remembrances like startled jackrabbits spring up and leap away, evading her efforts to hold them.

Shaking her head, she drives on past Murillo's Tastee Stop, where the crazy little Mexican regales passing travelers with his feigned foolishness—proffering wadded napkins and crumpled straws along with his burgers and shakes. She'd never forget the first time she accepted his offer of ketchup, only to have him squirt it on the front of her dirty river shirt. When she realized it was just a piece of red string coming out the end of the squeeze bottle, her delight had left her wet-eyed with laughter. Now, so many years later, her chest and belly constrict in remembrance of joy, wanting it back.

She stops to get gas on the edge of town. After paying for fuel, a soda, and some chips, she walks over to pet the scruffy burros that idle their time as local tourist attractions. A raven sits on the top rail of the corral, eyeing her purchase.

"Got any words of wisdom for me?" she asks. He tilts his head and blinks. "You knew all along this was going to happen, didn't you? Why didn't you warn me?" The raven stretches his neck and gives a croak. "Yeah," she says, "yeah, I guess you did." She tosses a potato chip in the bird's direction and heads back to her truck.

All day the sky has altered between rain and clouds, blue and sunshine, attempting, it seems, to transform her dark mood. As if on cue, a flock of mountain bluebirds rises from the road shoulder like a cloud of turquoise, moving out and arcing back to the highway, coursing and streaming past her windshield in flashes of azure till she's dizzy with blue and feels like a bird. Another flock rises before her and then another. Kallie's mind fills up with color, and a fleeting thought brings a smile to her lips. She'd been sure that when Evan left he had taken the magic with him.

On her right, the cloud-shadowed flanks of the Aubrey Cliffs rise like piebald ponies from the worn-out rangeland. The countryside spreads out and away, unadorned by any tree—nothing but sere winter shrubbery and the pinks and maroons of dried wild buckwheat. I can do this, she thinks; my life's not over. Switching on the radio, she taps out the beat, humming along with the oldies till one of "their" songs comes on. She snaps the music off in disgust.

She makes the turnoff at Peach Springs and drives north through the sleepy little Hualapai housing area. Apprehension coils inside her. She's hoping she won't run into any Indians on the road, fearing she might have to justify why she is here.

On the seat beside her is a basket filled with ceremonial objects, old photos, and the charred remains of her marriage license. In a veiled portion of her being, Kallie is brooding an ancient wisdom—something with the power to heal. How it will mani fest is not yet clear. She has no words to explain.

As the truck bumps down the poorly graded road that rises, falls, and twists into the canyon drainage, her senses are alert to everything. The sun is shining and the wind breathes fitfully, dancing the dried grasses. It has been a long time since she's been here. She drives under the branches of an old cottonwood that once was home to a Cooper's hawk. Many of the tree's great limbs are now missing, and her body resonates with the loss—so much has fallen away. The truck is almost crawling now on the washboarded road, raising huge plumes of dust that quickly gust away in the wind. In the distance she sees another cloud of dirt moving toward her and knows she's not alone. On she creeps, not sure if it's the terrain or her own hesitation that's prolonging her journey. The approaching vehicle draws closer, and her heart sinks to a new low as she recognizes a Hualapai with a business look on his face. The truck pulls abreast of her and stops. Kallie rolls down her window and nods.

"Are you with a river trip?" he asks.

Suddenly, she's furious; she wants to scream at him: No! I'm not on a fucking river trip! I'll never be on another river trip. It's all over. Don't you get it? "No, I'm just sightseeing," she replies.

"It's fifteen dollars to drive on the road. I'll take a check if you don't have cash."

Kallie sighs and pulls her wallet from the jumble on the seat beside her. She watches him from the corner of her eye as he methodically makes out the permit while she scribbles out a check. The final indignity. The Indian hands her the permit and she glances at it before giving him the check. "Thanks," she mumbles, and drives away.

It's close now, her destination. She can feel the energy of it and keeps expecting to see it around every curve along the dusty track—the gateway. It is only a gateway in a figurative sense. From the road it looks like nothing more than the crest of a hill, but from a distance it is obvious that this is no ordinary piece of earth. Like some relict monolith of another time, it rises from the floor of the drainage, nearly block-ing the wide expanse where two canyons converge. Kallie rounds a bend, and she is there. Heart pounding, she pulls onto the shoulder and stops, staring at the place where she first looked into the eyes of Evan.

Now what? she wonders as she climbs from her truck. Walking to the exact spot where she stood at their first encounter, she visualizes Evan squatting carelessly in the circle of eager would-be river runners. He radiates energy, magnifying the power of this place, and she is dazzled. When their eyes meet, it is electric. The wind kicks up and a cloud passes over the face of the sun. The vision fades. Kallie is shaking, and she's crying again, stumbling back to the truck. "Now let it end," she breathes, "let it end in beauty, the way it began."

A WOMAN stands alone on the hilltop, an abalone shell in her hand. Sage smoke drifts up and away on an eagle feather as she walks counterclockwise in a circle, stopping to greet the Four Directions. She speaks an incantation. In the south she places an image of the Goddess. In the east she places a ring. In the north she places an image of the God. In the west she places a photograph of two people, torn in half. Again she circles, this time sprinkling ashes, whispering a prayer. "It is done and it is so," she says, and turns to face the river.

LYING ON a smooth boulder beside the Colorado, Kallie lets her thoughts be carried downstream as the last of the ashes have been. The roar of the river soothes her and the golden sweetness of late afternoon sun on rock is gentle to her eyes, so tired now from weeping. Watching blue shadows creep toward their mergence with night, Kallie knows. Hollowed out, empty; loneliness leads her back to Source.

The cool rock beneath her begins to steal her heat. It is time to go. The mountains whisper now, calling, beckoning her home—to her son, her friends, her work. Gratefully, she begins the long journey back.

Heading south to the highway, she again passes the place of power, but she does not hesitate, doesn't look back. It is finished. She breathes in the beauty of her surroundings—chenilled hillsides of purple-hued blackbrush, gilded deceiving softness of staghorn cholla, fluffy dried flower-heads of baccharus backlit by winter sunset. The world has gone to velvet before her eyes, rounding the sharp corners of that piece of pain she will always carry. She breathes deeply and remembers the magic. Last light of day burnishes the land. The clouds are gone. Night is falling. She drives into the fading light of the eastern sky.

FROM *Picture Bride*

YOSHIKO UCHIDA

YOSHIKO UCHIDA, 1921–1992, was born in Alameda, California, and died in Berkeley. Taken from their home by the U.S. government during World War II like thousands of other Japanese Americans, Yoshiko and her family lived for a time in a horse stall at Tanforan Race Track. Eventually they were transferred to Topaz, a concentration camp in the Utah desert, where she taught second grade. She was an educator, secretary, and author, with a BA from the University of California, Berkeley, and an MA from Smith College. Her award-winning books include the children's title The Dancing Kettle and Other Japanese Folk Tales; The Invisible Thread *for young adults;* Desert Exile: The Uprooting of a Japanese American Family, *a memoir; and* Picture Bride, *a novel.*

IT WAS SUNDAY, AND Taro and Hana started out early for church. It took them at least twenty minutes to walk to church in the center of camp, since Taro walked so slowly, head down, watching the ground.

"Papa, must you always walk looking down?" Hana asked, not wanting to be late for church.

"Go on. I'll catch up," Taro answered.

Ever since he and Kenji had found two perfect arrowheads and a fine trilobite one day, Taro had succumbed to collector's fever. He never went out now without keeping a close watch on the ground.

"At least he's taken an interest in something," Kenji confided to Hana, "and that's good for him."

Hana was glad for Taro's new interest in his desert findings, but even more for his deeper friendship with Kenji. Taro talked often with him, and it was Kenji to whom he had taken Kaneda's letter.

"It's hard to know what God has in store for each of us," Kenji had said. "Perhaps there is work for Dr. Kaneda to do in Japan. He may find the fulfillment there that he was denied in this country. Accept his decision in peace, and try now to start a new life for yourself and Mrs. Takeda. Perhaps you could look for work outside. We must all think about going out beyond the barbed wire."

"To what?" Taro asked. "To the kind of hatred that killed Henry Toda?"

"There has always been hatred, Mr. Takeda. You've known it before in California. You survived in spite of it."

"I was younger then."

"And now?"

"I haven't the strength to go to a strange city to seek new roots. I want to wait here until the war ends, and I can go home again to Oakland."

"What will you do there?"

"Begin again. But at least I will be home."

Taro turned more and more to the desert for solace. It fascinated him in a strange way as it gave up its treasures from the past.

"You can be happy here in the desert then?" Hana asked.

"I would not call it happiness."

"What then?"

"Acceptance. There is no other way to find peace."

"Then you don't want to go out and find a job?"

"Picking sugar beets in Idaho or being a houseboy in Chicago?"

"I know you don't want that, Papa."

"Someday we'll go back to California," Taro said patiently. "I'd do any kind of work there. We could both work, and maybe earn enough to buy back my shop. Wouldn't you like that?"

"Yes, I would, Papa."

"Well then. Be patient. Accept what has to be. One day, perhaps this country will redeem itself."

Hana would not push Taro any more. He had had enough of her assertiveness in his life. She would try now, as Taro always had, to accept quietly what life brought.

So Hana tried to accept the desert, but she hated its brittle, dry growth and the creatures it sheltered. She was afraid of the scorpions that she sometimes found in her shoes, and she longed for the sight of something green, and for the sound of the song sparrows. One morning she had seen two seagulls winging their way across the sky, and the sight of them had filled her with so much longing for San Francisco Bay, she almost wept.

For several months, they had watched anxiously as trees were brought in and planted throughout the camp. But none had survived the heat or the hostile soil. Now they thrust barren limbs into the sky as their roots shriveled in the sand.

Hana and Taro passed dozens of these skeletal trees as they walked to church. When they arrived, the pianist was already playing the prelude. They quickly found a place on one of the benches, and Hana was pleased to see that Kenji Nishima was preaching that day. She thought he seemed particularly handsome as he stood at the lectern. His face was serene and his hair, now touched with gray at the temples, gave him a look of dignity. Sumiko's love had given him new dimensions and there was no one in camp who could not turn to him for sustenance or comfort. He had become a giving, loving person—a true man of God.

Hana felt proud of him and allowed a moment's pride in herself as well. He is one person I can truly say I have helped, she thought, hoping perhaps God might feel, at last, that she had redeemed herself.

As Kenji spoke, the desert wind began to howl and Hana found it difficult to concentrate on what he said.

"Dear God, please, not another dust storm," she prayed. The dust storms terrified her, and with each storm she feared Sumiko's mother would die of suffocation.

Hana could see the dust swirling outside, and soon the screaming wind caused the dust to seep like smoke into the church. The windows rattled, pebbles rained like hail on the glass, and garbage cans, boxes, anything not secured, were hurled against the building like toys. The sound of coughing rippled through the congregation, and people covered their noses and mouths with handkerchiefs.

Hana felt the building quiver, and instinctively clung to Taro's arm. Kenji, sensing the mounting anxiety of the people, stopped in the middle of his sermon.

"I'd like to read to you from the book of Joshua," he said calmly. "Please listen. 'Be strong and of good courage; be not frightened, neither be thou dismayed, for the Lord thy God is with you wherever you go.' He is with us here and now. Do not be afraid."

A woman screamed as the wind suddenly flung open the door and the entire desert seemed to pour into the building. "Mama, Mama!" a child cried out in terror.

Kenji rushed from the pulpit to help secure the door. Then, raising his hand, he hurriedly gave the benediction. The storm might last for hours, but when there was a lull, he knew everyone must try to get home.

"Those needing help to return to their barrack, please come forward. We will try to find people going back to the same block. I will go with anyone who needs me," he offered. And Sumiko gathered the older people who wanted someone to accompany them.

Hana tied her scarf around her head, covering most of her face, ready to leave the moment the wind subsided a little. They would certainly not be any safer in their own barrack, but an instinctive urge to be in her own room surpassed her fear of facing the storm.

"Do you want to go now?" Taro asked.

"Yes, I can't bear to stay here another minute."

They plunged out together in the sea of dust, feeling like two blind people. The powdery dust swept about them like great billowing veils of white and they could not see more than ten feet ahead. Hana felt the sting of pebbles and sand raining against her legs, and she gasped as they stumbled on. Every few yards, Taro would draw her toward a barrack where they would rest for a moment and then plunge on. Sometimes the wind pushed them, almost lifting them from their feet, while the next instant, it flung angry fistfuls of dust in their faces. Hana thought of seeking shelter as they passed a laundry barrack, but she could not open her mouth to suggest it to Taro. They clung to each other and struggled on, passing other huddled figures plodding in the opposite direction.

When at last they reached their room, it was smoky with dust. A layer of white covered everything. Hana tasted the dust in her mouth and tried to shake the dust from her clothing.

"It's lunch time," Taro said, looking at his watch.

But Hana could not think about food. She felt as though she had swallowed half the desert. She was dizzy and light-headed. Retching, she crept into her dusty bed and stayed there the rest of the day.

By evening, the wind died down, the stars came out, and it was as though there had never been a dust storm. Sumiko and Kenji came to see if they were all right, and brought news that upset Hana even more than the dust storm.

"The doctors tell me Mama must get out of the desert," Sumiko began. "They say we must take her out to Salt Lake City, where the air is clean and clear."

"And you will go with her?"

"I must."

"And Kenji San, you too?"

"Sumiko and her mother will go first. I will stay here and be useful as long as I can."

"But you must apply for permission to join them soon," Taro concluded. "Your place is beside your wife, no matter how much we need you here."

Kenji looked troubled and pained. "I cannot bear to leave all of you behind," he said. "And yet, maybe now my work is on the outside. There I could look for jobs and sponsors to enable you and others to be released from camp. You *will* give serious thought to applying for leave clearance before too long, won't you?" he asked.

Taro nodded, but said nothing. They all knew how he felt, and Hana knew that the two of them would probably remain in camp until the terrible war came to an end.

KENJI AND Taro bent together over the general camp registration form that everyone was required to fill out and sign. Taro had answered every question but one. That one he could not answer. He was glad Kenji was still here to advise him, for Sumiko had already taken her mother to Salt Lake City, and Kenji would join her as soon as a suitable apartment was found.

"Listen," Taro said, reading the question aloud again as he had done so many times. "'Will you swear unqualified allegiance to the United States of America and forswear any form of allegiance or obedience to the Japanese Emperor or any other foreign government power or organization?' If we answer yes, we would be left without a country, wouldn't we?"

"We certainly would," Kenji agreed. "Because this country denies us citizenship, we would, in effect, be left stateless."

"Then how can they ask us to do such a thing?" Hana asked.

"It is completely unreasonable," Kenji said, indignant.

Taro spoke as though he were addressing the unreasonable government itself.

"Japan is the land of my birth," he began, "but I decided long ago to make my home in America. I would gladly give up my citizenship in Japan, if only I were allowed to become a citizen of America. I must have one or the other. I cannot give up both."

"That is exactly what I will tell the administration officials when our committee meets with them this afternoon," Kenji assured him. "I will insist that we cannot answer such an eminently unfair and impossible question."

"Good," Hana said, relieved. "I know you will convince them."

"Well, I'm certainly going to try," Kenji said, rising to leave. "Now don't worry about it any more. We're going to work until we get that question removed from the registration form entirely."

Hana felt better, but the question continued to fester in Taro's mind. What was America trying to do to them now? It had already deprived them of their freedom, their homes, and their livelihoods. And now this.

Taro was as much troubled by what the country was doing to itself as by what it had done to him and his fellow Japanese Americans. He had learned well its early history. The principles and ideals on which the founding fathers had established this country were lofty and good. He admired them and had long ago determined to make those beliefs his own.

He believed that what this country had done to the Japanese Americans since the war was the result of fear and hatred and greed among bigoted and misguided men. He believed this was not the real America he knew.

He could understand its hatred for the militarists of Japan, but how much more anger and vengeance was it going to vent upon the innocent Japanese Americans who had chosen to live on its shores? The angry giant would destroy itself and everything it stood for before it crushed those it harassed, for the Japanese Americans, by not becoming embittered, had not yet allowed themselves to be destroyed. Taro longed to talk to Sojiro Kaneda of these things.

"Hana, I'm going out for a walk," he said, still troubled and unsure.

"Shall I come with you?"

"No, I want to be alone. I want to think."

"All right. Be careful then."

Hana heard Taro's footsteps crunching on the gravel walk. She knew he was turning to the desert for peace. There was still a little light left to the day. Perhaps the desert would be generous and allow him to find another of its treasures.

Hana went to the laundry barrack and filled her kettle with water. She put it on the pot-bellied stove and added a few lumps of coal to stir up the fire. By the time Taro returned, the water would be hot enough to make him a cup of cocoa.

Hana tried to keep her mind on the red wool sweater she was knitting for little Laurie, but she made so many mistakes in the cable stitch pattern, she had to rip out more than an inch. Finally, she put her knitting aside and decided to write to Kiku. It was still Kiku to whom she turned when she was most in need of a friend.

She longed to write to her mother, but the war had cut off those she loved in Japan. She wondered how they were and what tragedies the war had brought them. What would they say if they knew that she and Taro now lived in one small room, behind barbed wire, in the middle of a barren desert? She could almost hear her mother saying, "I knew you should not have gone off to America. If only you had stayed here. If only. . ."

"Dear Kiku. If only you were here, I could tell you how despondent I am. Did you agonize, too, over the camp registration questionnaire? Have you heard that Sojiro Kaneda is asking to be repatriated to Japan? We may never see him again. And now, Kenji San will be leaving us soon, too. . . ."

Hana tore up the page she had written. She would not burden Kiku with her troubles, for she knew Kiku must be lonely without her boys. Hana was rewriting the letter on a more pleasant note when she heard footsteps pounding down the path and then banging on her door.

"Mrs. Taro Takeda?" It was a young messenger. He was breathless, panting from having run so hard.

"Yes."

"Come with me quickly, please."

"What is it? What is wrong?"

The young boy had been instructed not to elaborate. "You're wanted at the hospital," he said urgently. "Please hurry."

Hana did not even put on her coat or scarf. She took the boy's hand and let him lead her along the path to the hospital. It was growing dark now and she had to be careful not to stumble.

They didn't speak as they rushed toward the lights of the hospital barrack, and when they arrived, Hana, with a pain in her side, was breathless. The boy led her to a door where a nurse was waiting for her.

"Mrs. Takeda? Come in."

She ushered her into a small room where a doctor and the camp director stood beside a single cot, their faces serious and grim. And lying on the cot, looking lifeless and ashen, was Taro.

"Papa! Papa San!" Hana called, rushing to his side. She knelt beside the cot asking, "What happened? What has happened to him?" Taro's eyes remained closed. His breathing was harsh and labored. The nurse put an oxygen mask over his face.

"There was an accident, Mrs. Takeda," the director began. "Your husband was shot by one of the guards. He was walking near the barbed wire fence and the soldier thought he was trying to escape."

"Escape? How could he? Where could he go? He was probably only looking for arrowheads!" Hana heard herself shouting at the director.

She looked now at the doctor. "Is he going to be all right?"

"His condition is critical, Mrs. Takeda."

"But can you save him?"

The doctor was young. His eyes filled with tears. "We're doing everything we can," he said.

Hana heard the director whisper to the doctor. "Are there relatives? Should someone be notified? Has the minister been called?"

The director put a hand on her shoulder. "The soldier said he called to him to halt. He said he aimed over his head. . . ." His voice drifted off, for Hana showed no sign of hearing him. She was not going to ease the soldier's guilt by saying she understood. "I'm so very sorry, Mrs. Takeda."

Hana was aware of nothing except that Taro lay dying. He was so still, he seemed already to be slipping away. She felt someone raise her gently to a chair and felt a hand touch her shoulder. It was Kenji Nishima.

He knelt beside Taro, and taking his hand, he prayed for him. He also prayed for Hana. Then he told her he would call Mary. "She will want to know and be here," he said gently. Hana simply nodded, allowing the decision to be made for her.

As the director and doctor left the room, the nurse whispered that she would be back shortly.

"Please take that thing off so he can talk to me," Hana begged. The nurse removed the oxygen mask.

At last, Hana was alone with Taro and the waiting presence of death. She prayed to the God whom Taro had taught her to love and trust.

"Taro . . . oh, Papa San. . ."

Hana held his hand in both of hers and watched his face, searching, waiting for a sign that he knew she was there. It seemed a long time before he finally opened his eyes, and when he looked at her, she understood that he knew everything.

"Hana," he whispered with supreme effort. "I'm sorry . . . I wanted to give you a better life."

Hana shook her head. "We had a fine life together, Papa San," she murmured. "Forgive me for all the times I hurt you."

Taro squeezed her hand slightly and closed his eyes.

Hana didn't know how long she sat there watching him, trying to find words to tell him how much he meant to her. The doctor and nurses came in and out, keeping a watchful eye on the feeble rhythms of Taro's life. And Kenji returned to pray with her, sustaining her with his love and concern.

"Your daughter is coming," he said quietly. "Sumiko is coming, too."

As the gray light of dawn slowly widened across the desert sky, Hana, her head still resting on Taro's hand, awakened with a start from a moment of sleep.

"Taro?" she called. "Papa?"

But at that moment, Taro died quietly and peacefully, without hearing her call to him.

Mary and Joe arrived the day after Taro's death, bringing little Laurie with them. "If only Papa could have seen her," Mary wept. "If only I had taken her to the station that night."

It was Hana who comforted her daughter. "Papa knows you have brought her to him now," she said. "Don't cry, Mary, your papa is at peace."

Hana sent three telegrams. One to Ellen Davis in California, one to Kiku Toda in Colorado, and one to Sojiro Kaneda in North Dakota. The answering wire from Kaneda was full of grief and shock. Ellen Davis sent loving words to embrace and console her. But there was no word from Kiku. Perhaps she was too overcome, Hana thought. Or perhaps she was not permitted to send a wire.

Taro Takeda was the first fatality of the Topaz Relocation Center, and the entire camp was infuriated by his senseless death. The maintenance men made a rough pine coffin for him, and the women of the church made lilies and roses and irises with crepe paper from the canteen. They shaped them into wreaths and bouquets on which they hung ribbons bearing Taro's name.

So many people came to the funeral that hundreds stood outside in the hot sun listening by loudspeaker to the words of Reverend Kenji Nishima. Sumiko had come, and sat next to Hana, giving her the support of another daughter.

"We gather here today in memory of Taro Takeda," Kenji began. "We deplore his needless death, but we can rejoice in the peace he finds now, far beyond the barbed wire that imprisoned him in life. He was a good Christian, a devoted husband, and a loving father. More than many who were born in this land, he loved America and what he believed it stood for."

Hana nodded as she listened. Taro would have liked what Kenji was saying about him. It was true, all true.

Yes, Taro, Hana thought, you were a good husband—steadfast and dependable—and you were good to me. You understood that I could not accept life in the quiet patient way you did.

"Mrs. Takeda." Sumiko was helping her to her feet. The service had ended. The mourners paid their respects. It was time to bury her husband.

Mary and Joe were horrified to learn that Taro was to be buried in the desert beyond the gate. "Must he be left out there all alone?" Mary asked.

Kenji told them there was no choice. "There is no room for a cemetery inside the gate," he explained, "and there will be others before it is all over."

"Never mind," Hana told her. "It's all right. Your papa had come to like the peace of the desert. He loved the sunsets and the great wide sky and the old treasures he found in the sand."

"Your mother is right," Kenji added. "Your father had come to terms with the life here better than most."

Hana nodded. "Better than most," she repeated.

A small wooden cross marked his grave in the desert, and the church women placed their crepe paper flowers around the cross. Their gaudy colors were vivid in the sun, seeming grotesque in the drabness of the surrounding desert. During the graveside service, the wind tore at the flowers, sending bits and pieces whirling into the desert to adorn the sagebrush and tumbleweed with the ornaments of death.

Mary, Joe, and Laurie stayed with Hana for three days. Laurie's innocent cheer touched her deeply, but through the dark days of numbing sorrow, it was Kenji who comforted her most. He had been through the darkest moments of life with her and knew her needs best. He made all the arrangements for the funeral and the memorial meeting that followed. He helped her fill out the papers and forms that were all the government wanted now of Taro's life.

Sumiko was there, too, going to the canteen for cookies and crackers, helping serve tea to the callers who came to pay their respects to Hana.

Through it all, Mary seemed dazed, an outsider, not knowing quite how to behave in the closeness of the Japanese American community. She did not know how to cope with death, nor did she feel the close kinship with the dead that the others felt from times past. She felt ill at ease among her mother's friends, and yet she admired their dignity and strength even in so desolate a place. She grieved bitterly, consumed with guilt, because she knew she had not been the daughter Taro hoped she would be. Each day Mary tried to persuade her mother to leave camp and return to Salt Lake City with them.

"They said you could leave if you had a place to go, Mama. And you do. Come home with us," she urged.

"We'd really like to have you," Joe added. "You shouldn't stay in this godforsaken place alone." He had been shocked to see the utter desolation of the concentration camp.

But Hana shook her head. "I can't leave Papa all alone in the desert," she said. "When the war is over, I'm going to take him home to Oakland where he and I both belong."

"I think that is what he would have wanted," Kenji agreed. "He would want to go home and be buried beside his son."

"I know," Hana said. "That is what I'm going to do. And I am going back to work so someday, one day, I can buy back Papa's shop." Hana straightened up, tilting her chin. "And if they ever let me, I'm going to become a citizen of this country just like Papa always wanted. I'm going to live the life he wanted, for both of us."

"Oh, Mama," Mary wept. "I've been such a miserable daughter to you and Papa."

Hana took her hand. "We must learn to forgive and to be forgiven, Mary. I had to learn that, too."

Joe saw Hana's strength and respected her resolve. "I understand what you want to do, Mrs. Takeda," he said. "We'll help you in any way we can."

"Thank you, Joe. Help Mary understand."

After they put Mary and Joe and Laurie on the bus returning to town, Kenji and Sumiko went with Hana to visit Taro's grave. A few crepe paper flowers still remained, but the wind had strewn the others across the face of the desert.

Hana knelt at the grave and brushed the wooden cross with her fingertips. "Ma Chan asked me to go home with her," she said softly, "but I'm staying here, Papa, until I can take you home."

They reached the gate to camp just as the incoming bus from Delta was arriving. Hana scarcely looked up, for only a few people were straggling from the bus.

"We'll walk you to your barrack," Kenji said.

Then they all heard the cry. It was shrill, like a child's call.

"Hana! Hana! Hana! I'm here!"

Hana turned, squinting into the sun. "Kiku? Is that you?"

Kiku rushed toward her with a suitcase in each hand. "I've come, Hana," she said, her face breaking into a broad grin. "I got a transfer to come live in Topaz."

"Oh, Kiku!" Hana hugged her friend, and they wept together. They wept for joy. They wept for Henry and for Taro.

"It's all right now, Kenji, Sumiko," Hana said brightly. "My friend has come. I'm going to be all right."

Kenji and Sumiko watched the two women go arm in arm toward the administration building, where Kiku would register as a new resident.

"It breaks my heart to think of leaving Mrs. Takeda here," Sumiko said slowly.

But Kenji told her not to worry. "They're strong, Sumiko, both of them. They each crossed an ocean alone to come to this country, and they're going to survive the future with the same strength and spirit. I know it."

They turned then, and began the long walk to Block Six. Sumiko looked back once more, shading her eyes. She saw Hana and Kiku deep in conversation as they walked down the dusty road. They did not even seem aware of the murky gathering of clouds in the sky or to feel the ominous gusts of the hot, trembling wind. They did not know that by the time they walked to Hana's barrack at the opposite end of camp, another dust storm would be coursing over the desert sands, enveloping all of Topaz in its white fury.

The Price You Pay

ELLEN WINTER

ELLEN WINTER, 33, grew up on the eastern shore of Maryland, a place as humid as the desert is dry. She received her BA in creative writing from Hampshire College, then came west to attend the University of Arizona MFA program in creative writing. "I hated the desert at first," she says. "Everything was either sharp, or poisonous, or it had been sitting in the sun so long it would burn you if you touched it." The harsh delicacy of the landscape grew on her, though, "because it's not unlike the characters I like best: tough and tender, full of contradiction." Ellen recently moved to Flagstaff, where she continues to write short stories and works at Bookman's Used Books. Her stories have appeared in a number of magazines, most recently Beloit Fiction Journal, Alligator Juniper, *and* Holland Cosmopolitan.

I'VE BARELY GOT MYSELF situated when he starts in. Tell me your story, he says, it's the price you pay. He glances over at me and the dog that sits between us looks at me too. You want a ride you gotta talk, he says.

He's not a clean-cut fellow and if I'd thought harder before I climbed in I might've slammed the door and let him keep going. But he was driving a Ford Falcon station wagon, brown as good rich dirt. Furthermore I'd been standing roadside for a half hour and I was tired of the way the hot wind pulled at my skirt.

I'm thinking, I say.

He's seen enough of me, so he turns back to the road. The little dog keeps its stare going, black nose jabbing at the air. It's brown and white with a bony head and paws the size of a cat's.

I look younger than I am and though I'm not a minor I can't prove it. My husband stole my driver's license when he figured out I was hitting the bars while he was at work. He took all my i.d. and I've got nothing on me that connects my face with a name. I can be anyone I want.

I tell him my name is Shane.

Funny name for a girl, he says. I can't tell whether he buys it.

I'm John Doe, he tells me.

I snort. You expect me to believe that? I say.

Believe what you want, he says.

The dog's name is Frito. His tail trembles when I say it so I guess that much is true. If I get a chance I'll yell John's name from a distance and see if he turns. I'll remember my own name, and his too. I think about the story I'm getting ready to tell. I want to seem tough, but I want him to feel a little sorry for me too. That'll keep him from taking off while I'm in the Ladies' like the last one did.

My husband hit me, I say. We'd only been married seven months when he started in. I'd show you the bruises but they're in personal places. Then I got pregnant. I didn't want him taking it out on the kid, so I stole his Visa and got an abortion. I threw away the first two statements. Then they started calling. I had to get away before he found out.

The pregnancy part's true, and the part about the abortion and the stolen card. But he never hit me. I threw a bread board once, and spilled coffee on purpose. But he never lifted a finger. He'd sit there like the pile of blubber he was, his brown eyes glistening. I actually thought he might *cry*. I don't know why you treat me the way you do, he'd say. His mouth would hang open a little, and his lips, too puffy and red for a man, would tremble.

That was in Kentucky, I say, making it seem like all this trouble is much further behind than it is. In truth I left this morning, and I've covered maybe fifty miles. I need this ride to last. I want a state line between me and home by sundown.

My husband is a Christian man, I say. He doesn't believe in birth control. He chopped my diaphragm in two on our honeymoon.

I still remember the way the pieces fell into the snow. We were staying in Snowflake, in his uncle's cabin. I'd left the diaphragm leaning against the hot faucet after taking it out and washing it. I was rocking in front of the fire when my husband came out of the bathroom.

What's this? he said, though it was clear by the look on his face he knew perfectly well.

I decided not to answer. He grabbed me by the upper arm and pulled me from the rocker. His fingers were long enough to reach around and meet with his thumb.

This sort of thing is for people who don't really love each other, he said. That's not us, is it?

What could I say? I shook my head. He pulled me outside, over by the chopping block. He put the diaphragm down, raised the axe high above his head. Then he brought it down, harder than he needed to. The diaphragm flew apart, neat half-circles coming to rest at a distance in the snow. The axe blade stayed where it was, caught in the wood of the chopping block.

John Doe takes out a cigarette and lights it. Seems to me a girl like you would be smart enough to get herself on the pill, he says between puffs. Frito leans toward me, away from the smoke.

Well, I say. I think about telling him I *am* on the pill, the people at the clinic made sure of that, but I decide to keep this news to myself. Fear of pregnancy might come in handy later. I crack my window and Frito sniffs the breeze. I will call you J.D. I announce.

WE TAKE 17 North out of Phoenix. I crane my neck, watching as the road to California passes over our heads.

Never said where you were headed so I figured you're just headed, J.D. says.

I was thinking west, I say. But north's all right, too.

Most people got a town in mind, J.D. tells me. Even if it's not true they tell themselves there's someone there they can look up.

I've been to California before, I say defensively. Like the whole state's waiting for me, practically holding its breath.

Fuck California, J.D. says. He pulls half of a submarine sandwich from under the seat, unwraps the white paper. The sub's a little worse for wear. Shreds of lettuce dangle from a withered end. J.D. takes a huge bite. Want some? he asks.

I shake my head no but he hands it to me anyway so I take a bite.

I was thinking Flagstaff tonight and we'll work from there, J.D. says. You sure it's not your pop you're running from? Trouble with the law I don't need.

Shit, I say, that old man wrote me off years ago. I pull my legs up under me and take a look at J.D. A piece of lettuce hangs from his overgrown beard. I'm wondering if he's taking a fancy to me. Men do, usually ones that like to play big brother. I'm a small woman and with my clear skin and wispy hair people sometimes take me for a child. Until they look me in the eye, that is.

We stop in Black Canyon City for gas and a couple of Cokes. Everyone we see knows everybody else; all of them sniff at us like we're something rotting in roadside grass. J.D. pays. I try to see how much money he has in his wallet but he holds his big arm in front of my face and I can't see a thing.

The highway climbs as we leave town and the station wagon, which held eighty on the flat, struggles at thirty-five. The temperature drops and I start to shiver. J.D. grabs a sweatshirt from the back and hands it to me. Like J.D., it smells of onions and smoke.

We stay in the slow lane with the RVs and semis and halves of double-wide trailers. We're surrounded by people prepared for anything, turtle-crawling beneath the weight of their shells. I have twenty-two dollars and a change of panties. When my husband gets home he'll figure I've gone for happy hour. He won't plan beyond what he's going to do to me when I get home. Last time, drunk as I was, he made me fry eggs for dinner. I haven't touched one since.

IT'S DARK by the time we get to Flagstaff and J.D. picks the motel with the brightest neon. I stay in the car while he checks in so we can get a cheaper rate. Frito lies across my lap. I'm already imagining the game of freeze-tag we'll play on the sheets tonight. But when J.D. opens the door the room has two beds, a double and a single. Someone's rolled the pillows in the bedspreads like tight little sausages.

Clean yourself up if you want to, J.D. says, so I do. I shut the bathroom door and lock it. It's not the first time I've been to a motel with a guy I hardly know. But in the past I always knew exactly why I was there. I come out dressed with my hair wrapped in a towel. My feet are bare.

Look at them teeny-tiny toes, J.D. says. He's lying on the double bed watching TV.

I sit on the little bed and pull on socks. J.D. heads for the bathroom. He leaves the door ajar and steam from his shower seeps into the room. He comes out bare-chested and I can't help but notice that he's not so bad. I halfway expect him to launch an attack but he doesn't.

Hungry? he asks.

I nod.

Let's go downtown and get us something to eat, he says.

What about Frito? I say.

Frito knows the rules, he says. We leave the lights on, and the TV in case Frito decides to watch.

He takes me to a place that's a diner up front and a bar in back. The good news is you can drink up front too, because that's where we end up sitting. We find our-selves a booth, and for the first time we really get to look at each other head on. He's got brown eyes, steadier than I expected. There are a few strands of gray in his beard.

Those eyes of yours sure are blue, he says. They're funny, he adds, and I know what he means. The rest of me looks about twelve, but my eyes are like a cracked sidewalk, worn by the weight of all that treading.

I hope you like Bud, he says, and he orders us a pitcher. I get the chicken and he gets meat loaf. Both of us get soupy string beans and rolls that are cool and smooth and doughy. We eat everything, including the crackers that come with our soup. We drink two pitchers of beer, and he tells me I do okay for a woman.

So what about your story, I say. I don't know a thing about you except your sup-posed name.

He plays with a bean, the last on his plate. Then he fixes me with a look so sad and direct it sends a shiver through me. I'm caught off guard. Everything between us so far has had a joking aspect to it.

You don't want to know about me, he says solemnly. No sirree Bob.

After that we go to a pool hall and J.D. wins a bunch of money off the locals. He gets me a beer every time he gets one for himself. He's twice as big as me and it's a struggle to keep up but I do. I expect him to start leaning on me when he comes over to deliver another bottle, but he keeps a polite distance. Most guys would be breath-ing down my neck by now. One of the locals makes a half-hearted pass, but J.D. doesn't seem to care. I find myself admiring his form as he leans over the table to shoot.

THE NEXT thing I know it's morning. The first thing I'm aware of is my throbbing head. Then I notice I'm pinned beneath something. I can't move an inch. For a second I think J.D. is lying on top of me. Then I realize most of the pressure is on my feet. I'm lying on my back with my arms bound close to my sides. I try to sit up but I can't.

I crack an eye. The motel room is filled with stale gray light that seeps through a gap between curtains. Craning my neck I see that Frito lies across my ankles. His skinny tail thumps when he catches me looking at him. J.D. must have laid me out like this, tucking the sheets tightly around my shoulders like an over-zealous mother.

I struggle to sit up. The room spins alarmingly. When things settle down I look over at the double bed where I figure J.D. will lie sleeping. The bed's empty. For a terrible second I think he's left me there. Then I remember Frito. The door to the bathroom's partway shut. It's a shame, too, because I need to use it.

I put on my shoes and J.D.'s sweatshirt. Then I head outside, leaving the door ajar so I can get back in. Behind the cinder block motel I hike my skirt. Frito has followed me and he makes use of the facilities too, cocking his leg over a tired-looking clump of grass. He finishes first, having put away less beer than I did last night.

As I make my way back to our room I can't help but admire the neat way the station wagon's parked by the door. Though I saw it for the first time only yesterday it's familiar to me in a way nothing else in this town is. A part of me's touched by the way its hind end sags, lower on the left side than the right, like a fat lady's riding behind the driver. A car like that doesn't have a spare, or if it does it won't have any air in it when you pull it out in an emergency. I've been riding in cars like that all my life.

Back in the room nothing has changed. The bathroom door's still three-quarters closed. Whatever J.D.'s doing in there's taking an awfully long time. I look around like someone who needs to gather her things. The fact is everything I've got is already on me. That's when I see J.D.'s keys nestled in front of the TV. They're attached to the kind of clip you'd see on the end of a dog's leash. A bent wedding band, sized for a woman's finger, is also fastened to the clip.

I don't plan this, I just cross the floor and reach for them. There are only two, and both look like they go to the Falcon. There's no house key. I take note of this, but I don't dwell on it.

Frito hops in when I open the station wagon, and I decide it's more trouble than it's worth to return him to the room. The Falcon won't be easy to start; there's probably some trick to it. I decide to treat it like my dad's old pickup, push the pedal to the floor once, turn the key, then three quick taps. It starts right up, the engine revving loud enough to shake a building.

The gear shift's on the column and I can't for the life of me figure out how to get the thing in first. While I'm struggling Frito's going nuts over something in the back seat. Finally I settle for second and the Falcon jerks across the lot, stalling twice before I get it on the road. All the while I'm expecting J.D. to come bounding after me, zipping his pants as he goes. A part of me almost feels sad when he doesn't.

We're stopped at the third red light in a row when I feel someone's hot breath on my neck. Must be hard to drive when you can't see over the dash, he says. He is just so pleased with himself. He bounces on the back seat like an out-of-control eight year old, hitting his head twice on the roof. Ow, he says cheerfully. Spurred by the excitement, Frito leaps back and forth over the seat, nails ripping at vinyl.

If there's one thing I hate it's being caught. I stomp the accelerator as we pull away from the light and the Falcon stalls, sending us all lurching. Want me to drive? J.D. asks sweetly. Neither of us is willing to get out of the car. He climbs over the seat. I have to crawl over him to switch sides. There's a point when I'm straddling him, my hands on either side of his shoulders, knees touching his thighs. Cars are honking as they pull around us but I don't care. It'd be nice if he'd at least look at me, but he just stares into the distance, eyeing the road ahead.

WE STOP in Tuba City for a late breakfast. Everyone else is Indian. I have never felt so white. All the way here J.D. has been going on and on. He can't get over it, the way I tried to steal his car. He calls me Shane now, as if I've earned use of the name. He says it again and again, and I almost tell him that my name's Sharon.

It turns out that my snoring was keeping him awake, so he decided to move to the car. That's where he usually sleeps anyway. Next thing I know I'm headed for Utah, he says. Shit, he adds. I'm the baddest woman he's ever known.

It'd be hard to take even if he wasn't so pleased about it. But J.D. is downright grateful. You and me got a lot in common, woman, he says as he polishes off a giant stack of pancakes.

Like what? I snarl. I've had a bunch of coffee and I'm starting to get agitated.

Neither of us knows where we're headed, but both of us got something we want to leave behind. His voice changes as he says this, a quaver coming into it like he's riding a washboard road on bad shocks. I glance up and he's got that look on his face again, eyes sad as Frito's when we told him he'd have to wait in the car.

What did *you* ever do? I say. I'm done eating and ready to get out of there.

You'd see me different if I told you, he says.

ALL DAY long we're buffeted by a hot wind. Things blow across the road: trash and tumbleweeds, reservation dogs so thin they're pushed sideways by the breeze. There are places where drifting sand covers the pavement. I imagine us losing our way and heading into the desert, bald tires slipping then burying themselves. My hot heels are braced against the dash. My husband with his crybaby face seems like a bad dream I had years ago. That he could be thinking of me now seems impossible.

I settle into my corner, leaning against the door though J.D. tells me not to. I'm feeling mean. The wind through our open windows has sucked the moisture from my eyes. I don't think I could ever cry again.

There's hardly any traffic. Every now and then we pass a pickup full of Indians who stare straight ahead like we're invisible. I wipe the sweat from the back of my neck and start in on him. Come on, J.D., tell me what you did that was so bad. What'd you do, steal someone's lunch in second grade? Bet you told everybody you fucked your high school sweetheart when you didn't. Shit, you probably never fucked anybody. Is that it, J.D.? You still a virgin?

He lights a cigarette with shaky hands and I snatch it from his mouth.

Girl, he says.

I take a long drag, put the cigarette back between his lips. Smoke streams from my nostrils.

You'll stunt your growth, he says, trying to be funny. His knuckles are white on the wheel.

I let my skirt ride up my thighs, move my hands up the bare skin that appears behind the sliding cloth. He keeps his eyes on the road but they narrow, squeezing out the sight of me. We filled a gallon jug with water when we left Tuba City and I've put away almost half of it. Better go easy on that, he says. I take another swig. And I keep it up, accusing him of dozens of small but humiliating crimes—everything from getting caught picking his nose to having special feelings for sheep. I tease, cajole, and demand. He tells me nothing.

The day stretches like old gum: stiff, chewy, and without much flavor. Everything around us glows white. Even the paint on the Falcon's hood seems to fade. With the wind blowing sideways and the heat waves rising there is motion all around us, yet we seem to be getting nowhere. Strange-shaped rocks rise before us on the desert floor, but they keep their distance. I lean over and check the speedometer. We're going thirty-five, and the needle on the temperature gauge is edging into red.

About ten minutes later the Falcon starts to shudder. We glide onto the sandy shoulder. The engine coughs twice, then dies. We sit in sudden stillness. Sun bores through the windshield, and droplets of water fall from the end of Frito's tongue. Then we all climb out and Frito turns quick circles. This is the best thing that's happened all day as far as he's concerned.

J.D. works at opening the hood, which is held shut with a twisted coat hanger. A hot wind pushes past us. There's not a tree in sight. The hood pops open and we stare at the oily engine. The radiator bubbles away, sending a smell heavy and sour-sweet as a drunk's breath into the dry air. There's nothing to do but wait.

J.D. walks away from me, out into the desert. At first I think he's going to take a leak, so I watch discreetly. But he just stands there slump-shouldered. The wind parts the hair on the back of his head. He's taking it hard. Men hate to be betrayed, especially by machines. I saw my husband lose it over a chain saw once. It wasn't pretty.

I walk over and put a hand on his shoulder. When he turns I give him the water jug. He wets his lips. My hand stays put. More honest than my smart mouth, it admits what I can't. There's surprise in J.D.'s eyes, and a caution. He kneels and my hand falls away. He fills his palm with water and Frito has a drink.

We end up sitting in the only shade there is—the Falcon's shadow. The car bubbles and ticks, then grows quiet. Its shadow swells, holding us more comfortably in its darkness. After a while J.D. uncaps the radiator, and we stare into its rusty depths. Way down deep a circle of light reflects back at us. She's pretty low, J.D. says. I can't help but think about all the water I put away.

We return to our places in car-shaped shade and wait for the sun to go down. Neither of us touches the water. My skin is dry and hot. I doze off and when I wake, J.D. wears the same expression. I deserve this, his fierce eyes say. He strokes Frito, who leans against him, humble and grateful. I'm alone in my half of the shade. I stare and stare, waiting for one of them to acknowledge me. When the sun balances on the edge of the earth, I get up and run into the desert. Holding my arms wide I spin in place until the ground rocks like a boat beneath me. I fall into the sand, which buffs a layer of skin from my knees.

You're a nutcase, J.D. says. Then he ambles over, offers me a hand.

WE'VE MADE it almost to a bench-shaped rock when the Falcon overheats again. By now the stars are out, but there's a faint glow behind us where the sun disappeared. J.D. tells me he'd like to get some shut-eye. He pulls a sleeping bag from the back of the wagon and heads away from the road. I follow. It's that or sit in the car. J.D. unzips the bag, spreads the whole thing flat on the sandy ground. He curls up facing an edge. You're welcome to join me, he says.

I sit cross-legged on the other side. The wind's still blowing and there's nothing to get in its way. It'll be cold here in an hour or so. I wait till J.D.'s sawing away. Then I lie down behind him, press myself against him while he sleeps.

Hours later I wake to find myself lying on his chest. His arms are around me. I'm hoping he pulled me here, that I didn't push myself beneath his hands like a sad but persistent dog. I snuggle in, and his arms tighten.

A shift in his breathing lets me know he's awake. I halfway expect him to shrug me off. Instead he finds my mouth with his. He kisses me gently, like someone who's been thinking about it for a while. The kiss is like the wind, it comes and goes in shivering gusts, darting here and there and teasing everything in its path. We are swept along by it, rolling and bouncing like a tumbleweed. But somewhere along the way I lose him; when I unfasten his pants and reach for him he's light in my hand.

I couldn't, he says, moving off me. You're so teeny-tiny I'd break you in two.

IN THE morning we're shifty-eyed. J.D. zips the bag back into a one-man pouch, then rolls it tightly. Frito tears around with a stick in his mouth. He's had breakfast, unlike the rest of us. The sun's still tucked beneath the horizon when we pull onto the road.

The way I figure it we got about fifty miles before we hit a service station, J.D. says. If we ride with the heat on she'll overheat once, maybe twice. We got about two cups of water. Go ahead and have yourself a swig. But remember, the sun'll be up soon.

I wet my chapped lips, give Frito a couple capfuls. I pass the jug to J.D. but he shakes his head. I don't want to spend a lot of time broke down on the side of the road, J.D. says. Here on the Rez it might be okay. But we don't need the Man stopping to ask a bunch of questions.

I nod.

J.D. pulls a bag of peanuts from under the seat and he feeds them to me one by one, flipping the shells out the window. A trail that will lead them to us, I think, though I know that the hot wind will scatter them in no time. As if anybody would actually look. My fat husband will miss me cooking his eggs, and the way I wiped the toothpaste from the bottom of the sink. But he won't come after me. It's much more satisfying to be sitting there wearing a look when I come dragging in.

If I was going to tell J.D. my story again I'd leave my husband out altogether. I like the idea of it: my past as flexible as my future. Three days ago I didn't know J.D. Three days from now I may be well on my way to forgetting him. Whether or not I'll tell the story we make remains to be seen.

The peanuts are making my mouth feel like a cement mixer, so I tell J.D. to stop. The sun rises in the middle of the road, squatting fat for a minute like someone summoning the energy to stand. Red light spills toward us and things glisten and gleam: Frito's moist nose, the Falcon's trim, the bent wedding band that dangles from the ignition. The heat's going full blast. You can tell by the smell that the engine's plenty warm.

I reach in front of Frito and touch the ring. There's a story to this, I say. There's nothing mean in my voice this time. It's just a statement of fact.

J.D. pats the pocket of his shirt, hoping for a cigarette. We finished them yesterday, crouched in the Falcon's shade. I'm sure there is, he says, staring straight ahead, but I don't know it. I found that thing in the parking lot of a Texas bar.

Yeah right *John Doe*, I say.

J.D. reaches for me, he takes ahold of the back of the neck and squeezes. It doesn't hurt, but it doesn't feel good, either. I told you girl, he says, tightening his grip, there are some things you don't want to know. He removes his hand, cracks a peanut with his teeth, and Frito snatches nuts from the air.

Leaning into my corner I know that there really is a story, and sure as I know the

Falcon will overheat again within the hour I know that I'll hear it, whether I want to or not. Until then the space the story will one day fill will hang between us. Like the desert around us its emptiness will make me want to shout, as if I could convince myself of anything by making my voice louder than the wind.

A little while later J.D. apologizes. I'll buy you a beer at the first establishment we see, he says.

By ten o'clock we're on fire. The Falcon's overheated twice. The water's gone and Frito's panting. The only thing hotter than the desert air is the heat that blasts from the Falcon's vents. It's the kind of heat that makes you want to throw yourself at someone's feet and beg for mercy, whether or not you've done anything wrong. And then it comes, moving toward us on the side of the road like something too good to believe: a yellow sign with a + on it. We're coming to an intersection.

When we get there the news is even better. Mac's Mini-Mart and Gas on the right, Brenda's Dogs and More on the left. We fill up on everything: gas, oil, and anti-freeze. We pour a package of something that looks a lot like dirt into the radiator. It's called Stop Leak, and when the engine gets hot it will melt and magically seal our leaks.

We eat a dog apiece, fill our jug with water and buy another. Then I go to the Ladies', and when I come out I'm happy to see that Frito and J.D. are still there. The Falcon's doors are spread wide like wings it's forgotten how to use. As I walk across blacktop the hot wind does a Marilyn Monroe with my skirt, and the guys at the pumps get a pretty good look at what I've got.

You coming? J.D. asks. He's seen, too, but there's nothing in his voice to give him away. His couldn't-care-less look is almost as convincing as mine. But way down deep in my stomach, mixed in with the peanuts and the hot dog and the water I drank too much of too fast, is something small and glittering, knocked out of round. I've swallowed it whole, my fear of what he's done, or what he could do.

Frito leaps from the passenger side and zips between us, punctuating the skidding stop at each end of his route with a sharp bark. I'm going, I know that. I like the way the Falcon pulls the road beneath it, spitting it out behind like tangled ribbon.

I climb in and we keep headed the way we're headed. Later that day, when J.D. and I are well into our second pitcher at the Lazy J Saloon, he takes my hand. I bet you're a dancer, he says, hitting on a truth about me.

PRESENCE

News from the Volcano

GLADYS SWAN

GLADYS SWAN, 61, grew up in New Mexico, the part of the Southwest in which many of her characters find themselves. "I've been looking for a territory of the mind where one might go in this era of the displaced person," she says, "when one can no longer bank on what held meaning in the past: spiritual certainty, a common culture, a sense of community, the structure of family." She has authored three collections of short stories (most recently A Visit to Strangers, 1996) and two novels and has received a fellowship from the Lilly Endowment, two Fulbright Fellowships—to former Yugoslavia and Romania—and the 1994 Lawrence Foundation Award. She teaches literature and creative writing at the University of Missouri, Columbia, and is on the faculty of the MFA Program in Writing at Vermont College.

RISING UP FROM LAND flat as sheet metal, the rock, sheer and huge, unprecedented, is a ship moving across the desert, its dark shape bearing straightaway, wherever it is headed, not to be put off course. Eons ago it rose towering above the land, lava overflowing from the molten core. Now the core is all that remains, the rest worn away by all that time can do. Only the core—a relic of ancient catastrophes, before any were present to know what they might mean. Hardened now and silent.

But now and then the moon rises blue in the dust of ancient memory. A haze of particles hanging suspended in the air, as though from that time when the volcano erupted. Who knows how they've gathered or where they came from? They gather above the rock, above the desert, above the occasions of earth below, as though reminded by the original disturbances of the air. So I see it now, as the moon rises three-quarters full. And with a light that comes from somehow beyond it.

It sends its bluish haze over a huddle of adobe houses, from which the small lights float in the surrounding indigo, and the smells of chili and beans and fry meat mingle with the evening chill. The light touches on the headlights of the trucks parked alongside, as though they were closed lids, gives a sheen to their metal casings and leaves the land beyond a dark sea. Prickly pear and yucca, ocotillo and scrub cedar raise dark silhouettes from darker pools. Along the road cars are moving, and among them is a stranger moving this way. He moves the way a shark moves toward a school of fish, a dark rush in the direction of the unwary.

Up the road a neon sign sets its glare against the landscape: a gas station–grocery–cafe, still open. Many times I have gone past, watched the customers enter and leave. Sometimes I've taken my loaf of bread and left change on the counter. Lupe I know from hearsay, for she does not speak much, at least to me. Perhaps she feels my gaze upon her and draws away, not wanting anyone to know too much. But I cannot get enough of certain faces, wanting to know what has shaped them. I only know I must not look too long. There is something frightening in too close a scrutiny. I keep close to myself and see things as they come.

Tonight Lupe sits inside as she usually does, on a stool behind the counter, waiting for Lorenzo to return to help her close up. He'd left her alone all that afternoon, away on some errand. He may have driven all the way to Gallup—he does that sometimes. She had already cleaned the grill and wiped the counter, totaled up the day's receipts. Whatever came in now belonged to tomorrow—it is good to begin the day with something.

A truck pulled in, three boys in front, two more sprawled out in the bed. Lupe knew the truck—Manuel's. They were headed to the dance in Farmington. She could hear them outside. "No, man, you're drunk already." "Look with your eyes, man." "It's the Russians—they've set something off." "Why them?—maybe it's us." "You're crazy, man. We'd have heard it." "It's from outer space. A spaceship—a huge one." "Not that big—don't you know any science?" "I know the moon when I see it—only that's different." "I want another beer."

It was a game, of course. But there was a difference in the cast of things. They could tell as they stood in front of the truck, looking at the sky. They broke their pose just as Lupe reached them. "See, look how strange it is," they showed her. And she stood with them, her arms hugging her shoulders over her thin blouse. She'd never seen the moon like that. Just now a plume of cloud fanned its surface, trailing across like a scarf. Splotches of light and shadow lay over the dark vegetation.

A different moon. Where had it come from and what did it mark? Perhaps it was a sign if she only knew what it meant. That is always the way—it could be this or that. Her grandmother had been one to know. She could read the world like a map of secret journeys—there are some who can do that, who seem to be born knowing. She could enter certain moments like a doorway and see what pulsed beneath, even if she could not tell the exact shape of what was coming. She could tell people where sickness came from, the violence in the flesh, and if an ill wind was blowing. It was something. Though perhaps not enough—perhaps it is never enough. One keeps looking for news; perhaps that's why I stare so at the things around me, waiting for them to speak.

Lupe's grandmother was dead now. Lupe had seen her lying at the threshold of her hut, left behind by the soldiers who carried off her chickens. They laughed as they caught the squawking birds. And the one who struck her down, who can tell? Or the others they left, scattered in the postures in which they had closed with death, set upon with the marks of whatever impulse or intention had overtaken them. Rumor caught these things and breathed them on the wind. But the soldiers had disappeared as they had come.

Lupe turned to go inside, and Manuel followed her in to pay for gas. It was his truck, he'd bought it used and took jobs hauling. He had a sister and a mother to support. Though he wanted to go off on his own, down to Albuquerque to look for work and perhaps for a certain freedom, he didn't stray, not even for better wages. Lupe liked him—he was older than his friends, held something in his face she could trust. "You going to the dance?" he asked her.

She gave a shrug. She didn't know, Lorenzo was so late in coming.

"We could wait," he said. "You could ride with us—in front."

She'd have liked to go with them. But she didn't like to leave when Lorenzo wasn't there. "I'd better stay," she said.

"I could come back," he said. He wanted her to go. "Unless," he said, "you have someone else."

"No, there's no one else."

Very likely it was Willie he meant. Willie was always asking her to go with him. He had a motorcycle and liked to roar down the highway with a girl at his back holding on with her arms around his waist. I've seen him many times, getting in his brags, you might say. There'd been a number of girls eager for the thrill, but Lupe was the one he wanted. It was easy to tell by the way he looked at her, as though he were trying to take her with his eyes. And she'd never sent a glance in his direction, was never lured by his roaring down the road.

He was trying to make a special link between them: They knew more than the others. They were above doing what the spoilers had done. He had found Indian somewhere in his blood, past the blue eyes and white skin that had corrupted the original purity, and he'd come west to find it. He brought his camera with him, and his power lay in that. He took pictures of road kill—that's what the hunter's skill had come to. Having left the buffalo to die by thousands, this was what civilization had brought—dead creatures in the road, and the effete beef steak. He took pictures of junked cars and litter and dumps and faces from which every dream had fled. Warnings and reminders.

There is always laughter in his eyes, when he turns his glance on Lupe, though when I've passed him I've caught something cold and sharp that goes right through and doesn't disappear. And he turns away as though he's already revealed too much. I too draw back. I have no wish to meddle. There is always something back of his expression when he's flirting with the girls, taking in their measure, taking the square root, storing things away for the next time—quite beyond them that perhaps he doesn't see himself. But his attraction works like a scent drawing to him all that might speak to his contempt.

Perhaps Manuel was relieved to know he didn't have a rival, for Willie was always asking her to go. "Maybe you'll come later," he said, taking up his beer and the change. "Save a dance for me." And he gave her a smile that she held on to after he had gone.

The truck started up, moved out onto the highway, and was gone. It was quiet now but for the refrigerator making cold, and the buzzing of the fluorescent lights inside taking the beer cans into their glare. She doubted she would go to the dance: Lorenzo would be too tired.

Once or twice a month he took her: She knew it was for her sake. He'd come through the door around closing time and say, "Let's go have some fun," and they'd climb into his pickup and go to join the crowd. Lorenzo didn't dance himself but stood on the edge among the spectators, drinking a beer and talking intently to whomever might be standing next to him, man or woman—he knew everybody. But he always kept an eye out for what was happening on the dance floor. If things started to get rowdy, Lupe had only to look for his nod, and they would leave. There were always those who hung around the edge, usually outside passing around a bottle, sometimes hooting and laughing, hoping for a fight. It was a question of whether they'd get bored and go off to further adventure or start something there. More than once the sirens came shrieking down the road, and someone got carted off to the hospital. Lorenzo kept a sharp eye in his head.

Lorenzo had had a wife once, but she'd run off to Denver with another man. Her lover had disappeared long since, and others had followed. But somehow she'd remained in Lorenzo's life, even though she never came back. If he went to see her, he never said. She called him at least once a month and told him her latest round of troubles and asked for his advice, and sometimes money. For a time he'd given her both, but the money blew away like scraps the wind had brought and would, as far as she was concerned, bring again. Now he gave neither but listened to her stories. From time to time, he was with a woman. Now he had no one, though there were women who'd have been glad to have him. He was a generous man, who liked people around him, but who kept back a certain melancholy he never imposed on anyone. People liked him.

A restless mood came over Lupe. The night was growing too long, and the lights were not strong enough to keep certain shapes from invading from the darkness outside, nor the cans of beer and the packages of snacks and loaves of bread solid enough to keep her solidly among them. She got these moods. And you could watch her struggle against them. I can remember when her look spoke only of this.

When they had first arrived, she and her mother, it felt strange to her to stop moving. She felt the moving still in her body, and a danger of falling over if she stopped. It was strange not to see one landscape shifting into another, whether they were on foot or in the waddling buses. She could not believe that if she closed her eyes the same objects would be standing in front of her when she opened them again or that she would wake in the same bed in the same room, the mountains beyond the window still solidly standing, and Lorenzo's place down the road.

She refused to go to school—they had to bring her home. She wouldn't be separated from her mother, though in many ways she was no longer a child. When the two of them came into the store, Lorenzo gave her sweets. When her mother sank into the drunken stupor that lay at the end of her pursuit of safety and could no longer take care of her, Lorenzo gave her credit. And when her mother went off with the man who took her by the hand and led her to his car, Lorenzo took Lupe in and taught her to make change and add figures and how to brew the coffee and cook hamburgers. She had finished growing up there.

The other girls envied her. Like one chosen, she had been given a place where she could earn her own money and put it in the bank. She had a future. She could go where she pleased, though she seldom left her place behind the grill or the cash register. She could lead her own life and didn't need a man if she didn't want one. She sensed their eye on her, their gaze as sharp as desire. But what was there to envy? The dark rush of her dreams? Sometimes she dreamed of animals devouring one another that lived like a menace just under the surface. She'd crossed boundaries where she'd had no wish to go, and who would care to follow? For she'd had experience, and no one could wipe it away. And what was there to be done with it?

She heard a car door slam and hoped it wasn't Willie come to lean over the counter to try to lure her in his direction. She had no idea why he continued to pursue her. Lorenzo never spoke to him. She was always pressed back by the tightness of a face that seemed to close behind some secret scorn, while his eye let nothing escape his notice. Then, unexpectedly, his face would break into a grin and he would tell her a joke, a bit of gossip he'd been saving up: who Manuel was sleeping with and which of the boys liked Lupe. He had something to tease everyone with, those he wanted to get the better of. He tried to tease her about Manuel, but she never blinked an eye.

He never had enough to do, it seemed. He was always around. Sometimes he showed off the photographs he took of mountains and desert plants to sell to tourists. Compliments made him smirk. There were times she saw Willie every day. He'd come in and pull down a loaf of bread, a can of soup, a jar of peanut butter, as if eating were a matter of indifference to him, slap some bills down on the counter and leave without a word, sometimes without his change. Or he might come in for beer and disappear for days on end. He'd be off in his room, chain-smoking, his music turned up loud so he wouldn't have to listen to the noise of cars. Sometimes he slept all day and went prowling out at night. Sometimes he stayed drunk until he felt like being sober.

But it wasn't Willie come to pass the time. It was a stranger. He stood with his back to her as he filled his gas tank, then replaced the hose and came inside: a tall man with a ponytail pulled back from a narrow, bearded, hawk-nosed face. He closed the door and surveyed his surroundings as though to take a reckoning. She caught the restless glitter of his eyes, a film of weariness over something leaden and driven.

He did not offer to pay but placed himself on a stool at the counter. The lights were off in the kitchen; it was too late for food, but Lupe did not tell him so.

"What do you have to eat?" he wanted to know.

"Omelette," she said, "or a sandwich. Ham or cheese."

He considered the choices as though they were the only things he'd ever be tempted to eat.

"Till tomorrow morning," she explained.

"I could be lying half-starved on the slope of Pike's Peak by then."

She didn't deny it. One could be anywhere, without so much as a piece of bread. He wanted an omelette with ham and cheese and coffee—lots of coffee. She put a pot on the Silex in front and went back into the kitchen to beat up the eggs, take out the cartons with the ham and cheese. She watched him while she worked. He drummed impatiently on the counter, glanced in her direction when any noise came from the kitchen. He took out a cigarette, lit it, took a long, deep drag and let the smoke out slowly. He set it in the ashtray and left it. She saw him reach toward his belt, draw a hunting knife from its sheath and lay it on the counter. She hadn't seen it under his jacket. It had what looked to be a bone handle with dark streaks, perhaps a design carved into it.

He gazed at it for a moment, then took it up, ran his thumb across the blade in a way that suggested that he wanted her to take notice. He glanced in her direction, but she'd felt his attention coming and had ducked away in time. This was something she had no business with, she knew it under her skin, but it would be hard to keep away from it. He turned the knife over in his hand, familiarly, as though he'd gotten it as a bargain and he could take pride in whatever the knife might bring him. A certain energy pulsed out of his weariness as he turned the knife back and forth cutting the light into metallic slices.

She didn't want to look at it, the way it cut the light, the restlessness of it in his hand, as though straining in the direction of what it had been shaped to do. It knew killing. Lupe saw at once. The knife had killed someone. It had leapt into the place where killing was and caught the secret scent. Who knew how it had happened? But it was glutted now with what it knew, even if it had blundered into that space, been caught blindly or risen up and driven forward in a flash. The man was hectic with the consequences, but he could not get rid of the knife. It was joined to him now like his flesh.

He set the knife down, then pushed it to one side when she brought him his food. This gesture was for her benefit, she was no fool—to show her it was subject to him. She asked him if he wanted ketchup, then came with his coffee. She wondered why he hadn't threatened her before, hadn't robbed the store of what he wanted and gone on his way. There was food enough to cram into his maw. The threat itself was enough to get him whatever he wanted.

But maybe he wanted to be reminded of something, the smell of cooking in the air, the aroma of coffee. She filled his cup. His hand trembled as he took the mug, raised it to his lips. A bit spilled over the edge. It was the knife—it had him in its power and wouldn't leave him alone. The knife had no interest but itself.

Every now and then he paused, his fork poised as though he were listening, perhaps for something that pursued him or something that had momentarily stopped, as though a buzz had been set ringing in his ears that wouldn't shut off. Till he was weary of it, sick to death of it. She could see how he was trying to push it away, rid himself of it as he tried to eat, as he tried to chew his food back into savor and to warm himself with coffee. He craved the ordinary and was working to get food to his stomach before it gagged him and turned to sawdust.

She breathed sharply. The knife was greedy too, as it strained against its moorings. It would spare nothing. In the fullness of its impulse it was trying to get her to form the image of her death, make it coalesce before her eyes. It wanted her to reach toward a source of terror, where its power lay. If she tried to run away, it threatened to pursue her. Not because of anything she would do, but because she was there and had seen it. It wanted her powerlessness. If Lorenzo wandered in, heedlessly, it could rise up against him. He could walk right into it. She saw that and stepped into uncertainty.

She put herself back into what she knew, those nights when the countryside had turned into the shadows of fleeing forms. They were all joined together in the shadows, pursued and pursuer, having shed everything but the one impulse that bound them. It lay at the bottom of the world. Out of it she could imagine her death. The absence of herself standing there—that was her death. It formed a space of stillness. The part of herself she was most familiar with would die. And whatever it was that lay behind it—that would leave her too. But she let go of that. She would not give it to him. It did not belong to him. Though she was looking at him, she seemed not to see him at all.

When he'd stopped eating and made a swipe with his napkin across the last of his food, he stood up and took his knife. "I'm finished now," he announced. "You can open up that drawer and give me what's in it."

"I'll give you nothing," she said. "You'll have to pay."

He looked at her like a snake risen in his path.

She did not let go. Neither did she pretend to innocence. She had passed beyond that long ago. She looked directly into his eyes with the knowledge of what he had done. "You have to pay," she insisted. "You've eaten, you've filled your car with gas. Now you have to pay."

She had no pity and asked for none. The knife had no pity. It was looking to make an excuse of her weakness, to bury itself in that. But she had let go of her life— it did not matter.

"I have no money," he said, as though it were a joke. "When you have this, you don't need money."

She stood there like a wall: He could kill her if he wanted.

He didn't move. Perhaps he caught a sense of what she knew and how the space between them joined them now. She was no accomplice. Or perhaps it was her voice that struck him, twisted inside him. It had found him out, gone to the bone. That can happen—I have seen it. It made him want to let go of all he knew, as if there were a moment in which both of them might rise above their images to something else. Everything wavered in that effort, that possibility. Then in a sudden movement he flung down the knife, reeled as though it had taken all his effort, and threw himself out the door. He stumbled and nearly fell before he reached the car.

Lupe did not move. For a long moment she seemed to stand outside her body. The knife had put her there, and now it was lying on the floor. She would not look at it. Dizzily she sat down, trying to regain herself. She tried to call to mind whom she'd seen that day, who had come for gas, for food.

She did not notice when the door opened again. And when Willie came up behind her, he startled her.

"You falling asleep?" he said with a teasing laugh. "Who's the guy who left—friend of yours?"

"I never saw him before."

Nothing to make a difference. "I thought you'd be closed up now. Why hang around? Let's go to the dance."

"No," she said. "Not tonight." She wanted to pull the grin off his face like a mask.

"You always dance with me. Just to tease, I bet."

"I dance with everybody."

"You don't trust me."

She shrugged. "Lorenzo would take me, but he's not back. I won't go till he comes."

"He's not your father—he doesn't own you," he said meanly. "What's he saving you for—himself? The big man." His foot struck against the knife. He bent down for it.

"Don't pick it up," she warned him.

"Why not?" He stood up with it.

"It isn't yours," she said. He turned it in his hand, watching her as he fingered the blade. "It's a good knife," he said. "You don't find one lying around like that every day. Finders, keepers."

"Fool," she said, turning away as he toyed with it.

"I've always wanted a knife like this."

She tried to ignore him.

"Look. Go with me," he insisted.

And if she went with him . . .

"Or you'll be sorry." Willie turned away, as though the threat would hold force without him, and strode out the door.

Now he had the knife. He would go where it took him. She would be sorry, he'd promised her that, when he turned again in her direction. He was asking her again to reach into the fear that filled the space the knife was ready to make. To live in that darkness. If she looked into the space, would she see only the blank tearing of flesh, the deep wounding that asks for revenge, the endless chain? What was to be saved, and what would save her? She stood for a moment as though waiting for news, for something else beyond her to come to speech, if it were there to speak. That was the question, the one that takes us to the depths, nailed by the moment, as though to listen for our lives. She could hear, she could almost see a great struggle roaring in the dark on the verge of some upheaval. She expected it to appear in front of her, but when she ran outside, into a brisk wind that was raising up the dust, the road was empty. The moon was still rising.

Indian Education

LINDA VOZAR SWEET

LINDA VOZAR SWEET, 42, fled adolescence and long eastern winters by moving to New Mexico to attend college. "I knew no one in my family would follow me there—no water, no trees, too far away. 'Mexico! You're moving to Mexico!' they said when I told them." For the past fourteen years, she has lived in Jemez Springs, where she makes her living as a studio potter who also writes. Her fiction has appeared in North American Review, Onion River Review, *and* Short Fiction by Women; *her nonfiction has been published in* New Mexico Magazine, Ceramics Monthly, *and* The Writing Self; *and she has sold her pottery in art shows around the Southwest. She lives with her husband, Roger, and son, Adam.*

DIEGO WAS NOT A healthy man. His face was purple, as if he was strangled by his own breath, and when he lowered his head to write I could see that beneath his shiny black hair, his scalp was purple, too. He was my student. I knew the sound of his light footsteps against the trailer floor, his youthful body as he settled into the chair. His black eyes were lively, full of vitality. Sometimes they would land on my breasts for a few seconds, and then he would gaze up, unthreateningly, into my eyes. It was a small pleasure, a little private moment between us.

Weeks earlier Diego had written about himself: *I'm an 11th grade drop-out from the hippie days. The army took me for two years. I had a chance to get a high school diploma but I just didn't care. Alcohol was my problem. I took the GED and they gave me money for college. Maybe one day I'll get a degree. I have been sober for many years now.*

Diego was the only man left in a family of women. His brother had died in Vietnam, his father of alcoholism. When Diego did not stop drinking, his wife left him. Now he lived with his two sisters and his mother in the center of the village, and he stayed home to keep the family together. "I am the glue," he said slowly, with dignity. The women in his family leaned on him. They had great hope for his success and called him the Scholar. He'd won a scholarship to attend college, but after his father and brother died, he dropped out.

Esther the Boss appointed Diego as my assistant. He only had energy for writing, and that made me trust him. I told him I was a writer, too. "What do you write?" he asked.

"I'm writing a novel about Vermont."

Diego nodded his purple head. "Vermont. Where it's cold."

I nodded, "That's why I left. Kind of."

"I'll have to read your novel," he said.

"I'd like that."

He was quiet then. When I said that one day he'd be teaching this class, he shook his head and said, "Only Anglos teach English here."

Esther had pale gray skin covered with freckles, and gray hair, short and choppy. When she invited me to dinner, I was happy to accept an invitation anywhere. I imagined we might become friends. She could teach me a lot. A Pueblo man had married her, and they lived by the school in new government housing. But Esther's house was any house in suburbia. I parked along the curb and walked up the paved driveway. I stood on the welcome mat and rang the doorbell. She served beans and chile, baked chicken, store-bought tortillas, a salad and bottled dressing. Her husband, Jimmy, was at a tribal council meeting and didn't eat with us. That disappointed me. I'd wanted to see their marriage up close.

Over dinner she spoke low, as if someone might be listening. "You have to work the system. It's a numbers game. The state won't fund us if we don't have the numbers."

"Numbers?" I said. Esther had promised me many classes, but she'd delivered only one. How could I think numbers with so few students? "What about homework?"

"You can always try, but they might not come back. Think numbers. One way or the other it always comes down to that. If they come to class once, that counts."

"What if they don't come back?"

"It counts. We can't expect much. I'm trying to recruit more students. I've got some things going—letters, phone calls to relatives. It's hard. I'll try my best, okay?

That's all I can say."

I knew I must not ask questions. Questions made me suspect. "I'll try, too," I said, but I didn't know what I meant by that. We ate Fudgesicles as Esther loaded the dishwasher, and then I left.

ENROLLMENT FOR the Wednesday evening class started out at seven, then dwindled to three. Sometimes only Diego came. As long as he showed up, I had a class. He must have felt my great relief because he always came, week after week, often the only one. I was becoming dependent on him. Just like his sisters and mother.

I am the glue, he'd said.

"We're up to forty," Esther told me, logging numbers in her book.

What if no one came to class? The possibility of sitting across from a sea of empty chairs with my stack of unopened composition books made me feel hopeless. I didn't want to end up back in Vermont or Pennsylvania.

I'd fled Vermont because I hadn't been living my own life; I'd been living my fiancé's life. He'd entered dental school in Pennsylvania, and I knew if I followed him I'd become a dentist's wife and nothing would ever happen to me. I wanted to be a writer. He laughed at me when I said that, throwing back his head and showing his perfect white teeth. "You? A writer? What have you got to write about?"

Now I'd been in New Mexico eight weeks. It was not green with grass; it was not neat and tidy with front yards and flower beds and white porch swings. All the big cottonwoods were growing far away along the banks of a river I could not see. I had strained my eyes looking for this river, but I could not see it. The locals ate green and red chile stew, a food I couldn't put to my lips. People owned pickup trucks, dogs, horses, cattle. They wore cowboy hats. I was free of my old life, but I was lonely, too. Where had I come?

I spent most of my time holed up in a tiny rental, working on my novel, or reading, or watching videos. I lived off my savings. The only people I knew were Diego, a few students, and Esther.

One day Esther rushed in from Santa Fe wearing a rust-colored pant suit—her conference clothes. Darting in and out of the trailer, she hauled in workbooks stamped *Indian Education*. She was frazzled and flustered, talking enrollment and meetings. She went to many meetings.

"How was the conference in Santa Fe?" I asked.

"A conference in Santa Fe?" She drew back her shoulders and blinked her eyes.

"Weren't you at a conference in Santa Fe?"

I was still asking too many questions. Lurking in the back of my mind was the fear that she could fire me at any time. I gave her a vague look, as if I were the stupid one, and then I shut up. Acting stupid around Esther was what bugged me the most about working for her.

Diego looked up from his writing. He was on to Esther's ways long before I'd arrived at the school, and he smiled at me as if we formed a conspiracy. Then he lowered his eyes and went back to his work.

Another student, Sammy, came into the trailer and spoke to Diego in Tewa. Sammy sat down in an orange plastic chair across from Diego and began to turn the pages of *Sports Illustrated*. I looked at the blackboard in the front of the class where I had written five grammatically incorrect sentences in yellow chalk. I was glad to see Sammy. I counted heads as if twenty students sat there.

"Hello, Sammy. How are you?" I asked.

He said hello quietly and went back to his magazine. Sammy had dark sleepy eyes and long legs. There was a pencil stuck behind his ear, but he hated writing. During class I gave him practice tests for the GED exam, but he was not too keen on test-taking. He usually fell asleep in the middle of them.

Suddenly Esther came in and talked out loud to no one. "It came parcel post, but it doesn't belong to me."

Then she said something important. "Agatha should be here tonight. I saw her today—she's coming to class. She promised. I haven't had time to recruit. They have a lot of doings at the pueblo so I can't follow up on people." Under her breath she was frantically counting papers, and then, to my relief, she fled out the brown metal door and didn't come back for the rest of the evening.

Agatha would make three tonight.

I worked with Sammy on the blackboard. He seemed interested so long as I was making the sentence corrections with him, but after he worked alone for a few minutes, I would lose him. He went back to *Sports Illustrated*.

Diego shuffled papers and showed me what he'd written. Nearly all his writing concerned his drinking days, and tonight, as usual, he wrote interesting stuff: *I started drinking when I was about 13 years old. First we would go buy gas for my grandfather's '52 pickup, and beer and wine for my uncle. Then we would start drinking. One day my uncle asked me if I would like a can of Hamm's. I was scared at first, then I tried it. The beer went tickling down my throat. Boy, that beer tasted good. It was just great. My uncle drank more wine and he got smarter and smarter. He started talking about stunt driving. I told him not to try it because if he did, my grandfather's fender would fall off. Early the next morning I saw my grandfather fastening the fender with bailing wire.*

I used to watch my uncle hide his beer and wine under the wood pile. I was about 15 years old. I'd go steal my uncle's booze and invite my buddy over. We'd have a party at the corral. Late at night we'd disturb the peace. We had sling shots and we shot at dogs. We knocked over outhouses. We got into fights. Sometimes I'd wake up in jail.

Finally one day I quit. How much of my life have I wasted?

"This is good stuff," I told him. "You should write a book about your life."

"'Who would read it?' he asked."

"Me."

I picked up the book I'd brought with me that evening, *The Names*, by N. Scott Momaday, which I'd dug out from the bottom of my suitcase. I wanted Agatha to hear this, but she had not come to class, and I'd waited up to now for her to show.

"I want to read something to you. It's about this place." I began to read out loud. Momaday wrote all about the pueblo—the narrow streets, the plaza, the secret dances, the men on horseback, the grisly "chicken pull," the day school that burned to the ground. They listened in disbelief, stunned that someone had written about their village. The descriptions stunned me, too.

MY LANDLORD was just someone I waved to as I drove down the narrow dirt road to my house. My other neighbor went to Alaska every year to make his money; he was gone now. A cow roamed the yard eating brown grass, and at night under the floor of the house the skunks made a terrible racket. There was running water and the outhouse didn't smell too bad. My suitcase remained only partially unpacked.

I bought groceries at Toya's Mercantile and the Circle K, and when those places were closed the Giant Gas Station was open twenty-four hours. I rented videos at Red Rock Video—a double-wide trailer that overlooked a field of chiles. I ate iceberg lettuce and frozen pizza and Coke and chips, and I got into a bad cycle of driving to the Chile Bowl Cafe every night and eating homemade ice cream. After a few weeks the Chile Bowl turned into a beauty parlor. By November it was a cafe again. I kept looking for hairs in my food and had to stop eating there.

Sometimes in the long light of sunset I would walk outside my house and watch the hard, dry ground change color under my feet. It would turn blue and pink, orange and lavender. A barbed-wire fence ran across my back yard, and looking across it, I could see an endless horizon of Indian land.

The pueblo sat in a dusty brown bowl. Off in the distance the earth rose into steep bluffs of red and gray and white mesas. I thought of them as the Lasagna Range because of how the land was layered, one color on top of another. I would look at that range of mountains and think: *English is the white layer.* It didn't blend in too well. To the north was a group of brilliant flat-topped red rocks, the brightest rocks I'd ever seen, and in the fields all around the village were acres of corn and chile growing against a clear blue sky.

I drove carefully in the pueblo traffic—loose cattle and unbridled horses on the road, children riding bicycles along the sandy shoulder, and short brown men hitch-hiking into town. Everything that wasn't moving in the wide open space seemed very still and full of belonging. Every field, every fence post, every piece of firewood belonged to this place. Even the mobile classroom, which someone had backed into and creased like tinfoil, turned a rosy beige in the autumn sunset. I heard a voice that was not purely mine, but came from inside me, say, Pay attention to all this.

On Wednesday I drove to the pueblo with my stack of books. I sat in my car, staring at the soft dirt, fine as bath powder. I wanted to walk through that dirt in bare feet and have it settle lightly over my skin the way it settled over the feet of the dancers on Feast Day. That dusty Indian dance had looked unexpectedly good to me. I listened to the radio and waited after watching the wide empty ditch and the round faces of children playing in the yard next door and the dent in the trailer.

When Diego arrived, he sat in *his* car, listening to the radio and waiting. We nodded hello, one succinct nod, and after a little while I got out of my car and went inside the trailer. That nod was the real beginning of class.

It was late autumn, but the air inside the trailer was hot and stuffy as summer. Sammy showed up a few minutes later. I wanted him to leave, but he'd just arrived.

He began turning the dry, crisp pages of *Sports Illustrated* as if no time had passed between this week and last. It made me drowsy and irritable. I wanted the evening alone with Diego.

I opened the window and looked out at the languid night, the soft, trampled dirt, the chain-link fence surrounding the building. I was only a visitor, I reminded myself, an outsider. I stood on foreign soil, where all the rules were different. What was I doing here? I suddenly longed for familiar landscape—my old house on the hill, green grass, water—even though only months earlier I had longed for a change like this one.

To wake myself up, I bought a soda. A sign on the refrigerator said *Please pay for your pop if you get one, 50 cents*. I dropped two quarters into a can and took small sips. Maybe Sammy would leave early.

Esther rushed into the trailer and made copies at the copy machine. Her hair was always windblown, as if she'd been fighting the wind all her life. She rushed out again, calling out good night and slamming the brown door. That's all she said to me that week: "Good night."

Agatha showed up, and I lost all hope of having Diego to myself. Her plump, brown body landed in the chair across from mine. She wore dark-framed glasses, an aqua-colored T-shirt, black jeans, high-top sneakers. Beaded earrings hung from her ears. She flopped open her notebook.

"English, English. For twelve years I have been talking and writing English," she said.

"I don't see a problem with your English," I said.

"They told me at the college that I have to take remedial English. They said I need a refresher course. I took their grammar test. Their comprehension test. I had to read about the atomic bomb! Why should I read about that? I'm not going heavy into the sciences. I want to be a school teacher. I want to teach *my* people."

I told her to write an essay about why she hated English, and she wrote for the rest of the night. She titled her essay "Enough English." She wrote: *I could vomit in English over and over again.*

Diego was sitting in his usual seat. He'd looked up only once to smile at me. Every so often he would stop writing and move his lips silently, then nod his head as if telling himself to go on.

Weeks earlier Esther had told me Diego was a good man, but he was very ill, and I shouldn't count on him for anything. "It's his blood pressure. He won't take his medication."

"Why not?" I asked.

"He just won't. He's very ill," she said, shaking her head. "He screwed up his liver drinking. Don't count on him."

Don't count on him? I couldn't believe he was as ill as she claimed. He looked handsome in his dark shirt and blue jeans and shiny boots. With his head bowed, he wrote in small fine script. Around him I felt connected and alive.

Three students tonight. I wanted two of them to go home.

At last Sammy put down the magazine and asked me for paper and pencil. "I can't spell," he said.

"Never mind spelling."

Sammy wrote about a time when he was pulled by a horse and wagon through corn fields behind the pueblo. The wagon bounced over deep ruts and lulled him to sleep in the hay. Next to him was a leaky barrel full of water. Every so often water would slosh out and cool him, while his grandfather sang songs into the wind.

"That's beautiful," I told him, but he didn't believe me.

After everyone left that night, I lingered in the trailer. I wasn't ready to leave. I read the newspaper that Sammy had cast aside, and sharpened the pencils in my purse. I scanned Esther's desk for evidence of her lies. Esther would live at the pueblo for the rest of her life, running the school like a bureaucrat, making good money, and driving all over the state to conferences at resort hotels. That day she had driven many miles to buy paper clips.

I turned off the trailer lights and went to my car. I drove through the center of the pueblo, up and down the crooked streets. The crumbling houses were like human shapes huddled against the cold night. I peered into windows. Televisions flickered, people moved quietly through the yellow glow of their kitchens. A woman sat at a table, her hands working in a bowl. I turned west toward the river. I wanted to hear the river go rushing by, but I was lost. I drove on. An antler fell off the roof of a house and startled me. Shadows moved in the night. I swerved left, away from the direction of the river, and drove through the maze of streets, up a steep embankment. Slowly I pulled onto the highway. I didn't want the lights of the pueblo to disappear too quickly behind me.

ONE WEDNESDAY night Agatha didn't come. Sammy didn't come. I asked Diego to read his work out loud. He said okay. In his hands he lifted his paper. I was surprised at how strong his voice was.

I got paid and went to Gallup by myself. I stayed there all day Saturday and I went home early Sunday morning. This was a long time ago. As I was laying there with the hangover, I was dreaming of ghosts. My saliva was sticky like honey and tasted like spoiled milk. My body smelled like a bunch of rotten apples in the sunlight. When I woke up I could hear the ringing in my head like hitting a big bell with a sledgehammer. In my dream I couldn't even open my eyes. Wild horses were chasing me. A bull! A wolf! Bang! went the door. I got up so fast I thought I'd been shot. I was shaking like a rattlesnake's tail, and sweating like a wild horse that got caught. Finally I opened my eyes, and there was my wife standing at the end of my bed. She was the bull in my dream. Her eyes were white and round with blood veins all over them. With little black dots in the middle of her eyes. Her nostrils were round and big with steam coming out of them. With a low voice she said, I see you been drinking again. I can see you got bloodshot eyes. I sat there for a while and I said, Not from this side of my eyeballs. It's like looking through a clear glass from this side. I told her she was the one with the bloodshot eyes. We just looked at each other for a while. I knew my marriage would soon be over because I could not stop drinking.

Diego put down his paper.

"That's good," I said.

"My wife—she just gave up on me." He didn't smile. "'I messed up, but things are different now.'"

"Don't change a thing," I said. "It's very good the way it is."

"I think I can make it better," he said slowly, moving the eraser across the paper.

"Don't change it."

He kept erasing. I was afraid he would erase the whole thing.

I didn't say anything else. It wasn't my story. After a while, our eyes met, and we sat looking at one another.

"I would like to see your river," I said, touching his arm.

"The river?"

"Yes, I can't see it from my place. It's too far away."

"Where do you live?"

I told him.

"The river is not some place I could take you."

"Why not?"

"That's how it is. Too many eyes." He widened his eyes, moving them back and forth in his head. We laughed. Then his eyes stayed on my face.

THAT SATURDAY night as I slept in my bed, I was startled awake by a sound on my front porch. I lay very still under the covers, listening. The sound was low and deep like a bear, prowling. Or a bobcat, or raccoon. I got out of bed and stood in the dark, too frightened to move. I clutched my pounding chest. After a few moments the sound went away. Then it came back—loud and ragged, rising and falling in steady rhythm. It seemed to come through the walls. It was inside the house. I grabbed a broom, flicked on the porch light, and looked outside the window.

A man was sleeping on the bench on the front porch. He was snoring, curled up on his side. He wore only a thin T-shirt and blue jeans. It was cold out. I stared at him. My heart still pounded. I couldn't see his face, but his hair was very dark and in the dim yellow light, I saw the purple scalp.

"Diego!"

He stirred on the bench. Slowly he lifted himself and sat up, shaking the sleep from his head, and wiping his hands over his face. We stared at each other, frozen and bewildered.

"What are you doing here?" I asked.

"I shouldn't have come."

"Why not?"

"Because."

"Come inside. Why didn't you knock?"

He didn't answer.

In the living room, we both hesitated. I was wearing the flannel nightgown my mother had given me years ago, and warm socks. My hair was a tangled mess and needed washing. I offered him some coffee, and he nodded yes. We stood by the heater, warming our bodies.

"Where do you buy your propane?" he asked me.

"I don't know."

"Probably from one of us."

We stayed up all night, talking mostly about his life—his favorite horse, his days as a drunk, his ex-wife, the fields he planted with corn and chile. Then he walked around the tiny house, looking at the books on the shelf.

"What do you do all day?" he asked.

"I write."

"All day?"

I was embarrassed. I thought I was not spending my time well. I curled my toes against the floor. What could I tell him about myself that would not embarrass me? That would make my life seem normal, and not what it was—out of place in a land where I hardly knew a soul.

"It's good you came here," he said.

"It's different from what I'm used to."

"Maybe you will get used to it. Maybe you will stay."

"Anything can happen."

Night air seeped into the thick pink walls, and the whole house was very still. Dawn seeped into the deep windows of the little adobe. I thought how love seemed impossible but true. We were both holding back, standing far apart, and neither of us could do anything about it.

Diego moved outside to the front porch and sat down on the bench where I'd found him the night before. I sat down next to him. Lasagna Range was turning red with the sunrise. English is white, I thought, and I'm only a visitor here. I saw the layers of Lasagna Range; the white layer was very thin and in places it disappeared altogether. We sipped our coffee and looked at each other.

"Let me read your novel," he said. "That's what I came for."

I gave it to him. He put it under his arm, and then he left, whistling.

DIEGO DIDN'T come to class the next week. No one did. Not even Esther showed up. I sat in the trailer with my composition books stamped *Indian Education* and waited for my students. You can wait a long time for someone, even when you know he isn't ever coming. I looked at magazines, at a book of poems. At the newspaper and the clock. At eight-thirty I went home. I stopped at Red Rock Video and rented *Back to the Future,* looking for Diego down the narrow aisles.

The next week I told Esther that no one had come to class the week before.

"Not even Diego," I said.

"Diego's in the hospital."

"The hospital?"

"I told you he's very sick. You can't count on him for anything."

"How can I reach him?"

"You can't. If you have a message, I'll tell his family."

I couldn't trust Esther to speak for me.

The next day I couldn't write. I couldn't eat or sleep. I watched the sky. It was so big, acres and acres of sky that nobody owned. Except Esther. She owned a little piece, she'd made it hers, and it would never happen for me the way it happened for her. I hated Esther then. That was how it was. I could not, even for one second, put Diego out of my mind.

SNOW FELL early December. White flakes smashed against the windshield. I drove to the pueblo and found Diego's house without looking. There were many cars and trucks parked out front. His mother was sitting on a low stool against the wall, crying. I introduced myself, and she sobbed in my arms. "He was our leader," she said softly. "He was all we had. The last one." His sisters made room for me on a bench by the fireplace.

On the dark floor was a shroudlike altar made of a blanket—a faded red cloth folded up with cornmeal sprinkled around it. I stared at the shroud.

The room was full of food and women, a few children, and fewer men. A black pot of water was boiling in the fireplace. Across the room sat shiny galvanized tubs of bread. An old woman stirred a big pot of bean broth, then another woman came from the kitchen and poured the broth into smaller pots on the floor. They knelt around the fireplace, pouring and stirring. I watched their broad backs working.

Diego's sister led me to the table. It was crowded with bowls of chile and beans and Jell-O and cookies and chopped lettuce and potato stew.

"I want you to eat. This is our custom. Eat good," she said.

At the table, Sammy was eating. He looked surprised to see me, and I felt like an outsider then. He didn't look my way but kept his dark head down, moving his mouth as he ate. I wanted to say: *I knew him, too. I knew him better than you.* But it wasn't true. I'd only just met him, and now he was gone. The table seemed very small with no room for me. I ate quickly, then went back to the fireplace and sat on the bench. His sisters were gone.

Finally, I stood to leave. The older sister came from the back room holding my novel. "Here. This is yours. He was reading it."

"What did he say about it?" For a moment I thought we might be friends. I might not lose him entirely.

She shrugged, "He was reading it."

I didn't want to leave, not now, but his sister was standing at the door, waiting for my departure. "He must have said something about it. What did he say?"

"He didn't talk about it."

I went to the cemetery. More snow had fallen. It took me a long while to find Diego's grave.

It was in the corner, a mound of freshly dug dirt, gently sloping on all sides, and piled high with pink carnations, poinsettias, and green ferns. The early snow was covering the flowers. My body began to shake. I couldn't stop crying. I looked down at my hands in fists, at my feet sunk into wet clumps of dirt at the base of his grave. My face was hot with tears and cold with falling snow. Then some men came out of the church and led me away. I shook them off, but they followed me to the car. I was still holding my crumpled manuscript. The pages were wet with snow. The men opened the car door and put me inside.

"Can you drive?" one asked me.

I didn't answer. I just drove.

MORE WEDNESDAY nights came and went. Sammy and Agatha didn't show. It was too close to the holiday, Esther told me, and so many doings at the pueblo. Food to prepare, wood to chop, decorations, and tribal meetings. Everyone was getting ready for the dances; they'd dance twelve consecutive days, rain or shine. They'd done it that way for centuries. I sat in the trailer, staring at the empty seats that stretched across the room.

Eating for Theodora

MELISSA PRITCHARD

MELISSA PRITCHARD, 47, lives in Tempe, Arizona, with her two teenage daughters, Noelle and Caitlin. She is an assistant professor in Arizona State University's creative writing program and author of two short story collections, Spirit Seizures *(which received Flannery O'Connor, Carl Sandburg, and James Phelan awards) and* The Instinct for Bliss *(the title story of which was reprinted in* Pushcart Prize XX: Best of the Small Presses*), and a novel,* Phoenix. *In 1995 she received the Claudia Ortese Memorial Lecture Prize in North American Literature at the University of Florence, Italy, where she nodded graciously as she was introduced to the large, Italian-speaking audience. To this day she has no clue what the laughter, and the ensuing solemnity, was about.*

HER MOTHER LEANS ACROSS, snaps open the car door.

"Where were you? I'm late again."

"Swimming."

She gets in the car, its white leather smelling sharp, new. Her stepfather is a credit-card daddy, buying cars, furniture, vacations. Hah. Picked her mother up dirt cheap.

"I haven't time to drop you home, you'll have to come to class with me. Here's an apple and cheese. Eat. God, you're thin again."

BACK PRESSED to the wall, Toni watches an aerobics class of elegant, sweating women. Her mother is appallingly beautiful, a fact Toni is impatient with, the unfair effect it has on men, women, and, less noticeably, children. Her mother's defiant ambition is to preserve her looks. It used to make Toni desperate; she would ache for the new wrinkle, the thinning in the neck. Now she hunkers, in military boots, ripped jeans, and a fuchsia T-shirt that says, "Nuclear war? There goes my career!" her dark hair cropped above one ear, past her chin on the other side, magenta crisscrossing the top. She's observed these ladies for some twenty minutes, taking one chomp of apple, the pulp in her mouth, a contaminant, gushy brown. Cheese slices stick in a little bag on her thigh, melting tiles. She feels sick; chlorine fumes off her damp hair and skin keep her from throwing up. Her mother winks at her from the front row.

Toni leaves to find the bathroom, spits the pulp into the toilet, abandons the apple, the cheese, on the sink. No one expects less from this world. She gluts on air; her own breathing stuffs her.

HER MOTHER drives them home, past houses Georgian or Tudor, imitation Frank Lloyd Wright, trees linked and stately, lawns vast and immaculate. There is cold distance, a dark iris of privacy surrounding this pale, almost divine wealth.

"How was school?"

"Okay."

"Just okay?"

"Yeah, it was okay."

Her mother, Clarice, tilts her wrist prettily to read her new watch.

"Oh, sweetie, I've got decorating class tonight. Would you fix us a couple of Lean Cuisiners so I can shower real quick? Those chicken whatsits, Marsalas, are decent, let's have those."

Clarice has a boyfriend, a lover, for whom the decorating class, they both understand, is a euphemism. This boyfriend recently gave her a sweater, an ugly sweater, which Clarice waved at Toni, thinking they would be like girlfriends, make fun, have hysterics.

"Do you have homework?"

"Sort of. We're reading about the War of the Roses."

"Wow. I remember that. Studying that."

Her mother snaps out the Sting tape, takes it in the house while Toni goes out to see the pool, calm herself, think about being underwater. Anytime.

WITH A wooden spoon, she keeps the plastic bags of chicken Marsala and rice pinned under boiling water. With effort, she manages to slit the hot plastic, squeeze sweet, wet chicken into two bowls. Her mother appears, in the boyfriend's ugly sweater, her hair sexily mussed, her makeup borderline vulgar. She pours a glass of low-calorie wine.

"Gee whiz, Antonia, I dis-like intensely that mah-roon hair. You had, have, such pretty hair. I wish I didn't have to work out and could stay half as thin as you. You're too thin again. Your bones are seesawing straight through your skin."

They're at the kitchen table having this meal neither of them especially wants, when the phone rings, and Toni gets it. "It's Daddy."

"Raymond? You mean Ray?"

Raymond is Toni's father; since the divorce, he's lived in New Mexico, and, according to Clarice, has gone eccentric, totally bizarre.

"Oh, lord, what can he want? I'll take it upstairs."

Her mother returns to the kitchen just as Toni's done trashing her Marsala down the disposal.

"He wants you to come out for the summer. I thought we'd planned summer school. God knows what sort of *dump* he lives in, who his friends are. I bet he has at least one girlfriend."

"Mom, I want to go."

Total piece of cake. All her mother has to do is figure how much more time she'll have with her boyfriend. Clarice is like one of those library books with extra-huge type.

"Honey, let's discuss later. I'm super late. Eat a bowl or two of ice cream, something fattening, promise? I'll be home about eleven. If anybody calls, I'm at decorating. Thanks, sweetie."

IN THE pool, the dirt and drag of this world cannot master her. In water green and chlorinate, she drums through softening ribcages of saints, their faces dolorous, ivoried beads. Her flesh works, diminishes; they swarm, feeding.

LATE, FROM her window, from behind curtains, she sees Clarice and this younger man in the water, legs wrapped around one another, her mother shh, shh, laughing, probably drunk, fooling she's a girl. The water bulky as tar, the saints put away.

In her striped bathroom, Laura Ashley—striped to match her bedroom, all her mother's pink and white controlling, she razors her bangs in a **V** over her eyes, nudges the scale out of the closet, mounts it like a guillotine. No breakfast, skip lunch, sixty laps at the pool.

SHE HASN'T seen Raymond in five years, not one picture. Clarice, who has, will only declare he looks bizarro (if he wants to be a pathetic, aging hippie, fine by her). So when Toni gets off the bus at ten o'clock at night to wait primly beside her luggage in front of the tiny Taos station, she expects to have difficulty recognizing her father, she doesn't anticipate his utter absence. After ten minutes, she's panicked, thinking taxis, motels, the next bus to the airport, a pay phone, but Raymond doesn't have a number, he doesn't even own a telephone; she's still panicking when an old black pickup with a face like Pluto bounces up, two people inside and two identical dogs wagging tails in the back.

Raymond is short, stringy; under streetlight she sees jeans, cowboy boots spackled with mud, hair in a flat, toad-brown ponytail to his waist. Toni ducks her head around to see who's left in the truck. A girl.

"Toni. Holy shit. Great to see you. *Tapestry* suitcases? Your mother's remained her socially hauling-ass self. I'll put these bourgeois embarrassments in the back of the truck so they'll get thrashed sooner than later . . . what are those, red stripes in your hair? All right."

"Who's that?"

"Who's who?"

"In the truck."

"Oh. Amalia. She's been helping me clean. She's probably your age. How old are you?"

"Fifteen."

"Godbless. I remember fifteen."

Toni's scrunched between them, between her father and this Spanish girl, Amalia, who's so plump and perfumed it gives Toni nervous nausea. Ray grinds the gears like hamburger, punches into the street as if he's pissed, which he isn't, it's how he drives.

"Hungry? McDonald's is all that's open."

Toni's no is reflexive, Amalia's soft, tempted. Toni feels her appraisal, taking in the postpunk haircut, the black ankle-length dress and ballet slippers. Toni has invested her clothing allowance in black, it has the advantage of being both worldly and occult. In black from her wrists to her ankles, no one can tell how thin she is. People have to consider its slimming effect.

Raymond follows the main road through town, turns, turns again, bounces into a gullied dirt area in front of a long, mint green warehouse that says ANGLADA'S BUILDING—it looks to Toni like a funky auto garage.

"You live here?"

"Ho, Miss Snarky Remark"—Raymond's grinning—"we've been cleaning all day. Maybe not what you're accustomed to, but it's been sweet home for some time now."

Half of Anglada's (Raymond has no clue about Anglada) is a dilapidated roller rink; on Fridays, one guy rents it, skates around for hours by himself. Without music.

TO GET to the rest of the old adobe building you have to push through molting drapes, red velvet stage curtains, to locate Raymond among his stinky jumble of oddities, old carousel figures, sculptures from jar lids and coat hangers, green elk antlers, scuzzy pelts, old bicycle parts, busted teepees Ray scavenges for sale or trade. The place has a hallucinogenic flow, claustrophobic, entangled, liberating. There is this space of Raymond's, a closet-size kitchen with a woodstove, rickety blue table chairs, then Toni's room, a wood crucifix on one wall, an iron bed with a shredding blue quilt, a small corner fireplace. Raymond thunks her suitcases down, shows her a leather trunk at the foot of the bed. The single deep-set window has a mayonnaise jar stuffed with fat roses. The dogs trail Raymond slavishly, scratching the linoleum floors. Borzoi wolfhounds he got in exchange for a dentist's chair. *Très* weird animals, high, flat, dimensionless. Like they got squeezed in one of those flower presses, Toni says. Pressed dogs.

"Yeah, they bark flat, come to think of it. Amalia brought these roses from her grandmother's garden, right out that window"—Raymond points—"about fifty feet away. Sweet old lady, Theodora. So how's your mother?"

"Okay, I guess."

"She says you're having trouble eating again?"

"For a while. Not anymore. I feel fine."

"Well, that counts. How about some ginseng tea and fortuneless cookies? This bag I got, so far all the little papers are blank."

She watches Raymond two-step around his kitchen; he has a spot, a large, moist freckle, laid into the white of one eye, his ponytail is cinched by a piece of leather, his teeth are tobacco stained. He wears a wide silver concha belt. In a million years and for a million reasons, she cannot picture him with her mother. Last time she saw him was at a wedding. He'd worn a white tuxedo and let her dance the old funny way, her feet parked on top of his. She'd been a baby when Raymond and her mother divorced, and Clarice refused to discuss it. An error, she'd say. A tragic, Shakespearean error on my part.

"Is there a pool in town?"

"Yup, indoors. You can walk or ride my bike. You like swimming?"

"Pretty much. Can I go tomorrow?"

"Hey, babe, it's your summer, go for it."

TONI TAKES Raymond's old mountain bike down parched, serpentine roads, past cattle blotched in alfalfa like sullen flies. Downtown, in the Spanish-style plaza, she walks the bike, navigates through tourists, following Raymond's directions. Coming in from dry glare and pinkish dust, she feels she has slid under a rock, into this dark, indoor pool smell, green light, heavy chlorine odor. The water long and turquoise, the pool blank. In the dressing room, Toni takes off her black pants, the wrist-length Chinese blouse. Her suit's solid white except for Minnie Mouse waving pink daisies across the butt, one of her fat, red shoes kicking up. Toni relies on mirrors to tell her things, keeps two in her purse, pulling one or the other out to affirm some piece of herself, her earthly presence. In a full-length mirror, she sees her upper arm is bony, like an animal's, spooky and flat from the back then dipping in, getting tiny, some shank a dog might worry. She walks out, paying her dollar to swim, liking the way the Spanish boy stares, fascinated then withdrawn . . . she likes dominating his field of curiosity, inviolate.

THE POOL is warm, a summer pond. Her contact lenses are out, everything has lost clarity but water, where life is complex and about survival, surviving through motion, through the repetitive motion of swimming. Her arms row, pulling the root of her body, water breaking in through her ears, into the center of her head like glassy splinterings, water dressing the surfaces of her opened eyes. Long black Ts wobble and shake along the bottom of the pool; she increases her stroke to the speed where she is a bird, arms winging, elbows cocked; when she raises her head, rainbows haze the windows and doors, the Spanish boy who guards her. Colors of oil slick radiate from the doors and windows, from the Spanish boy, who sits, silent and dry.

Later, she bikes to the library, an old rambling adobe with turquoise doors and windows, flagstone porches with treelike sprays of pink geranium. She finds *Lives of the Saints* in the reference room, sneaks it into her big straw purse, not theft, no—she'll return it someday.

On the way back to Anglada's, Toni stops for cappuccino and biscochitos, local cookies spiced with anise. In a courtyard, on a canary yellow chair, its legs half-sunk in gravel, her book of saints opened, the sun like heretical fire on its print, Toni feels guilty, eating, feels the fat filling her shoes, bunching up her legs, how bloated she is, out of whack from these cookies whose taste takes her power, the anise hypnotic, rolling over her tongue, up the sides of her mouth like wine. To punish herself, she rides past Anglada's up a long, unshaded incline and back down, though her legs are weakening and she is on a current, an eddy of exhaustion so profound she is weightless and the cars mirages, honking, wavering like the black Ts in the pool.

She practically lunges into the cramped interior of Anglada's, escaping the thorny glare of outside. Raymond has gone off to one of his girlfriends', leaving her a note to pick up their laundry at Amalia's, along with five dollars to pay the grandmother for the use of her machines.

THE LADY opening the door is skinny, dark, and sour; sponge curlers bunch like pink fruits on her head; behind her, a washer thrashes, chugs, presumably with their clothes.

"I'm Antonia, Raymond's daughter? He asked me to pay for our laundry."

"Yes, come in. It isn't finished yet."

"Are you Theodora?"

"No, no, one of her daughters. Come in. We're cleaning from lunch."

Toni has never stood in a house this small and, by Clarice's standards, this poor (migawd, she hears her mother). But there is a scrubbed cleanness, a sense of objects honored for plain utility. The kitchen has canary yellow walls, copper pans lined up, red geraniums profusely clouding windows, yet Toni feels purity covering heartbreak, some persistent sadness darkening, however invisibly, this house.

A woman with a square, jowled face stands up from a red Formica table.

"Sit. Sit down."

The daughter rinses a sinkful of dishes, Theodora closes her crossword book, and Toni sits.

"Would you like an empanada? We baked this morning."

"I'm not sure. What's an empanada?"

"Pastry with meat, spices, raisins."

"Sure. Gracias." Toni grins. "Whatever."

This first time, meeting Theodora, so many people come and go from the small house, aunts, uncles, daughters-in-law, cousins. She thinks of her mother's house, enormous, decorated with expensive, untouched objects. How no one is ever there.

AMALIA AND her boyfriend have their arms around each other's waists, staying to one side of the refrigerator so the grandmother can't see the boy with his black, curling hair and thick, polished arms sending his hands squeezing around Amalia's butt. After a while, they take the aunt for groceries. Theodora still sits with Toni, who has not touched the empanada, maybe an insult, a waste of food, so she raises it to her mouth and scrapes a few flakes of browned pastry off with her teeth. Its flavor intrigues, repels her; then she sees Theodora's hands tremor, she looks up to see grief blunting her face, and Theodora drying her cheeks with a dull punching of one fist. What has she done? Has she done anything wrong?

"What?" Toni asks, apprehensive.

"No, not you. It's not you."

Silence, weighted, alarming, swerves the chemistry in the room.

"Not you . . . it's my sadness. My husband was murdered."

The empanada turns to weight in her hand, homely, greasy.

"Oh, God. I'm sorry."

"Shot to death. Here." She places her hand against her chest. "This is how I see angels. Five years now."

Telling, she cries. Toni wants to but has not known raw, traumatic loss. She begins to understand the desperate work, the compulsive scouring of household objects.

They sit, the clock ticking over the sink like water dripping. Toni accepts the napkin Theodora passes, done with talking, done crying, her face almost quiet.

"You are too thin for such a young girl."

Toni brushes her lips with the napkin, ashamed.

"I was ill. I lost a lot of weight."

"The Devil helps himself when you are weak, finds his way into you. Do you eat now that you are better?"

"Yes," Toni lies, "I do. The empanada was very good."

"No, you haven't touched it."

Toni takes an apologetic bite. It stops in her mouth, at the back of her throat.

"I believe in angels," Toni confesses, swallowing. Why is she saying this? Why? "Whoa. I've never told anybody that. I mean *nobody* knows what I believe."

"Of course. Angels are always present with God. But the man who took my husband's life is out of prison, I pray God finds him, this man." Theodora rubs her hands down her thighs. "I pray for it, then feel bad about this hate in me. Five years of this hate."

IN THE little squared flower garden, Toni shifts the laundry basket from stomach to hip. Theodora, pulling up weeds, piling them in wilted heaps, moves with the immodesty of those with no one to please, in dark baggy pants, a print smock, her face stern, pulled down. In Theodora's presence, around her lack of vanity, Toni feels strangely calm, as if she can almost breathe. She thinks of her mother's anxious self-absorption, of her father's string of girlfriends. Toni has met three since she got here; there are, he says, several more. Raymond is often gone, coming in at unpredictable times, in unpredictable moods.

"I was born in this house, my father, too. I've been here seventy-five years. I can remember when Doctor Cetrulo was the only person in town with an automobile. Now people are in a hurry to get I don't know where."

"I starve myself."

"Anyone can see you have chosen to do this. To be angry in this way."

"I think I'm trying to be like the saints, like the angels. The less I take from life, the closer I can be to God."

Theodora seizes the grasshoppers off the rosebushes, one at a time, squashes them inside her fist.

"The one you're hurting is yourself, not the world. This is taking, this starving, and God wants us to give, Antonia. Don't you think I asked for death back then, waited for death like a young woman wanting her husband at night, again and again? No. God puts us here to give. No matter how it hurts."

TONI SWIMS, rides Raymond's bike around, visits Theodora. Fridays, she sees the therapist, a thing Raymond and Clarice agreed on—if Toni visits, she has to See Someone.

"WHEN WAS your last menstrual period?"

"I don't remember."

"Six months, a year?"

"I don't remember."

"Antonia, you're uncomfortable with the idea of sex, with yourself as a sexual person?"

"I'm not a sexual person."

"What about love?"

"I love God."

"Have you been getting along with your father?"

"He's pretty cool. He doesn't try to change me."

"Have you met anyone here you especially like? Are close to?"

"No."

The therapist works with Toni's addiction to swimming, her lapses of time sense, how she plays with food, manipulates it, punishes herself for putting anything in her mouth. These sessions are predictable, narrow in scope. Toni passes reassurance to this therapist like salt, promising to eat, confessing misplaced pride, denying her flesh.

It is only in the long, yellow kitchen, the flower garden, the dark, lilac-smelling bedroom with its rosaries, pictures of Jesus, the Pope, the saints, that Toni breathes and begins to eat, tomatoes from a neighbor's garden, mountain raspberries, mostly for Theodora, who feeds her, insistent, nourishing.

THEODORA ASKS Amalia to drive them to Chimayo, to the santuario, saying it will do them all good. Amalia borrows her uncle's blue Ford truck with the rosary wrapped around the radio dials, and with the three of them lined up in the cab, Toni studies their hands, Amalia's plump and brown with oval, sugary nails, Theo's roots, puffed and dark, her own hands, limp and freckled, tentative. This drive through mountains is long. Toni feels a certain panic, hurtling through mountains too immense, indifferent. Relentless rollings of pine and piñon, tough, uncompromising sunlight she cannot get used to, timelessness, a disorientation; she has never swum in open water, never entered water with no graspable boundary, always kept to pools with hard defined edges that could save her. These mountains have a maniacal open-endedness, a grandiose power over the human and the weak. They devour her.

Then the road curves, drops until they enter a valley of orchards, pastures with cattle, sheep, black and chestnut horses. Amalia turns down a dirt lane shaded by arching cottonwoods with heart-shaped leaves; on Toni's side, water pushes slug-gishly through an irrigation ditch choked with red willow.

Getting down from the truck, she follows Amalia and Theodora across a gray, warped footbridge into an adobe-walled courtyard with tall, conical evergreens, a flagstone floor with gravestones, a skinny wood cross. Toni enters the dark, empty santuario, imitates Amalia and Theodora, tracing a cross on her face with sour-smelling holy water.

To pass from the linen mildness of summer, the heart-leaves of old cottonwoods, air gold, solid with roses, to enter a place rough as a cave, formed out of mud and wood and trapped air, lit by candles, watery white ovals with charred wicks, hun-dreds, each a misery or supplication, two deep-set windows pulling in sparse, laven-der light, this is divine, intended assault on the deadened human spirit. Theodora crosses herself twice with holy water, her sandals slapping up her bare heels, down on the reddish stone floor. She and Toni sit on a wood bench near the altar, in dim-ness like cloth, in cloying, waxen heat. The altar has a gilt screen with primitive figures in faded cobalt, faded ocher, worn gold, Christ centered between painted curtains, a puppet theater, the puppet on a dark green cross. Doll figures sit on either side of the altar, a blond, curly-haired boy in a pink satin dress and gold crown, an arrow-faced man on a starved horse in a glass case. When she looks to the side, Toni's heart does a fish-jump. A second wood panel, this with ocher and black warrior-angels and apostles and at its center, a carved life-size man in an ivory satin robe with gold trim, hands crossed, ribs leaking red, his large, almond eyes black-rimmed, Egyptian-looking.

A terrible sensuality thickens the air in this plain Spanish church. Toni, kneeling, stares through laced hands. Theodora prays, rubs her swollen knees. When Amalia goes up to the altar and stoops through a little door on the left, Toni and Theodora get up to follow her.

In a dark, thin room, stifled in sweet warmth from tiers of lighted candles, she ducks her head through a second warped doorway, enters a second, tiny room, where the cement floor has an open circle of dirt. Theodora kneels, pushes her pained fingers in this dirt. Toni trails hers, too, in cool siltiness, crossing herself. A window with an iron grill lets in a hard block of light—Toni sees horses ripping alfalfa, is conscious of the bright constancy of birds, sees the world green and golden. But God is here, dark, thick-smelling, pressed liquor, dressed up in dolls, put into amateur paintings and plastic flowers, a glass box with Jesus in there on a black cross, in a pale satin gown, the reins of a rosary on his wilted neck. Snapshots of infants, children, families, couples, all Hispanic; a man, naked, reclining in bed, laughing, his black mustache shiny and potent, for what reason, pinned under the tendriled legs of a small crucified Jesus.

She walks back to the first room, one wall solid with crutches, canes, orthopedic shoes, names and dates scratched or inked on them. A handmade white chapel, inside a baby king in a rose satin dress, baby shoes curling around his tiny, chipped feet, a broken basket with three pennies. The other walls, floor to ceiling with oil paintings, velvet paintings, pictures made from sequins, gold and red glitter, carvings from cedar, sculptures from tin, of Jesus, Mary, the saints, so many bloodied submissive Christs—and everywhere letters, photographs, testimonies of souls, tributes of the healed, prayers for the dead, the murdered, the missing, the failed. The wavering heat, perfumed stench from hundreds of candles, the dozens of doll-holies in pastel gowns, beads, plastic roses, and Our Lady of Sorrows, long in black, face behind veils, body sealed in an opaque plastic bag, intercessor for sorrow, hanging in one dark corner.

Theodora and Amalia have gone. She studies every picture, reads every letter, in its smeary pencil or perfect ink, in its Spanish or English, some words misspelt, all put down with painful effort. Bloodied wings flash out of her head, angels pack the place, tread the walls and air with holiness, made giant by humility and stark belief in magic, in idolatry, in baby shoes set before a little red-mouthed doll with yellow hair. Such gothic naiveté is Truth to her, Grace to her, serving the ache to be released.

At the end of the dark aisle, wood doors slope open to the glaring courtyard. She finds Theodora and Amalia at a picnic table drinking Cokes, talking in Spanish, laughing. How did they so easily reenter the world? Toni may never speak again, or it will be tongues and babble, for God is all over and in her body swarming, His wings clap her face, deafening.

Amalia, seeing her, waves.

"Hey, Toni. I need to use the restroom. Come with me. Eeei, I thought I was pregnant for sures. Then I prayed and took some of that dirt and guess what, sitting out there with my grandma, I felt the blood starting to come."

Amalia is beautiful, glazed with sexuality, fertility; if she is not pregnant now, surely she will be, her womb irresistible. Toni feels dry, deficient of the sorrow and theatrics of sex. Her passion is in the undetected, her lust holds out for Spirit.

She hears Amalia in the toilet. "Thank you, God. Hey, Toni, I'm *bleeding*."

Toni, digging into her arm with fingernails, pressing red out of her famished, blue arm, says, "No, I am," and leaves to find Theodora.

TONI IS biking back from seeing her therapist and swimming. The therapist was pleased by her weight gain; swimming, Toni was once more alone, the black crosses on the floor of the pool showing faces pale like beads, sad, oblong beads strung along the mournful, black cross she churned above.

Toni is thinking no matter what Theodora wears, it looks black. Her anguish, stubborn as blood, turns the fabric.

The white Cadillac is parked like a boat, like a damned yacht across the dirt in front of Anglada's. A week early. A week before they were supposed to pick her up. Shit. She drops the bike against the chipping green wall, shoves the velvet curtains, and goes inside. Clarice is at the kitchen table, sipping something.

"Your father doesn't keep coffee, not even instant. God, I'm trying this herbal stuff, it's like gargling cologne. I don't know, Tones," she says, looking around. And Toni sees how shabby this place is with Clarice here, the magic shut off, concealed. Her mother looks worn, even in this shadowed kitchen, even with her sunglasses on, meaning she knows she looks terrible. She is wearing a white silk pantsuit with bunches of turquoise around her tanned, lined neck.

"This is such a berserk setup, how did you last this long? You should have let us know. God. We're in this gorgeous condo in Santa Fe. We thought we'd get up here a few days early, surprise you, rescue you, I'd say at this point. We have opera tickets for tonight and want you to come with us."

"Can Dad come too?"

Clarice frowns, mashing her tea bag with the flat of a spoon.

"I don't know. We only have three tickets and I'm positive they're sold out. Maybe another time," she says with familiar cheerful deceit. She wouldn't be caught dead with Raymond.

"So, what do you do here: I haven't gotten one word from you. No postcard, no letter, *nada*."

"Ah, swim, bike around, stuff."

"Oh. Great. Sounds fun. Right." Clarice sighs.

"So where are the dads?"

"They walked down the road to buy beer, I guess. Well, Tones, how about showing me your room. Gee, do you have a room?"

THEY ARE sitting in the middle of the roller rink, on the dusty floor, drinking so much beer her mother is actually beginning to have fun, to laugh with Raymond enough so Toni can imagine the attraction at one time, maybe. Her stepfather is trying hard, in his madras sport coat and gold bracelet, not to make waves for anybody, his face more florid than usual. Toni excuses herself to go through the quiet garden with its intricate white flowers, bridal lace, to knock at the door. After a little while, Theodora answers.

"My parents are here for me. I was afraid you'd be asleep."

"No, no. I laid down and couldn't sleep. So. Tell me how next time you visit, you'll be so fat, so big, I'll need somebody to introduce us."

"Yeah right. A real pig. Snarf." Toni makes a pig sound.

"Remember to eat for God, and if that doesn't work, then eat for me so I won't worry."

Theodora cups Toni's thin fingers around something bunchy, cool, in her hand. Kisses her.

OUTSIDE ANGLADA'S, where Toni hears her parents, all three of them, laughing, practically choking on their own wit or whatever, she opens up her hand. Dulled black beads, the thin silvery Christ, caught like a tiny fish on Theodora's rosary. Taking her in. Feeding her. One hunger exchanged for another.

In the air-conditioned Cadillac, Toni persuades them to take the high mountain road to see the santuario. It's the most famous church in northern New Mexico, she says. Clarice sniffs, she has no interest in churches, but Toni's stepfather, not unkind, says, Let's stop, what can it hurt, Toni says it's something special.

But when they get to Chimayo, there are tour buses, the parking lot is full of cars, rows and rows of cars, a watery polish across their hoods. There is a gift shop Toni doesn't remember, selling holy water, medals, religious articles, souvenirs.

She's self-conscious beside this elegant woman who attracts lust, envy, beside her stepfather in his gold jewelry and white leather shoes. The church feels absent, the church is not there, although tourists crowd its shell, take pictures, set up picnics outside its walls. Toni wants the holy water but stops herself, avoiding her mother's ridicule. Already Clarice is stage-whispering, You brought the camera, did you bring the camera, her husband hissing, Yes, yes . . . Clarice yakking on, oh charming, so primitive, folk art is very collectible, all the while instructing her husband what pictures to take. Toni doesn't want them in the special rooms, but Clarice notices people going in there and wants to see.

Inside, the three of them watch an elderly Spanish woman dribbling dirt into a paper bag, most of the dirt falling over her shoes, she is so feeble, praying Our Father.

"Poor thing," Clarice whispers to Toni. "Superstition is so fascinating. This type of ignorance."

"I'm dying from these candles," her red-faced husband says. "There's absolutely no air. Can we go?"

"I'll be out in a minute," Toni answers.

KNEELING, FAMISHED, tongue lapping God's dryness. Feeding dirt into the tin she's taken from her purse, mouth working God, crossing herself with soured water down her meager face, all mixed with earth.

¡Missss Rede!

DENISE CHÁVEZ

DENISE CHÁVEZ, 47, lives in the house in which she grew up in Las Cruces, New Mexico, and writes in the room in which she was born. "It's a living presence," she says of the influence of the southwestern landscape on her writing. "In the mountains [of New Mexico] you can almost see the outline of breasts, or people, or faces." Her BA and MFA in theater have guided her in the writing of more than twenty plays and influenced her poetry and fiction writing styles as well. Her books include the short story collection The Last of the Menu Girls *and* Face of an Angel, *a novel; short pieces and excerpts of her work have been published in numerous literary magazines and more than a dozen anthologies.*

STOP THAT NOISE! STOP that and listen to me. You have no right to do that. To go off. When will you be back?

Did I ever tell you about my honeymoon in El Paso? No, not to your father. To Bucho Faver. Your sister's father. He was accidentally poisoned.

Every day we went to a little restaurant. On Mesa Street. Every day we ate oysters. I didn't like them at first. But Bucho did. We were happy, Bucho and I. He was a kind man and shy. And he was very clean. He would bathe two and three times a day.

It all started when I told my cousin Toña I was going to marry Bucho Faver and she told someone and someone told Bucho. Delfina Rede says she's going to marry you. Shafter, Texas, was a small town and I was a teacher there. But I was more than a teacher.

One night I was called to deliver a child. The partera was gone. As the teacher I was expected to know, to serve, to do. I knew nothing about babies, but I boiled the water and brought that child into the world, his bright body slithering, the umbilical cord cut with a knife. He lived! He lived to grow and thank me, Miss Rede.

Later on, there were other births, other children. This crying child was my first, as I scrambled up the hills near the silver mine, to the little house. I was a school teacher, not knowing about life, not knowing anything real. But how could I tell them that?

Like the time I taught at Indio Ranch. Like the time I lived in exile, on baked earth swept clean each day. I decided to go for a horse ride. Les dije a los muchachos, get me a horse, but they were busy, so I got one myself. The horse was stubborn, mean. I struggled with him, and he still wouldn't be calmed. But eventually I got the saddle on. And that was just the beginning. That horse kicked and danced and wouldn't be still; he bucked and ran, wild-crazy through the mesquite and over the cerro and then by the river, like a fever driven, and finally, exhausted, came back to the ranch. I was tired, but I wasn't going to let that horse take charge. Rede, I said, you can do it! And, what's wrong with this horse?

When I came back to Indio Ranch the men flocked around me, incredulous and worried. ¿Que has hecho? they demanded. What have you done? This horse, Diablo, was unbroken, untried, Missss Rede! What have you done? Didn't you know?

It was the same person who walked into the night to deliver Ismael Contreras Junior when no one else would. The same person boiled water, tore strips of cloth, and cut the umbilical cord with that sharp knife.

If anyone had asked me, Delfina, can you be any happier, I would have said no. No. No. No. With Bucho I was happy. Now it's in heaven that we'll embrace.

Bucho got sick. He told me, "Fina, me han matado. I'm going to die. They've killed me. The druggist gave me something. I didn't want to take it. They forced it down my throat."

It was I had told him to go to the doctor. It wasn't there things went wrong, but with the druggist. You know, I could have sued. But in those days, who sued? Who sued and for what? They had to hold him down it tasted so bad.

Later he came to me. I was in the other house, our rooms, across from Mama Gumersinda's. I was about to give birth to your sister, Faride. Bucho said to me, "Fina, I'm sick. I'm really sick." He knew. I was in bed, and I could see him coming through the window. He was tired and stooped and sad. It was twilight and in September. Today is the anniversary of his death.

I wasn't able to do anything. I was able to give birth to your sister. What else could I do? Bucho got sicker. Every day sicker. And he kept telling me, "Fina, Fina, I'm dying." Until one day he couldn't walk and he stayed in the big house. I looked through the window. The lights were on all the time. He didn't have anything to say anymore. He didn't have to say anything anymore. He was in bed at the big house and I was across the courtyard in our little house waiting for our child to be born. Our child. September the tenth. Three days later Bucho died.

I could have sued, but in those days, who sued?

Everyone I've ever loved . . . I've cried over. Why is that? Everyone.

That was 1942. Today. In Shafter, Texas.

Everyone I've ever loved. I've cried for. I cried myself to sleep every night for nine years. I taught school, I traveled to México. Thirteen summers. I raised Faride. But there were always those tears. Until I met your dad. I met him and when I thought about it later, I remembered. It was the first night in all those years I hadn't cried myself to sleep.

This is the first I've told you about that time in Shafter. All day I've been thinking about Bucho. All day. I've got to stop. I'm tired now.

All this loving has worn me out.

Roll up the window.

The man told me he'd be here soon to unlock the storage unit.

Bucho used to bathe two or three times a day. He was very clean. He used to ask me to scrub his back. He begged me, but I wouldn't. I was too shy.

Now I regret not washing his back. It would have made him so happy.

Roll up the window. It's getting cold. Where is that man? Where? Where? How long do we have to wait out here? How long?

I was just thinking.

Today is the anniversary of Bucho's death.

I wish you weren't going so far.

I know, I know. But that doesn't stop me from crying.

When will you be back?

Until then, your things will be safe. Don't worry. They'll be home.

Home.

Come soon.

There he is now. There he is. The man. Isn't that someone, in the darkness, there?

I can hear someone coming.

Maybe that's him.

Waiting so long, so long. I don't know. I don't mind. I don't. Mind. Not really.

I'm used to it.

Living on the Border

BETH LAURA O'LEARY

BETH LAURA O'LEARY, 44, teaches at New Mexico State University in Las Cruces, New Mexico, where she lives. For the last nineteen years she has worked as an archeologist at New Mexican excavation sites, looking for evidence of the past. Artifacts she has found range from ten-thousand-year-old arrowheads to a children's cigar box wagon with tiny crown bottle caps for wheels. Her archeological work includes the publication of her study of the Tutchone people of the Yukon Territory, where she spent five years doing fieldwork. She is a new writer; her other publications include pieces in Mountain Passages, Rio Grande Writers Chapbook, *and* Hudan Hude.

MOST OF THE TIME it's quiet. The illegals don't bother me. I see them go through the property once in a while on their way to El Paso. Sometimes they're even going the wrong way. Those canyons can get awfully dry; even the cattle tanks don't hold much because no one's here to keep them up. Up at Santa Teresa some surveyors found a dead Mexican under a mesquite. He had an empty plastic jug with him. It's hard to think that these people struggle so hard to cross that border. It takes a lot of guts to come across miles of old mesquite dunes tearing at your clothes, worried about walking on roads, camping without a fire at night. They must have a real powerful urge to get to the other side. I don't know if I could make the trip if I was them. I'd want to know that I could survive once I got there. To cross over all alone must be scary.

I live in Fort Hancock, Texas, three miles from the Mexican border. It doesn't have a fort. It has a Pic-Quik, a gasoline station, a dry goods mercantile, and Angie's.

Angie's is where I go for lunch. I need a hot lunch since I don't eat right. One hot meal. Today the food was bad, and I told Angie. She's usually a good cook, but today it just didn't turn out. Tomorrow it will be better since we told her. I see all my friends at lunch. My best friend is Mary McGuire; we call her Mary of the Mountain because she lives over in the Findlays. She's by herself too. She's a pistol. I'd like to go to Angie's for dinner but it's a long way to the ranch and Scott isn't here to drive at night so I don't go.

Last time I drove after dark I smashed the Ford into the cattle guard and I called for a long time on the CB after I woke up on the road to the east cattle tank. A neighbor man came. Scott knew him. I knew his face when he showed up to find me yelling into the walkie-talkie. He said "Sarah, it's John." He drove me home because I was a little stunned. I didn't drive in the dark after that.

Last week some archeologists came up to the ranch to study the old rock drawings. They even took pictures of the ruins where Scott's grandpa had lived. Scott had carved his name on a rock near there. It says "Scott Passmore 1922." They told me that was an historic document. Imagine that being historic! I remember 1922 real clear. The archeologists want to get the drawings registered so they can't build the waste dump down near Diablo dam. Scott had been all fired up about it, but it doesn't much matter to me, though I suppose if they build it I'll have to keep that gate locked all the time so I don't have anybody wandering in. I like to keep it open.

I guess people think I'm crazy for living out here by myself. Sarah, they say, what if something happens? I told them this is just as good a place to die as any. We built this ourselves. Though I had to let most of the cattle go last year, I still have a few, maybe twelve or eleven head. They're up in Flat Canyon now. Jack O'Brien looks after them for me. I tried living in town, but I felt all cramped up in an apartment. It's just too small. After we found this hill we just came up here and camped. There wasn't a thing here. The house isn't much but it's paid for, and besides the Border Patrol guys come by at least once a day. They stop in and I fetch them a cold drink.

My kids come once in a while, but they don't want this ranch. They come at Thanksgiving and I get to see all the grandbabies. But they're busy. My baby Josh is a stockbroker in Dallas. He makes lots of money. When he comes he likes to wander around with me. We take off in the truck while his city wife stays in the house worrying with the kids. She thinks I'm a little crackers. Josh knows I am so he never has to worry about my going senile.

I can still find the first spring Scott found on the property and now it's so dried up there isn't even a bush marking it. Like my dog Hazel, I just know the way there and I can tell exactly where it is because every time some animal has dug up the sand to get the water that oozes out. Animals must smell that water because they have to dig at least a foot before it even gets damp. All the times I've been to that spring I've never seen an animal there. Josh laughs when I tell him we have to sneak up because we may catch a little mule deer scraping around. Scott and I used to go here with Josh when he was little. I once made the mistake of telling Josh, even though I know it can't be true, that I expect to see his father there one day. Maw, he says, he ain't even tap dancing in the same room. I know it makes us both sad. He doesn't want this ranch now that his daddy is gone.

I like having Hazel around even if she is only a dog. Sometimes in the middle of the night she wakes me. She's spooked and she spooks me. I can't sleep much anyway. Some nights I just wish night didn't happen. Hazel starts in moaning. She won't let up until I go outside with her. I think she hears the coyotes. The nights are usually very still even if it's been blowing up from hell and back. I can see each star as clear as specks on a windshield.

One time I went out with Hazel and fired my pistol. I always keep a loaded gun in the house, but it had been a while since I'd shot it. It was so loud in the middle of the night I could hear the echo all the way down Diablo canyon. Just me and Hazel standing out in the desert. Me in Scott's old bathrobe and Hazel jumping around like her paws were on a hot pan. After I shot in the air, Hazel calmed right down. Now I have to do it every time.

When we were younger Scott and I used to go to Juarez. It wasn't bad then, no drugs. Everything was nice. The people looked better, not all tore up like they do now. Before it was just one bridge and you'd see people walking across on Sundays with their families. The little girls were all dressed up. Before I had my babies I always wanted a little girl with long dark braids and black eyes like those Mexican gals had. I think I married Scott because he had dark brown eyes and I wanted to have dark-eyed babies. We even thought of getting a Mexican orphan because it took me so long to get pregnant. One August we tried every hour until I thought I couldn't hold any more of his seed even if we were staying in the best air-conditioned room in the

El Presidente. I went to Juarez to pray at Nuestra Señora de Guadalupe Mission and I wasn't even Catholic. All those poor little skinny Mexican ladies were kneeling beside me praying not to have one more niño while I was praying to have one. A little while after, I got a baby. I haven't been back since but I would have gone back if it wasn't so far.

It's been awful dry here. Not one drop of rain in one year. It was really dry too last July when we're supposed to get most of our rain. Scott would have fretted this year. He even fretted when he was in the hospital last June. He was all tubed up in the bed after his heart went out on him. I didn't know what all those tubes led to. I knew it was real bad because they took off his Santo Domingo ring. I gave him that ring. He wore it all his adult life except that day when I walked in and saw the nurse with it pinned to her chest on a big safety pin. I know he hardly gave that ring up himself.

He couldn't talk because they had a tube wound around inside his neck. He looked up when I came in and his eyes were real bright. He struggled to talk but he couldn't. The nurse came over and calmed him down a little and put her hand out with the palm open. He took his finger and spelled out "Rain?" I just wanted to cry because I had to shake my head.

Sandstone

(In memory of Russ King)

REBECCA LAWTON

REBECCA LAWTON was among the first female river guides in California, Utah, Idaho, and Arizona. She spent several seasons guiding on the Green and Yampa rivers in Dinosaur National Monument, where she also interned at the dinosaur quarry. Rebecca has a BS in earth science from the University of California at Santa Cruz and an MFA in creative writing from Mills College. Her short fiction, mostly pieces of a longer work entitled Leaving Felliniville: River Tales, *has appeared in* the Acorn, THEMA, *and the first* Walking the Twilight. *She returns to the Uintah Basin in dinosaur country every chance she gets, to camp by the river, take her family boating, and smell the fresh-cut alfalfa in farms along the Green River.*

THE PALEONTOLOGIST TAUGHT ME that bones in a river settle parallel to the current. I hadn't figured that out, though I'd worked at the quarry for twenty years before he came, green as corn, from graduate school at Yale. I'm not saying I hadn't noticed things about the bones I'd been finding in the rock all that time. For one, they showed up in little piles—or big piles, I should say, seeing that they're dinosaur bones. For another, most of the long bones—femurs, tibias, fibulas—lined up west-to-east in the rock. But until Dr. Case showed me the rock was old river deposits and the bones lined up the way the current left them, I didn't see the connection between dinosaur days and the nowadays rock.

See, I knew it all meant something, but my job was just to dig. I'd been hired because I knew my way around a rock bar and sledge and how to handle a jack hammer at any damn angle. No wonder I was good—I'd started work at the gilsonite mines when I was sixteen. My dad had left home, and though I may not have been ready to, I dropped out of high school to work full time. When I got the quarry job years later, I learned to detail the bones right where they lay, with ice picks and soft-bristle brushes. Lord, that was the meanest work, the hunching over with tiny tools for hours at a time. It just about did in my back and legs. Still, I outlasted the whole string of men who ran the quarry over the years before the paleontologist came along.

It took me some time to get over my first impressions of him. For good reason. For one, the man ran from the housing area to the river every day—rain, snow, or summer heat. Evenings I saw him in my rearview mirror as I headed back to town and he jogged along the quarry road. He called running his meditation.

"You mean medication, Dr. Case," I said, thinking of the pills Betty had taken to relax when she was my wife.

"No, meditation." It was the first time I'd heard that word used outside of church. Sometimes, Dr. Case's young wife, who'd also gone to college, pushed their baby daughter in a stroller while he ran ahead. I remember seeing her out there even when afternoon winds blew up the river and kicked up dust and little bits of rock. Couldn't have been too good for the baby, and I'm not sure what the wife got from it.

Another thing—and this rankled me, because I grew up Latter-Day Saints—was that Dr. Case used to invite in the missionaries just to argue with them. He studied the Book of Mormon enough to figure he'd found the loopholes, and then he'd ask those kids into his home and debate their faith. He teased about Jehovah, who he called the "God of the quick and the dead," and he got a big kick out of the land of Moron and the angel Moroni, who led Joseph Smith to the golden tablets. Those things don't seem funny to me, and I sure never questioned them. But a man of science probably can't be called on to trust in the church or the mysteries of the spirit.

At work, Dr. Case got to watching me close during the detailing. He put names to everything. I'd clean off what I knew to be a shoulder bone; he'd put on his goggles and say, "Look Erv, Apatosaurus scapula." Or I'd finish up a string of tiny neckbones: "Cervical vertebrae from a juvenile stegosaur." I liked hearing the fancy names, and I remembered them. Sometimes though, he'd hover, saying I should use a smaller-sized pick, or a bigger one if I needed to be working faster, or that it was time to clear away the debris. Then, one day: "Careful, Erv, you'll gouge the socket."

"I know it, sir, I'm being careful."

"Shouldn't you be using the number six pick?"

"No, Dr. Case, I shouldn't. Believe me, I've done over a hundred ribs this way."

"Maybe so. But let's get this one right."

That did it. I peeled off my safety glasses and threw down the pick, walked past the office and out into the parking lot. He followed me all the way, asking where I was going, what I was doing. I was too mad to answer.

He followed me to my truck. "Erv, stop! Where are you going? I didn't mean it. You know me—I'm a paleontologist. I can be boneheaded."

I leaned against the bed of my truck and pulled out my smokes.

"Erv, I shouldn't have interfered. You're the one who knows your job. Really, I need your expertise."

That stopped me. Though I could teach him plenty, I knew the man would do fine if I chose to quit, which I didn't, because I hate like hell to look for work. But he was getting on my nerves on the rock. I lit a cigarette and turned to him.

His dark hair blew in the afternoon wind. Behind him, Split Mountain stood out in the sun, bright and clean as you please. His eyes looked that deep blue color the river turns late in the afternoon.

"Dr. Case, I'm not going anywhere. But we've got to get a few things straight. Number one, Jehovah is not the God of the quick and the dead. He's the Eternal Judge of both quick and dead."

"Oh, Erv, I've been teasing, I—"

"And we say Morun, not Moron."

"Fine, Erv, but—"

"And I hate to say this, Dr. Case, but what you don't know about detailing bones could fill your library in there."

He just stood a minute, squinting in the low-angle light. He looked at me, then down at his feet. To his credit, he said, "You're right, Erv, and I know it. I was wrong."

He held out his hand. "No hard feelings?"

"No, sir, I guess not."

I took his hand and shook it.

AFTER THAT, Dr. Case began to spend more time with me, asking questions and telling me things. Surprised him, I think, how I picked up names. He didn't expect that from a guy who'd never been farther from this valley than Salt Lake. Who'd had to quit school in the eleventh grade. See, I could tell when I found something special, like the crocodile scute nestled behind the Camarasaurus toebone, and the almost intact skeleton of the baby stegosaurus. I called his attention to those things. He put the names to them. He was a whiz, and I filed his facts in the back of my mind.

One day as I was enjoying a smoke, taking a break from the pounding of the jack-hammer, he sat near me and dug quietly in the broken rock.

"Look at this stuff, Erv," he said. "All sandstone, but all different. Layers on layers of sandstone."

"That's so?"

He nodded. "An old river bed. Millions of years of sandbars building and shifting and changing."

I pondered that. "But dinosaurs didn't live in rivers. Where'd the bones come from?" All these years I'd figured the quarry was an ancient dinosaur burial ground: a swampy place where the big lizards dragged themselves to die. Dr. Case's river theory blasted that idea.

"Carried down from upstream. The beasts probably lived and died throughout the basin, and the river in flood picked up their bones and moved them."

I thought about that. "But bones don't float, Dr. Case."

"No, but they do roll on the bottom. Or they float if they're still in a carcass. And a lot of these were probably carcasses shunted into eddies by side components of the main current. Picture it, Erv." He reached out his arms like he was showing me the Milky Way. "A river of floating dinosaurs."

"Ah," I said. "I can picture it all right. You mean bloating dinosaurs. You wait until spring—you'll see enough puffed-up cows in the Green to scare you off steaks."

That night after work, I walked to the public library to read about rocks, because I couldn't get the notion of sandstone out of my head. Me, who'd been digging in the stuff for two decades. I found three good geology books and spread them on the wooden table near the magazine racks. I read about sandstone: that it forms in rivers and oceans and desert dunes. The rock can be full of calcium or quartz, tough or crumbly, gray or buff. In my digging, I'd felt the changes in hardness, and those were just in river rock. I couldn't figure how ocean beach or desert sandstone would feel.

On my way out of the library at closing time, full of thoughts of minerals and rivers, I walked smack into my ex-wife near the "Latest Arrival" shelves.

"Why, Ervin," Betty said, hugging a hardbound book so close I couldn't see its name. "What are you doing here? I thought you'd given up books."

"True. But I'm doing a little research."

Her eyebrows lifted slightly, and her mouth formed an O. She was tan and lovely, just the right amount of plumpness in her pink summer dress. Her hair looked grayer but wasn't permed as tight as before. It seemed soft and easy around her face.

"You look great," I said, in spite of knowing I shouldn't.

She blushed.

I walked her back to the house, where I'd lived with her for almost twelve years. At the edge of the valley, piles of black-bottomed clouds and short curtains of rain hung over the mountains. The scent of sage blew in from the desert outside of town. I heard soft whinnies from the Searles' horses beyond the high school baseball field and sharp zaps from the neon bug killers in the Rasmussens' garden. As Betty and I passed under the quiet rustling of elms, I told her about Dr. Case and how the quarry was once a riverbed.

"There's sandstone there where a river used to be, maybe even a big one like the Green." She didn't answer, but she was giving it some thought.

At the house, the lawn looked green and neatly trimmed. A single light shone in the downstairs window, where my reading chair once was. I wanted to open the door, walk inside, and sit and read as if time and disappointments had never pushed me from her. Instead I said, "Goodnight, Betty."

I left her in the half-darkness, knowing that she was beautiful and tender, but not knowing what to do about it.

IN TIME, Dr. Case lost his pasty grad-school look. Maybe it was his meditation or just living in country with a wide, blue sky. He took up fishing: Every weekend he'd fish Flaming Gorge, or a mountain lake, or some part of the Green. He went after it whole hog, like he went after everything. In the lunchroom, I found an article he'd clipped from the *Vernal Express* about Utah's legendary, oversized German browns. Fishing catalogues covered his desk. He bought hip waders, a canoe, one of those khaki vests with all the pockets, and a hat with the lambswool strip for keeping flies.

"I'm in heaven, Erv," he said.

"No, Dr. Case, it's Utah."

He grinned, and I couldn't help but grin myself.

He was pulling in support for the quarry, too, calling professors and finding money for our work. I figure a man doesn't get all the way to a Ph.D. in paleontology without a burning interest, and Dr. Case was on fire. He'd travel to conferences in Laramie, Phoenix, or Las Vegas, or invite guests to the quarry for his witty talks that earned standing ovations. Every time, he gave me credit: "the man who knows the rock," he'd say, asking me to stand, or "the fellow who does all the real work." After a while, I got used to it. Pretty soon I looked forward to going to his talks at the quarry, to swap tales with the visiting professors. And I looked forward to going to work.

One afternoon near quitting time, as I was working the jackhammer, Dr. Case waved me over. I shut down the hammer and took out my earplugs. We hunkered near a pile of ribs. "Look, Erv, see that little tail of sediment trailing east? That means the river right here flowed from the west."

"That seems likely."

He pointed to a big legbone. "And this stopped every other bone in this pile."

"How so? Like a little jam-up on Main?"

"Right," he said. "When one unit stops, it almost always causes a pile-up. Or the bones can settle in an eddy behind a rock. Not a lot of isolated bones here, are there?"

"No, sir, I had noticed that."

"Well, it's no coincidence, it's physical law." He called the piles waves, so named by a geologist at Berkeley.

That got me thinking. I climbed to a pile of bones I'd been detailing. "Here's another wave, Dr. Case." I pointed to the two huge sauropod ribs stacked against an end-up vertebra.

"And another, Erv," he yelled from the top of the quarry, where two femurs, each about five feet long, leaned together easy and neat as dominoes.

"Here's the best one yet." I kneeled near a string of neckbones that curved around a nest of skull plates.

"Wait," said Dr. Case. "Don't move! I'm getting my camera." He climbed down the face of the quarry, trotted along a poorly lit ledge of sandstone I'd been digging in all week, and—as I watched—stepped off the edge of the rock and tumbled fifteen feet down the steep path that bordered the quarry's west end.

I scrambled to help him, but he was already sitting up really tall, dusting himself off, by the time I reached him. "No sweat, Erv," he said, as I helped him stand. "Just a little problem with my eyes."

"Sir?"

"I don't understand it myself, but I can't see much in the half-light."

"There's an eye doctor from Salt Lake who gets to town once a week, Dr. Case. You ought to go see her."

"I'll do that." He fetched his camera from his office.

We stayed at the quarry until well after midnight, logging the waves of bones and understanding for the first time what they meant. "This is it, Erv," said Dr. Case, his face weary, but his eyes bright. "This is the beginning of something. Don't you agree?"

"I sure look at this rock a whole new way."

He was quiet for a moment. "Erv, I want you to come to Denver with me in September."

It took a minute for that to sink in. "Oh no, sir, I'm no professor. I've never even seen the outside of a conference hall."

"No matter. You know more about detailing than anybody I've ever met. You could contribute a lot to the meeting."

"Well, I'd love to, but—"

"Then it's settled. I'll authorize travel for us both." He checked his watch. "Oh, jeez, I'm out of here. Tell you what—take tomorrow off. I'm going to. I feel like going fishing."

We agreed to that, and I gathered up my things and walked outside. Dr. Case was still in his office when I turned from my truck to admire the quarry lights against the Utah sky. Then the big lamps switched off. In the starlight, I saw Dr. Case lock the gate and cross the parking lot.

"Erv? You there?" He stood near his car.

"Yes."

"It's a beautiful night, isn't it?"

"Sure is, Dr. Case."

"I could almost believe there's a heaven up there on a night like this."

"My God, you mean you don't?"

"No, Erv, I don't think so—I haven't been able to reconcile religion with my work." He opened his car door. "What about you? You quit the church, do you believe in God?"

"Oh, yes, sir. Of course. I always have, especially in hard times."

"But what about the bones, Erv? You believe in fossils. Aren't they an indication that life evolves? That earth wasn't made in six days?"

"Dr. Case, those are the details. I figure God's big enough to work them out. Or that the evolution itself is His doing. To me what counts is prayers. I couldn't have gotten through any other way when Dad left and I had to quit school. Or when my wife and I split up. The church might've got on my nerves, but I'll always believe in the Almighty."

"You're lucky, Erv." He waved good night. I watched as he climbed into his white station wagon and drove off down the hill—to his young wife and child and their three-bedroom home in the housing area.

I stood by my truck a minute. Cool air from Split Mountain washed down around me. Below the light burst of stars I spotted a satellite on a north-south course and remembered what Dr. Case had said about the conference. And that he'd called me lucky. "Thank you," I said to the heavens that were up there above the darkness.

THE PHONE call from Sheriff Hatch came after our day off, before dawn. I was sound asleep in my apartment. Hatch said he'd heard from Dr. Case's wife: The paleontologist had gone to Flaming Gorge and wasn't home for dinner. It had happened once before, she'd said—he'd stayed out fishing after dusk, too excited to quit, and he couldn't see well enough to drive home. He carried a sleeping bag in the car, just to be safe. But he had a CB radio, too, and this time he hadn't called in. The wife was beside herself by midnight. She told Hatch to phone me.

I'd spent the day in the library reading paleontology papers, sent in at my request from the University of Utah. Toward closing time, I looked up to see Betty standing opposite my reading table.

"Hello, Ervin," she said. "You've been spending a lot of time here."

"More and more." I removed my reading glasses. "I'm preparing for a paleontology conference in the fall. Dr. Case invited me."

"My. Well, it's good to see you reading again."

I walked her home. We passed lawns and sprinklers and water-filled gutters. At the house, lilacs filled the air with sweetness. The same light brightened the window where my chair used to be.

"Betty," I said. "I'm feeling better."

"I know."

"I'm thinking maybe I can be somebody."

"But, Ervin," she said. "You are somebody. I tried telling you that."

"Uh huh. Drove us both nuts telling me."

She looked startled for a moment, then leaned back her head and laughed. "Not that you ever listened."

"Well, you know me—too thick to plow."

When I bent to kiss her hair, she looked startled again. It felt soft and smelled of the same lavender shampoo that I remembered. Then it was all I could do to step down off the porch, with her only half hidden behind her front door. But I wasn't sure, and I wasn't ready, so I walked across town to my place. I sat up reading more of the dinosaur papers until early morning.

When the sheriff called, I'd been asleep just a few hours and I woke kind of panicky.

"Erv? It's Jim Hatch. I need your help. There may have been an accident."

Rays of sunlight had just touched the mountains when I met Hatch and his search-and-rescue team downtown. They were standing in front of the station in their hunting colors, drinking steaming coffee from Styrofoam cups. We rode together in a van to Flaming Gorge. I listened to the police radio, its static and garbled messages, and tried to calm my stomach. Hatch asked me some questions, which I answered as best I could.

"Do you know where he'd be, Erv?"

"What kind of fishing does he do?"

"His wife said he's got bad eyes—did he tell you that?"

"He's pretty new in the valley. How well do you know him?"

We parked near the dam, right next to Dr. Case's white station wagon. Hatch had guessed as soon as we saw it that no one was inside—the windows weren't at all steamed up. We wiped a little bit of dew from the windshield. The CB was turned off and hung up on the dashboard. The sleeping bag sat on the front seat, rolled up in its blue cover. We used Hatch's megaphone to call for Dr. Case, with no luck, while the sickening feeling grew in my stomach.

Hatch headed to the lake while I led a few men downstream.

A little fog hung on the river. The water smelled fresh and cool. Below the dam, the Green's fast and shallow, with narrow eddies. There are sudden deeper spots behind boulders, which Dr. Case would have known better than anyone but maybe not seen if he'd been fishing at dusk.

The first thing we found was his plastic lunch cooler, right by shore, with just an apple core and sandwich wrappers inside. I called again, and tried to run, but the boulders were slippery with dew. So I walked near shore with the other men, calling for Dr. Case, hoping to find him sitting up really tall, brushing himself off.

I did find him. See, I knew where to look—he taught me. Sure enough, he'd been pulled down near one of the deeper spots, his waders full of water. He'd washed into an eddy, where his arms trailed upstream parallel to the current in the backwater. I pulled him in and turned him over. An eerie paleness had settled under his new tan. And his eyes—which for a while I'd figured missed nothing—were open, but the light was gone.

THAT AFTERNOON, I called Betty. She said, "I heard."

We met at the museum and sat out back at the picnic tables. The air was full of the sound of cars cruising Main and the smell of fresh-cut alfalfa from beyond the neighborhoods. My stomach hurt the way it had since morning at the river. I kept seeing those young blue eyes with nothing in them, a sight I wish I hadn't seen.

"He was it," I said. "He was the engine. I wasn't ready for him to leave."

Betty picked pieces of cottonwood fleece from the picnic table. "I'm sorry, Ervin."

"And there'll be no conference now. No being somebody."

She didn't speak right away. When she did, her voice trembled. "I think you're wrong, Ervin. I think he'd want you to go to the conference."

"By myself?"

She nodded.

We sat for a time without speaking. I was grateful for the silence, which she never used to allow.

After a while she stood and smoothed her skirt. She asked me if I'd like to come for coffee later on. Then she walked home across the big lawn behind the museum, brown arms swinging, flowered skirt swaying. Beyond her, light changed on the buff-colored cliffs of sandstone. I couldn't stop staring at them—would I ever? They stood this side of Flaming Gorge, with its legendary German browns and its cold, rushing stream below.

ERUPTION

Tortoise Watch

SHEILA GOLBURGH JOHNSON

SHEILA GOLBURGH JOHNSON, 57, a dedicated birdwatcher, gave up teaching twelve years ago to devote herself to writing and birdwatching. She spends months each year hiking in the Catalina and Chiricahua mountains of southeastern Arizona and has seen such local rarities as the Elegant Trogon, the Rose-Throated Becard, and "a dazzling array of hummingbirds." Her combined interests led her to edit an anthology of bird poems, Shared Sightings, *and her short stories, essays, and poetry have appeared in a wide variety of publications. Her novel, titled* After I Said No, *won the Sydney Taylor Manuscript Award from the Association of Jewish Libraries in 1995.*

Life is not a tale of progress; it is, rather, a story of intricate branching and wandering, with momentary survivors adapting to changing local environments, not approaching cosmic or engineering perfection. And success in natural selection is often a result of producing more surviving offspring.

> —From narrator's old ecology textbook

WALKING IN FRONT OF a grader watching for desert tortoises is not the greatest job in the world, but the money's good and they put me up in a motel in Barstow. There's even a food allowance: another twenty a day.

The heat is hard to take. Here in the Mojave Desert in June it's over a hundred by ten o'clock in the morning—and dry. It's so dry it hurts to breathe. I can feel the air rasping along the vessels inside my nose every time I inhale.

The tortoises survive in it, but they only come out to graze in the morning and late afternoon. The rest of the time they stay underground. Smart. We're supposed to be watching for burrows, too, and warn the driver. You can't dig up the burrows, since the tortoises are listed as an endangered species.

Such species and population stocks should not be permitted to diminish beyond the point at which they cease to be a significant functioning element in the ecosystem of which they are a part.

—Endangered Species Conservation Act, 1969

THERE'S ANOTHER person out here working for the state Environmental Protection Agency. Rick told me he was a graduate student in classics—Greek, Latin, and Sanskrit—the first day we walked in front of the tractor. He looked a little old to be in school, and uneasy. Mid-thirties, I guessed: tall, thin, with a stubbly red beard.

He read my look. "I was an engineer. An electrical engineer. I was making fifty thousand a year, and saving some."

I shrugged. "Why'd you give it up?"

"You have to be married and play golf to get ahead. Next thing you know, you've got a house in the suburbs, a wife, and two kids. You're stuck for life." He batted at his head lightly with his hand.

"So you chose dead languages?"

"They're not so dead. A lot of our ideas about law and government came from that period."

"Does anyone speak or write them anymore?"

"No. But there's a lot of research being done in them. There's great stuff in classic languages that's worth reading in the original. And it's fun figuring out what their lives were like. Not so different from ours. After all, they gave us Oedipus."

The roar of the machinery behind us died and left a deafening silence. I looked back. The driver popped open a can of Sprite, drained it, and tossed the can. I struck out for a wash bordered with tamarisk and flopped in the shade. Rick folded his long legs under him so that he was sitting cross-legged in the sand. He reached for the canteen slung over his shoulder, took a deep swallow, then batted at the side of his head.

I fished a can of apple juice from my backpack. "So what are you planning to do after you get your degree?"

"Who knows? I gave up thinking everything has to be useful. Look at the tortoises. What do they do but scrabble around in the desert chewing leaves and grass? But we watch out for them while we're digging up the desert to lay cable."

"The guy who hired me said the cable contains hundreds of filaments of optical fiber that carry messages by light beam. Is that a telephone call?" I asked.

"Your voice is coded into light when you speak into the phone. The optical fiber carries thousands of messages at the same time. It converts back into sound at the other end. They'll be able to transmit calls across the country at the speed of light. It's incredible."

"Do you think they'll survive?" I was really talking to myself. "The tortoises?"

"Well, we're trying," he said. "The fact that the EPA pays us eighteen dollars an hour to make sure the graders don't dig up burrows kind of gives you hope, doesn't it?"

"Maybe." I heard the rumble of the machine starting up and scrambled to my feet.

> *Tortoise signs in the form of tracks, droppings, and skeletal remains are found more often than the animals themselves. A resting tortoise can easily be overlooked because of its resemblance to a stone.*

THAT EVENING, paddling slowly around the dinky motel pool in Barstow, I thought about the tortoises. We didn't do all of it, of course; species have come and gone on this earth since long before man appeared. They evolve and fill some niche. When conditions change too much, they die out.

Maybe it's a good thing. How could life evolve if extinction didn't open the way for novelty? If the dinosaurs hadn't died out, we mammals would have remained a minor group of small creatures living in nooks and crannies the dinosaurs didn't fill.

It's the same with family arrangements, I thought. Marriage used to be an important goal for women, but now that we have other niches we can fill, it seems to be dying out. A year ago I walked out of my marriage when I was offered a chance to do graduate work here in California. My husband had refused to move his law practice from the East Coast.

"You expect me to start all over again?" he had asked.

"I'd do it for you," I said. "If it were important."

"I'd have to take the California Bar Exam. The laws are different in California."

"I would do it for you," I said again. I couldn't think of anything else to say. I had put off having children so that I could be an environmental biologist. It had been a hard choice for me, but he hadn't felt strongly about having children. Compared with that decision, moving to California seemed like a small thing.

"You don't have to do it at all. You don't need the grant. I make plenty of money. I'll pay your tuition. Study someplace here."

"This is my own thing," I said. "The university at Irvine is willing to pay me to go there because they're interested in my honors' thesis. I'll get to work with some of the best people in my field."

"So commute." It had the sound of a cell door slamming shut.

I clambered out of the pool, grabbed the too-thin towel, and wiped off my face. Some of the water was tears—after a year it still hurt. My project was going well, but the results I was getting from my experiments in cell adaptation were dismal. Some of the pollutants we've been pouring into the atmosphere have far more devastating, long-term effects on human cells than we have imagined. But it would be years before anyone could convince the powers that be.

It didn't help my state of mind. Sometimes I wondered why I was spending all those hours shut up in my lab when I should be running up and down the streets waving a sign: "Save Yourself!" Sometimes I understand the lunatic fringe.

And the loneliness still got to me. Eating dinner alone after some years of marriage was devastating. One night I wolfed a peanut butter sandwich in my studio apartment and I took a shower. Standing there with water pouring down on my head, mixing with the tears, I felt such a visceral urge to end my life that I had to reach out of the shower and grab the sink to keep myself upright. I literally reeled. I turned off the water and took a long, deep breath. I looked into the mirror. My lips moved. Don't do it. Do something else. Fast.

I pulled on clothes and rushed out of the studio. I ran a long way until the pounding of my heart was all I could hear. I felt better when I got back, but after that I understand why people take their lives. The impulse, when it comes, is as strong as the impulse to live. I've managed to keep myself steady since then, but sometimes I wonder what for. I need a little joy now and then. Some sign that I did the right thing to resist, a reason to go on working.

The turtle group is one of the most distinct of the orders of reptiles more ancient than the dinosaurs, and its representatives are immediately recognizable by the enclosure of their bodies in bony shells, usually covered with scale-like plates, combined with the complete absence of teeth.

JUST AFTER Rick and I arrived at the site the next morning, we saw a tortoise. It was feeding on the stiff leaves of a desert mallow, chewing with great concentration. Its round dome of brown plates with yellowish centers blended perfectly with the colors of the desert.

"Do you think we should warn the driver?" Rick asked.

"No . . . it's pretty far off our path." I giggled. "They don't exactly dash out in front of machines, you know."

We marched along in front of the grader, trying to keep ahead of the rising dust.

"It's amazing they survived this long," Rick mused, "considering how much activity goes on here."

"And how specific their needs are," I said. "The animals with the best chances are the ones who can adapt easily. Sharks are one of the most successful groups. They can survive in warm or cold oceans, and they'll eat just about anything. If one food source dies out, they switch to another."

"Hmmm. Maybe that's why they keep attacking surfers," Rick said.

"Who knows? We probably look delicious to them."

He batted lightly at his head. I wondered if it were a tic he developed when he moved from one niche to another. "How did you get into tortoise watching?" he asked.

"Well, mostly it seemed like a good chance to pick up some money and get out of the lab for the summer. But now that I'm here, it's depressing." I looked at the tortoise heading toward a burrow with his particular waddling gait. "They're an anachronism."

"They'll make it. We have to save little pockets where they can survive, because everything is getting so crowded," he said. "But we can. We're the bridge between what was here to begin with and what we're creating."

"What we're creating may do us in," I said.

The grinding rumble of the grader had been building up and finally reached a crescendo. We both turned around. The driver killed the engine and swung from his seat to the ground with a gesture that signaled his irritation.

"He's hit some kind of snag," Rick said. "Want to find some shade?"

I lifted my hat and fanned my face with it. We headed for a little arroyo about thirty yards off, with a few acacias at the edge.

I was just about to jump down when I caught a movement near the opposite bank. I squinted into the glare reflecting off the sandy ground. The figures I was looking at suddenly took shape against the surrounding brightness. I turned to Rick and grabbed his arm to signal him to be still. Silently, I pointed.

A male tortoise approached a female with his shell held high and his head bobbing. He bit at her back legs and shell and then lunged at her again and again, retracting his head at the moment of impact. She flattened her foreclaws against the ground and raised her hind end slightly. In a few moments he fell behind and mounted her from the rear, balancing on his scaly hind legs. She fell still and arched her neck back toward him. He continued to pump against her with his mouth open.

I looked at Rick. He grinned and raised his canteen in homage as a harsh, hissing cry rose above the sigh of hot desert wind with a kind of ancient bravado, a primordial declaration of being.

Sheila

KATHRYN WILDER

KATHRYN WILDER, 40, is the editor of the original Walking the Twilight *and author of a children's book,* Forbidden Talent. *She has a BA and an MA in creative writing and has taught writing privately and at Northern Arizona University and Coconino Community College. Although her family has lived in California for a hundred and fifty years, Kathryn has let her spirit roam the West and find home where it would—on ponderosa-clad mountains, in lupine-filled meadows, in red and yellow canyons, on the river. She currently lives with her son, Tyler, in a cabin on the fringes of Flagstaff, Arizona. Her other son, Kenney, lives on a California ranch with his father.*

LET'S SAY MY NAME'S Sheila and I pick up road kill. Let's say that maybe my friends have been known to find such things as a flicker or a tassel-eared squirrel in my freezer. And let's say my kids don't live with me, that they live in another state with their father, a hunter, a man who, in another lifetime, may have taught me to hunt. Who may have taught his kids, who did their teething on buck jerky, how to spot game and put the sneak on a black-tail deer when they were barely out of a car seat.

Let's say the kids' names are Cal and Tex, and that one 117-degree day I was driving across the desert to meet them and bring them home to my house for a not-long-enough visit, and that I found a bobcat, fresh-killed, somewhere on Interstate 40. Let's say he was so fresh that his blood had not yet coagulated on the hot-enough-to-fry-an-egg blacktop, that it was still running from the wound at his right ear in little rivulets east, with the slope of the hill. Let's say he was still warm, not from the 117-degree day but from his own blood and breath and heartbeat, recently stopped, and that I, Sheila, mixed tears with his blood as I lifted him, gently so as not to disturb the departing spirit, and wrapped him in an old towel and placed him on the back seat of my car.

Because of the heat, and the long drive still ahead, let's say I stopped in the next desert town and purchased a cooler and a couple of blocks of ice. Let's say I put the bobcat, who was now stiffening slightly, in the cooler on ice, right there in the parking lot of Kmart. And that I continued on my long drive with the bobcat on ice on the back seat of my car.

And then, mid-Mojave, I got my kids, meeting their stepmother under the only tree for miles around like I always do, and as Cal and Tex and I, Sheila, got back on Interstate 40 heading in the direction from which I had just come, let's say I told them about the bobcat, who was now sitting on the floor at Tex's feet—he's the younger one, only six, and so has the shorter legs of the two—in the cooler on blocks of ice, of course.

Let's say the kids said, at once and in unison, "Mo-om!" because, let's say, they think I am Sheila and that I stop for road kill, and sometimes they get tired of it.

"Wha-at?" I may have said back. And then let's say I explained that I hadn't gutted the bobcat yet because I was in a hurry to meet their stepmother and get them, that I hadn't wanted them to fry in the shade of that one tree for miles around in the now 120-degree desert afternoon.

So let's say one kid, Cal, the older one, said, "We better gut him, Mom." He looked into the heat-waving distance and pointed off to the right. "See that dirt road?" let's say he said. "Take that road. We can gut him out there in the desert."

"Turn up there," he maybe said as he eyeballed the lay of the creosote-covered, rock-strewn land.

And let's say I followed my nine-year-old boy's directions, and that we drove down the dirt road, which was sand, really, until we found some taller creosote bushes and a little ravine, and that I turned the car onto the faint tire tracks in the sand where somebody else had stopped to do something else they wished unwitnessed by other highway travelers. Not something unpleasant to discover, let's say, like you often find in ditches and large culverts near the Interstate, but something freeing and full of desert spirit on a maybe not-so-hot desert day. And there, like members of many an American family—though not like the two who had used this spot to mix air and flesh to make love—we pulled the cooler from the car, plopped it in the minimal shade by the back tire, and opened it up.

And then let's say the boys said, "Wow!" as I pulled forth the bobcat and unwrapped him from the old towel I had found in the back of the car earlier that day, when the weather was only 117 degrees hot. And even though the cat was on ice, he had stiffened still more, so that, let's say, he was somewhat difficult to manage, but my older boy, the nine year old, who has gutted a lot of deer with his father, helped me stretch the front and back legs apart to expose the slightly bloating belly. And let's say that even though my knife was a bit dull and I a bit rusty, Cal and I managed to gut out the hypothetically road-killed bobcat near a sand road, once ridden by lovers, in the middle of the desert on a now 121-degree summer afternoon, while my other son, Tex, the six year old, searched under creosote bushes for alligator lizards.

Let's say Tex came over to watch at the very end and the three of us offered the guts to the ravens, or turkey buzzards, or the lone coyote who might brave the heat hours after the sun went down in search of just such a treat, and that we each said a prayer of thanks and of happy traveling to the departed bobcat spirit before we wrapped him back up in the old towel, and put him on ice blocks in the new cooler, and headed toward home in the direction from which I had earlier come—my two boys, I, Sheila, and a freshly gutted, road-killed bobcat, whose spirit might have been any of the heat-wave shimmers dancing above the desert floor like lovers in the night.

So let's say we made it home to a cooler clime before it was too late, and that we pulled the old towel from the bobcat like a skin, wrapping him in plastic instead and settling him into the freezer for his next life before settling into ours. And then, because maybe picking up road kill is illegal in some states, or maybe it is in all states, I don't know because maybe I'm Sheila and I don't pay attention to such things, I went down to the drive-through liquor store near the alternative bookstore and bought a hunting license.

One afternoon in this cooler clime after my kids had returned to another state, let's say I went to a taxidermist's shop near the train tracks, the bobcat riding stiff on the seat beside me. And after placing the furry frozen rock—that maybe used to be a living, breathing animal spirit until black rubber stopped its life at the edge of the freeway—on the countertop, I turned around.

And then I'll say that what I saw was half an elephant. Bisected at the girth, I'll say that he stood against the wall of the warehouse on his front feet only. That the tips of his ears reached where my head would if I were twice my height. That his ears were set as if he were flapping them at flies, or bullets. That his tusks were longer than a tall hunter's arms. Whiter, too.

And let's say that at that moment, the smell of fresh death reached my nose, twisted on my tongue, settled in my throat. That my nostrils had clamped down on it one 117-degree day when I leaned over and stroked the fine fur of a just-dead bobcat, when I lifted his warm and sagging body to my heart. And that another day long ago, when I brought my first buck to his death, the blood I smelled was my own, my broken-by-the-rifle-scope nose a cover-up for the tears that fell. But this day, in the taxidermist's shop, the smell of hides being stripped from bodies could not be blocked, the smell of raw meat cooling and blood congealing could not be stopped.

Let's say I turned around slowly, as if in a dream or a bad commercial, images reeling. Gazelle and antelope, bison and water buffalo, cougar and African lion lined the walls. Bear, bobcat, black-tail, white-tail, and mule deer decorated the morgue. The elephant held up the wall the way he could no longer hold up himself.

"Where will he go?" let's say I said, and that this conversation ensued:

"To a six-thousand-square-foot house north of San Francisco," a man answered. "The trophy room."

"I've never hunted what I wouldn't eat," I whispered.

The man peeled the plastic off the bobcat. "Oh?" He eyed me across the counter. "Do you have something for me?" he said. I shrugged—the bobcat was intact. "Like a hunting license?" he added.

I found my wallet and handed him the crisp new piece of paper. As he marked me down in a column, penciling "bobcat" beside my name, I wanted to explain to him that my name is Sheila and I pick up road kill. But I was as silent as the animals covering the walls.

Outside, sun and air flooded me like memories, or nightmares. And I'll tell you the truth: Children teething on venison jerky aside, I am not Sheila. I am just another desert spirit. And when I shimmer in a desert dance with my lover, with my children, I breathe life back into the bobcat. He is already a part of me.

Fire

TERRY TEMPEST WILLIAMS

TERRY TEMPEST WILLIAMS, 40, lives in Salt Lake City, Utah, where she is naturalist-in-residence at the Utah Museum of Natural History. Her books include Pieces of White Shell, Coyote's Canyon, Refuge, An Unspoken Hunger, *and, most recently,* Desert Quartet. *In addition to studying and writing about the natural world, Terry is actively involved in protecting it. She and her husband, Brooke, are currently engaged with Utah citizens in the creation of America's Redrock Wilderness Act, HR 1500, which would define 5.7 million acres of Utah's canyon country as wilderness.*

I STRIKE A MATCH and light the shreds of kindling I have cut with my knife. Juniper. I fan the incense toward me. The smoke rises, curls, coils around my face. It feels good to be in the desert again. Home—where I can pause, remain silent. There is nothing to explain.

I break twigs and lean them against each other in the formation of a teepee. More smoke. On hands and knees in red sand, I blow at its base, blow again, add a handful of dried cottonwood leaves, blow, they ignite, flames engulf the triangle.

I sit back on my haunches, pleased that the fire is growing in the desert, in me, so that I can dream, remember, how it is that I have come to love. It is fate that determines the territory of the heart. I add more sticks, blow, the fire flares in darkness.

The wood opens.

Flames rise, flicker. My eyes blur. I hold every detail of love in my body, nothing forgotten, put more sticks on the fire. It surges, sputters, and purrs. The fire holds me captive, charismatic flames wave me closer. I add two more sticks like bodies to love. They are consumed instantly. The fire shifts, then settles with new intensity; it shifts again, adjusts. The wood pops like vertebrae. The silver bark of juniper burns black, turns white. A spark breathes.

I crouch down and blow on embers. They flare and quiver. I blow again. They become rubies. I reach into the coals, believing, and burn my fingers, blister their tips, pull back in pain and bury my hands in the sand. The fire wanes. I cannot bear its absence. I lower my head and blow. The fire ignites. My longing returns. When we want everything to change we call on fire.

I fetch more wood. Bones of piñon and juniper lie on the desert floor. Even in darkness I see them illumined by the moon. I gather them in my arms. This time they are larger. I must break them over my knee and feed the fire once again. The fire is aroused. The flames reach higher. I stand before them with my arms raised, my hands surrender and come down to caress the heat and mold it into faces I love. Do I dare to feel the white heat of my heart as prayer? What is smoldering inside me? And how is it that pleasure exists between such beauty and violence? Feed the fire. No. Yes. My fingers touch the blaze of bodies in flames.

The fire implodes. Flames become blue tongues curling around each other. My eyes close. I step forward. My legs open to the heat, the tingling return of heat, inside, outside, shadows dance on the sandstone, my ghostly lover. I allow myself to be ravished. My generosity becomes my humiliation. The hair between my legs is singed. My left hand shields my face from fire. Fingers open. It is a shuttered scape. Fingers clench, I hold a fist before flames, loyal and disloyal at once.

Above me, free-tailed bats circle the flames like moths. Moths frighten me. I hate their addiction to light. But bats delight in darkness with their ears wide open. What do they hear that I am missing? Gifted in the location of echoes, they listen twice to all that is spoken in the desert. They are dark angels who register our longings and pinpoint the cries lodged within our throats.

Heat. More heat. My face flushes red. The fire's hands are circling. I sit inches away from something that tomorrow will not exist. The blue-eyed coals I gaze into will disappear. Ashes. Ashes. Death is the natural conclusion of love.

But tonight it remains alive and I know in the shock of my heart that love is as transitory as fire. The warmth I feel, the glow of my body and the force of my own interior heat, is enough to keep me here.

It is our nature to be aroused—not once, but again and again. Where do we find the strength to not be pulled apart by our passions? How do we inhabit the canyons inside a divided heart? One body. Two bodies. Three.

Beyond the junipers and piñons of this starless night, I face the deep stare of darkness. This wildness cannot be protected or preserved. There is little forgiveness here. Experience is the talisman I hold for courage. It is the desert that persuades me toward love, to step outside and defy custom one more time.

The fire now bears the last testament to trees. I blow into the religious caverns of wood and watch them burn brightly. My breath elucidates each yellow room and I remember the body as sacrament.

I have brought candles with me. I take them out of my pouch and secure them in the sand. With a small stick I carry a flame from the fire and light one, and another, and another. They threaten to flicker and fade. I shelter them with my hands and watch the way the wax trickles down the side of each taper. Once away from the flame, it hardens. My body reflects the heat. I dip the tip of my finger into the small basin of heated wax shining at the base of the wick, bring it to my lips, and paint them.

I turn toward the flames.

Desert Rhapsody

LIZ BESMEHN

LIZ BESMEHN, 35, grew up in "the sticks" in northern Minnesota, "pretending that all things in the woods could talk, that even rocks were alive." She moved to Utah fifteen years ago and discovered the voice of the Colorado Plateau. She's been listening ever since. She lives with her husband, Bruce, and her sons, Josh, Luke, and Dusty, in Salt Lake City. Her fiction has appeared in Visiones, Shades, *and the first* Walking the Twilight.

THE DAY BEFORE I ran away from home I dressed in combat boots and a ratty tie-dyed skirt. I went to a biker bar, ordered a shot of water and some change for the jukebox. I played an old Eagles song seven times. A couple of bikers toasted the West before it was lost. A couple more got up and left. Some of us sang the last line together: "Call someplace paradise. Kiss it good-bye."

A long thin man with starched, colorless hair and a pale, puffed face was sitting beside me at the bar. I don't know why he was in that bar on a Wednesday afternoon. He didn't ride in on a Harley, but neither did I.

"Are you real?" he asked. He put his laptop computer in a brown briefcase and looked at me like I smelled bad and should leave. "Are you insane?"

The day before I ran away from home I might have been crazy. Fear can do that—make otherwise invisible people leap to center stage with unabashed autocracy. I wanted to tell the man with two pens in his pocket that I was leaving in the morning, would probably die out there for no good reason, and sometimes music, a particular song, can make it all make sense. I wanted to say this, but instead I looked at the floor.

The man without eyelashes asked the bartender for "Jack, no ice," and would she change the song on the box before he paid for the drink? I felt him stare at me. "What are you, a tree hugger?" he asked.

"I've hugged a few trees," I said politely, just over my breath, still intent on the floor. "But truthfully, I prefer to run naked in the night with a dagger, chanting Celtic words and slashing the tires of polished gray BMWs. I kidnap the firstborn children of corporate executives whenever possible, shake chickens over their heads until they promise to plant trees and grow mandrake on the White House lawn."

"You're sick," he said.

"Could be," I told him. "Is that Beamer in the parking lot yours?"

THE DAY before I ran away from home I was thrown out of a biker bar for disturbing the peace, for pouring water on a paying customer, and for playing the same song too many times in a row. The day before I ran away from home I was feeling a little crowded.

THAT NIGHT I painted purple lines on my face, braided beads into my hair, and wore my father's moth-eaten, World War II Air Force jacket and cap. I hung a harmonica and Grandpa's old skinning knife from a twine-string belt that wound around my waist and dropped to the ground like lost reins.

I stood in my back yard, close to the fence, faced a corner I call The Wild Garden. I took off my wedding ring, burned this year's school pictures of my kids, cut a braid out of my hair, and buried it all together beside the grave of my ferret, Mr. Wheeze.

Around here, things that matter end up in The Wild Garden. It's an unruly piece of ground thick with morning glory, thistle, and knee-deep grass. There are two unpinned rosebushes, one red, one yellow; a dead peach tree; and some purple iris, remnants of the manicured garden that was here before I moved in. I let the garden go its own way to remind myself that life takes care of itself, to provide an everyday place for wilderness in a landscape that depends on routine.

Inside my house, I've given up rights to the kitchen window above the sink. It's a no trespassing zone. No glass cleaner, no dust rag, no motorized vehicles for any reason. In the eight years I've lived here I've watched the window transform from a sterile piece of clear glass in a painted wood case to a complete ecosystem. Ivy has slipped through the cracks and moved inside. Enough dust has settled to form soil; moss grows. The window supports a community of ants and a couple of wolf spiders. Things change in my window now and doing dishes has become a hobby.

The night before I ran away from home I climbed the peach tree in combat boots, a tie-dyed skirt, and an Air Force cap. I stood on a wind-worn branch and saluted my white-brick rambler house. I played "My Country 'Tis of Thee," "America the Beautiful," and "Jesus Loves Me" on a C-chord harmonica Santa left in my sock twenty-six winters before.

Over the fence, in the yard behind my yard, the sound of a person clapping hovered in the branches of my tree. "Nona, is that you?" I asked.

"They say they'll lock me up if they find me out here again."

I imagined her ninety-year-old body in a pale yellow nightgown, thin wisps of translucent gray hair brushing her collar while she searched the sky above her fence looking for me, or airplanes, or the sweeping arc of a spotlight selling cars from a lot beside the freeway. Her mouth would be open, milky blue eyes squinted for distance, almost lost in the folds of her face.

"They'll lock you up, too. They'll lock us both up if they catch us," she said. "But will you play one more? Will you play 'Greensleeves' for me?"

The day I ran away from home I sat on a black and hot-pink jacket in the driveway, wrapped in a wool blanket, sorting white socks, surrounded by a fortress of camping gear, and cried. The sun was remarkably warm for the first week in March and I couldn't remember anymore why I wanted to go.

My husband was working, the boys were in school, my fat cat, Paws, washed his face from the top of my sleeping bag and watched me fuss over fabric and pick at the groceries I'd bought for the trip.

"What do you think, Paws? You want to come with me? We'll shit-can our efforts to harmonize in this mega-metro-pseudo-scum-dog-eat-dog-stinking-livetrap and we'll escape. We'll go to the desert and live without evil; no hyped-up missionaries trying to sell stained-glass religion; no Prozac mornings, neutralizing the brain's panic in order to cope with the ten P.M. news, everybody's damn opinions, and the freedom-stealing laws that are born from them; no too many people waiting in lines, breathing together on the highway, in the bank, at the ice cream shop, even the bathroom; no more trying to avoid the inevitable 'moo' some jerk always bellows from the open window of a passing car while you walk down a sidewalk thinking you look good."

WHEN I was seven I pretended my bed was a boat and I was at sea. I packed jelly sandwiches, a cat, the thick blue pencil I brought home from school, and a tablet of brown paper. I hid under the quilt, away from four sisters, three brothers, worn parents, and I weathered make-believe hurricanes, pirates, true love, and sharks till I was nearly fourteen. At thirty-six, I've traded jelly sandwiches for rice and black beans, the sea for desert; the rest is the same.

The day I ran away from home I didn't say good-bye to my family. I filled my car with premium unleaded, hesitated at the gas station, hands shaking, crossed my fingers, and drove south until the world turned red around me.

THE DESERT isn't the terrain for a low-riding sports car. I drive as far back on gravel as I can go without serious damage, then I leave it and hike in another mile. I choose a canyon my mate and I found a year ago, in December while we were stumbling through another cactus patch in our marriage.

We found the canyon two hours before our weekend was over. I wore a black velvet dress, open back, plunging neck, with pearls and a large feathered hat. I carried a gold sequin clutch and strolled over frozen sand in gold stilettos. He lit a cigarette for me and I smoked half of it while I leaned into a rock and watched him skate on the blue glass of a desert pool encased in brilliant pink walls, icicles hanging, glittering in half sun like a ballroom adorned with white diamonds. He laughed, we danced on ice, and I left the petals from a single red rose to be scattered like hope through the canyon.

TODAY, THE canyon moves me with its silence, its creek, the hidden pools and waterfalls. The place is sacred, is spiritual in its lack of human habitation and quiet desolation. Towering salmon-colored sandstone walls, red sand floor, piñon pine, juniper, cliffrose, and sage dress this slice of earth in a wardrobe of wildness.

I find a sheltered gateway between two junipers, a front door into a circle of trees and twisted brush above the creek. I walk in, look around as if exploring an abandoned house, throw the tent on the ground, and call this place mine.

With the sunlight left, I gather firewood, set up the tent, put together a kitchen, and while my dinner cooks buried in the coals of a comfortable fire, I sit on a table of crimson stone and realize I'm smiling.

I'm not any of the things I'd prepared myself for. I'm not lonely or cold or stranded and as long as there's daylight, I'm not even afraid. I haven't been stung by a scorpion, bitten by a snake, eaten by a lion, or fallen into a river and drowned. My tent went up easy, fire lit easy, cooking is easy, and I feel safe enough to unlace my boots, walk barefoot on powdered red sand.

Just in case, I put a ring of salt around my camp to ward off spiders and snakes, vampires or monsters, that might be in the area. I build a small altar and leave bits of food, a sprig of sage, and some purple vetch I find growing by the river. I do this to win favor with the spirits of place I know live in the canyon.

The first night away from home I eat my dinner alone and listen to myself chew food. I watch as the day turns twilight and then the twilight turns black. I put more wood on the fire, try to force myself to look at the stars, but the stars are scary. They're right on top of me. The sky is big and unfamiliar without its pink, city-light glow.

I want to be brave, like when I was small on a boat at sea, like when I'm camouflaged in one of my costumes, but at night, alone in the desert, costumes come off and all coyotes have rabies and every sound is something hunting you. I wonder how long it will take a big cat to shred the tent and if death will come quick.

I build the fire to a roaring blaze and crawl inside my tent, light two candles, and watch the fire from inside. I listen to water rush and wonder if the creek runs faster at night. I listen deeply to the desert, half in terror, half curious. I note sounds, snapping twigs, wind, the hiss of fire.

Why do women run away from home? If I were my husband, this wouldn't be running at all; it would be camping, simple as that.

The first night I'm away from home, I'm scared and I wish I had brought my dog. I watch the fire die and feel blood ooze from my body into the floral cotton print between my legs. I don't want to leave my candlelit tent to wander in the black night to look for something I can use to catch the red wetness that unexpectedly stains my only pair of thermal underwear. I sit cross-legged in the open-flap door of my tent, rocking, holding my crotch with one hand and biting fingernails on the other until my fear of blood-scented wind drawing the company of bears outweighs my fear of the dark.

I take my first bath in a freezing, fast-running creek at night. The moon rises while I squat over knee-deep water, holding a branch with one hand and splashing myself clean with the other. I watch as the moon, a huge, orange-glowing orb, rises above the mountains that rise above the canyon. The moon lights the night and the water sparkles. I can see both sides of the canyon, the rim and all the way down. I can see my shadow on the ground while I walk back to camp, and stillness grows inside me.

I sleep curled around my shovel, my fingers touching the safe handle of my axe. I decide if I'm attacked, I'll fight. The first night I sleep alone, I feel alone, and it's not romantic, and Robinson Crusoe can kiss my ass. The temperature drops to twenty-eight degrees and I finally let go of the axe to bring my hands inside the sleeping bag. I burrow in deep.

I have one dream. I dream I wake up to listen for noises outside my tent and hear rain falling. I dream I hear thunder. The sky lights with lightning, the bolt strikes the tent and my forehead. I dream it splits my head apart; I'm dying. I wake in the middle of a prayer, alive, and to dawn. I wake knowing the first night will be the only night I spend sleeping with a shovel.

I SLIP quickly into a routine that makes camp feel like home:
Stoke the fire in the morning, put coffee on to cook.
Go pee, don't worry about scorps and snakes.
Check the altar, feel unfamiliar delight when the food left the night before is gone.
Look at the sky.
Listen to moving water.
Feel the red walls.
Feel strangely alive with joy.

I STAY eight days. I forget that I worry about being fat and become lovely. My body moves without effort, performs every task without argument or pain. I bathe daily in the afternoon when the sun is high and hot. I bathe on a flat rock that rests in the creek. Naked in daylight, alone in the canyon, I feel as pretty as the land around me.

I stay eight days and forget that I have a name. Words like woman, wife, mother, daughter lose their significance. In the desert I'm not anybody and being nobody I can spend two hours perched on a rock halfway up the wall, looking into my canyon, singing made-up songs about all of it. Things I see and things I sense. I sing about it all.

Every morning two hawks circle and scream in the same corner of sky that the Big Dipper hangs from at night. Every night the moon rises a little later and Orion hunts behind me. A jay has lost his fear and shares camp with me. The salt I circled myself with has mixed with sand and gone away.

One day it rains. The creek turns red. I fish a deep hole by a snag, never get a bite. One day I walk so far I don't make it back to camp until the next day. One day I find a raven feather.

I WANT to stay forever and forget that I live in a world that wakes up inside of houses. I want to stay until my bones bleach white and I become one of the ghosts that whisper from the rocks, a bit of memory and history that haunts wild places.

I might do this, but on the eighth day the desert sends me home. I sit by the fire and sip hot coffee. The sun rises warm and delicious as spring in a desert can be. The hawks make music in a sky so blue it hurts my heart to look at it. Real pain. The kind that comes with unreasonable love. I scratch words on paper, caught up in contentment, and then I see the new path to the creek, the one my feet have made.

I look around and know I'll have to go farther for firewood. I've taken it all from here, every piece of cedar, piñon, and sage that will burn. I've killed a couple of plants that were living close to my fire ring. A yucca, a tiny cliffrose. The color of the sand is different, tinted with ashes.

"Call someplace paradise . . ."

It hits me like an anvil falling from a cartoon. I am just one person, someone who practices ecology in her kitchen, a "tree hugger," and my presence in the desert is changing it.

I break camp as gently as possible. Put back the charred rocks I used for my fire, bury the ashes deep. I sweep away my footprints with a branch of sage. I take a piece of juniper with bright blue berries and put it in my medicine bag. I take a blue feather the jay left in the desert holly by the creek. I take one stone.

THE DAY I head home I dress in cut-offs and a red flannel shirt. I stop in town on my way back to the city, pick up a newspaper, and buy an iced latte at the new coffee shop on Main Street. I sit on the patio and watch traffic slide over the highway like so many ants on their way to the hill.

The small town I knew is gone. The honest little town with her quiet streets and clean air and one local natural foods co-op is lost behind a face-lift of bright Navajo color, fake adobe, and real estate offices. There is a plastic water park close to the river, seven new motels, and a peculiar yellow haze above town.

I can think of many words to describe what I feel as I sit in the spring sun on the swarming patio. *Silence, stillness, peace* would not be among them. *Wilderness* would not come to mind.

I open the paper. There's a half-page ad. It says, "Entrepreneurs wanted. Come grow with us. Recreation abounds. Quiet lifestyle in small town." I think of rivers dammed for roses and thirsty green lawns, as if the desert has water to spare and scarcity means nothing at all.

There is a picture of Kokopelli playing a flute, skipping across the rim of a cliff. The ad says, "RED DESERT PARADISE." I think of stone cathedrals that scrape blue sky redecorated with asphalt. I think of slickrock whose voice is lost behind the clatter of construction, of bicycle tires, hiking boots, and all sorts of peace seekers, land lovers, tree huggers, and folks who come to play.

A billboard at the edge of town says, "FUNPIGS WELCOME!"

I'm sorry. Damn sorry we learn so slow.

I TAKE my time driving home; stop to watch the sun set behind the swell, to think about the footprints I swept away this morning.

I know I'll leave footprints where I walk. I can walk more gently. I can look for the sun every day, the Big Dipper at night, and I can make The Wild Garden even bigger, until every street is wild, until, even downtown, hawks fly at dawn.

A River Runs Through Them

PAM HOUSTON

PAM HOUSTON, 33, has lived in several western and southwestern states, including California, Utah, and Colorado, where she now resides with her horse, Deseo, and dogs, Hailey and Jackson. Her best-selling collection of short stories, Cowboys Are My Weakness, won the 1993 Western States Book Award; other stories and articles have appeared in such magazines, literary reviews, and anthologies as Outside, Mademoiselle, The Mississippi Review, Quarterly West, and Best American Short Stories. A licensed river guide, Pam can be found floating southwestern rivers for pleasure or on writing assignment on distant rivers like Africa's wild Zambezi. When not adrift, she is at work on her second short story collection.

DAY ONE: LOOKING LIKE beekeepers in floppy hats and mosquito netting, long pants and long sleeves, the urbanites will arrive at the put-in, arms full of gear, most of which the guide's letter told them to leave at home: one carefully washed and pressed T-shirt for each day, brand new Teva sandals, still hooked together with small plastic twistee, and, in the case of both the stockbroker and the literary agent, a tiny cellular phone.

Although the dermatologist from the Twin Cities will assure them that after No. 15 it's all the same, they will each wear three bottles of sunscreen around their necks with numbers ranging from 24 to 65. Given their choice, the women will all get into one boat, the men in another. The boats will maintain this junior high school dance configuration an astonishing eighty percent of the time.

The guide will name the ever deepening rock layers in the canyon walls, explain the various stages of desert varnish, point out cacti—prickly pear, barrel, and hedgehog—and find a group of desert bighorn ewes and lambs. The passengers will only want to know about the rapids, when will they get to them, how bad are they really, is it true that last year somebody died?

Despite the heat, nobody will jump into the water on the first day: There are too many clothes to be taken off and put on, and they are afraid they'll look ungraceful trying to get back into the boat. They will be ashen-faced and cotton-mouthed in the small opening rapids, where the guide will assure them she couldn't flip the boat, even if she tried.

By the time they get to camp, the acupuncturist, the infectious disease specialist, and the guy who will only say he's "in oil" will all be sunburnt, and the ex–poet laureate of the United States will have been stung by a bee, three hats will have gone overboard, one pair of Tevas will have been left at the lunch spot, and at least one of the vegetarians will be hungry enough to eat meat.

Over dinner (orange roughy Mexicana, fresh asparagus, parsley new potatoes, and Bear Lake raspberries with real whipped cream), they will each tell the story of the last time they slept on the ground. The guide will look at the cloudless night sky and suggest sleeping under the stars. There will be urgent whispering about snakes, scorpions, and rain. The tents will be pitched, and before bed the guide will give a lesson about finding their way by constellation.

By day two they will all have realized several things: that they really do have to shit in something called a "rocket box," that there aren't many mosquitoes in the desert after all, and that it probably would have been okay to sleep outside. The bee-keeping nets will be packed away, and most people will have traded long pants for bathing suits, long-sleeve shirts for Bain de Soleil. The clinical psychologist from Chicago will make the first splash, and before lunch everybody will have had a life-jacketed swim through a minor rapid.

They will have exhausted the surface information about each other's lives and will begin to ask questions about the things they see. After dinner (barbecued chicken, fresh spinach, corn on the cob, and pineapple upside-down cake), the ex–Flying Tiger will drink just enough rum to tell everyone about what happens when he travels in space and time.

By day three they will realize there is no point in trying to get their finger-nails clean, that washing dishes is the best job (momentarily clean hands), and that closing up the toilet after everyone has finished is the worst. They will realize that swimming in the silty river makes them feel a little dirtier than before they went in, that everybody's hair gets greasy in three days, but not equally, and the two Berkeley computer guys, unshaven, will start to wear bandannas around their heads and look like members of a gang. The rapids will get bigger and bigger, and they will realize that when the guide says she thinks they should zip up their life jackets for this one, she means it.

By this time, everybody will know the difference between a cliff swallow and a sandpiper. Geology will have stopped being just the title of one of the sections of the guidebook and will have started to mean time and wind and water; they will see it all there in the record of the rock. They will notice the way the sunlight colors the canyon differently, every hour from the time the sun rises until the time it sets. In the morning, the talk will be about opera, deconstruction, monogamy; the time traveler will admit that the planetary federation on Venus was supporting Ross Perot.

By late afternoon they will have figured out it's okay to be quiet, and they will drift through miles of deepening canyon without a word, or cough, or laugh. Tonight, there won't even be talk of setting up tents. The military policeman and the Hungarian film producer will begin a joyous, clandestine affair and will fool no one. After dinner (linguine with clam sauce, salad, Dutch-oven brownies), *they* will show the guide which star points north.

On day four they will run the biggest rapid of the trip, and something will happen to somebody that makes it seem to them all that they almost died. What will follow this is a lot of serious discussion about making the most of their time, about how fragile they all are, about how being outside puts them in touch with some essential part of themselves. They will start planning which river they want to float next year, they will speculate about what it would cost for a cabin and a couple of acres in the area, and when the guide tells them will say, always, "Damn, I pay more than that to park my *car.*"

By now, they are turning a nice rusty river color. They are forgetting now, in the morning, to change into their carefully packed shirts. It's hard to keep them in the boats, in and out like seals all day long, burnt and peeling and burning again. They will begin to say things like, "Coming out here has made me like myself again," and "It's amazing how much living in the city makes you forget." They will say, "This is so very beautiful"; they will say, "My God, the things I've missed."

By the fifth day, they will start seeing literary shapes in the rock formation—there's Don Quixote and Sancho Panza; there's George Jetson's dog, Astro; there's Roddy McDowell as he appeared in *Planet of the Apes*. Fear long gone, they will whoop and holler in the rapids, and say, "Wow! Please, can't we go back up and do that again?"

When they stop for the night, the stockbroker, the shamanic healer, and the actress will work together like a chain gang unloading gear. The psychologist and the computer brothers will have the kitchen assembled and the salad made before the guide finishes pumping water out of her boat. It's the last night on the river, and they won't even be talking about showers anymore; they want, they will say, the trip to go on forever.

They will emerge from the canyon and arrive at the take-out by noon on the sixth day. They will stand between the deflating boats and the running bus that will take them back to their rent-a-cars like so many Persephones, the pomegranate bitten, the world beckoning, neither enough. There will be more hugging than anyone would have anticipated after only five days.

The guide will thank them for their hard work and good company. She will tell them that nearly every wild river in the world is threatened by something: power plants, pollution, drought, development, irrigation, recreation, corruption, greed. She will hope that they will carry whatever piece of themselves they found on the river back to the cities with them. She will hope they will make decisions that will keep the rivers flowing for the time when they want to come again.

Tailings

KAREN SBROCKEY

KAREN SBROCKEY, 46, says that for her writing is a tool of reclamation. Her fiction, interviews, and articles have appeared in publications such as The Seattle Review, Folio: A Literary Journal, The Bloomsbury Review, Changing Woman, *and* HomeOwner. *Although she has lived in Denver, Colorado, for the past seventeen years, she has spent much time in Arizona and New Mexico, drawn there by "the rough dry country of wide open skies." Her story, "Tailings," was inspired by Arizona's copper mining industry.*

DRIVING TO TUCSON, I go over it yet again, that last time we were together six years ago. Molly, Bilbo, and me, at their table like we'd done so many times since college. Twenty-one years' worth of apartments and houses, moving from wobbly kitchen tables to oak dining sets. Conversations—variations on the same themes and dynamics, worn smooth by familiarity, expectation. Until that last time, the schism.

I'm on my way to see Bilbo in the hospital. Not him, really. Won't see him, hooked up to tubes and monitors, in intensive care. Going to see Molly. If she'll see me.

I flew into Phoenix and rented a car. Decided to drive to Tucson instead of flying in from L.A. I wanted to take a side trip through Miami, where Bilbo had been working that last time. And I wanted a few more hours to think.

Miami, Arizona, is a cruel joke of a name. No moist ocean air here. No white sands. Unless you count the tailings, mountains of dune-like waste left over from gouging two billion pounds of copper ore from the earth. The white dust blows across the highway, settling on cars, houses, clotheslines full of shirts, underwear, and bed sheets.

Behind the tailings, out of view, are the operations of Inspiration Mine. Inspiration: another name arising from heat-dulled senses or plain deceit. Inspiration has created a huge open-pit mine, a crater reamed into the earth for the extraction of copper ore, the livelihood of most of the men in Miami.

Behind Inspiration is Sleeping Beauty, a range of rugged buttes on the horizon, framing the landscape between here and the sky.

These are the things I needed to see, examining the terrain of our friendship.

Driving through Claypool, right outside Miami, I recognize Molly and Bilbo's "starter" house, which used to be painted a brazen yellow that hurt your eyes.

We're making a fist at the sun, Molly had said.

When I first visited them after college, Bilbo was an engineer for the mine. He took me on a tour explaining the process.

First we dig out the overburden.

Overburden?

The dirt on top that contains no ore.

You mean, what the cactus grows on? The regular dirt?

Yeah.

You don't use it?

It's overburden. We get rid of it.

BILBO AND I have always maintained an edgy balance of civility. We are not people who would have chosen each other as friends. Even now, when I know he is dying, my heart is cold. I don't want to think about him.

AFTER THE tour, drinking margaritas on their patio, I held him personally responsible.

How do people feel about those tailings?—It was easier to challenge him with Molly around.

Hardly notice them!—Molly blurts out.—You'd think they were real mountains or something!—Sideways glance at Bilbo.

We've become more efficient with the leaching process.—Bilbo, ever the company man.—We can now *re*-process those tailings, run them through again, to get other minerals and more copper ore.

So what I see along the road is *really* useless dust.

Not a hundred percent. We can't get everything out.

Hey!—Molly jumps up.—How about Mexican food? I'm starving.

THEN AGAIN, we were young. Arguing was a newly learned skill, a way of flaunting our individuality. We all knew there was nowhere to put the waste. We'd seen the earth from the moon on TV. There was nowhere to run, nowhere to hide. Not yourself, not your trash.

IT'S BEEN twenty-seven years since I first met Molly, freshman year at Arden Hall, Arizona State University. I've known her through my marriage and divorce, through the birth and childhood of her two kids, through my abortion and teacher certification, through her breast biopsy and PTA presidency. Her oldest, Bethany, is probably in college now. Trevor, in high school. Last time I saw them, Bethany was getting her braces off, Trevor had taken up the drums.

Molly and I were fast friends as soon as we met. She was one of those fresh-faced girls who makes you think of handmade quilts and canning peaches. Tall, pretty, easy laugh, deep shining eyes, and a soft seriousness. We wore each other's clothes and heard each other's dreams.

But the surprise was the wild streak that ran through her, forceful, uncharted, like an unexpected river at the bottom of a canyon.

I suppose we fed that streak in each other. *I* didn't come to college that way, either. We had each been the consummate good girl. Honor student, student council, church fellowship, et cetera. But classes, homework, grades—we could do that stuff with our eyes closed. We had come to partake of the Big Adventure.

Together we created our own magical reality, with the help of the late sixties, where anything was possible and we never got hurt.

I hadn't known that kind of reality before, and I haven't known it since.

YEARS LATER, sitting in her back yard drinking apple juice, watching the kids squirt each other with the hose and splash in their plastic pool, we'd shake our heads.

Remember when we were on our way back to the dorm that Friday night?—

Molly rubs sunscreen on her legs.

I know what you're talking about. That time we left the Watering Hole when they had that shitty band.

And we saw those two cute guys on the corner, drunk out of their minds.

"Beautiful girls! Hey darlins! Come over here!"—I act it out to make her laugh.—You took the straight-looking one.

Ben.

I took . . . what was his name? That shaggy hippie.

Gabriel.

Yeah, Gabriel. There was a troubled soul.

You always liked that type. Bethany! Honey, bring that hose over here, Mommy needs to wet her arms. No, don't squirt me. Bethany! Stop it! Do you want to go to bed now?

And that shack!—Another time we would have analyzed my taste in men, but today we want to relive this memory.—How long did we stay there?

Friday, Saturday, Sunday.

Seemed like forever.

I had an abnormal psych test first thing Monday morning. Ben drove me in. I aced it.—Molly stands and stretches.

The details were savored like a fine meal that someone else cooks and cleans up. Three days of playing poker and gin rummy (me unable to get past the face cards: What does it mean? The king has a scepter, the queen is raising her palm), eating peyote, Gabriel playing guitar, dancing, cooking eggs and toast and spaghetti, drinking Mad Dog 20/20.

But that was all BB, Before Bilbo.

After Bilbo, she was still my friend, but I had to share her. And the wild times were over. Bilbo held the scepter.

IT'S A long drive from Miami to Tucson, even in an air-conditioned car with a tape deck. I get tired of singing, so I give a lecture, out loud, to my ideal high school classroom. The students are enrapt, attentive. No one is sleeping, throwing paper wads, or tapping a pencil to drown me out. They listen, they learn. They will make the world perfect, like we failed to do.

I tell them: Here's your basic recipe for copper mining.

First, you dig tons of earth out of the ground. Use some huge motor-driven shovels, about the size of your living room. Discard the overburden, the topsoil that has no ore.

Dump the ore-laden earth into gigantic crushers, about the size of your house.

Crush the ore until it is pea-sized. Add water. This makes what we call slurry.

Next, pour the slurry into huge swimming pools.

Add diluted sulfuric acid, enough to cover the slurry.

Let it soak until the copper leaches out (dissolves) into the sulfuric acid solution. The solution may also contain gold and silver, an added bonus.

Your liquid solution is now heavy-laden with what we call precipitate copper. It can be sold this way or further refined by smelting.

Smelting is a hot, messy process involving furnaces and heat. It makes the precipitate copper more pure. After smelting, it's called blister copper. You can see why. What's left over in your smelter is like a red-hot lava that turns black when cool, called slag. (We won't go into cleaning the smelter today.) Remove the slag and pile it up somewhere. Along railroad tracks or streams is a common choice.

Now I'll digress a moment, back to leaching. What about what's left in the swimming pool?

It's leached *again*, for other minerals, such as zinc. Now you've really got a mess in your pool—ground up, gritty, depleted ore. This you will pipe out onto the tailings, named so because this is the "tail end" of the process. You'll have a good base for them, since they've been accumulating for about ninety years. When a tailing reaches about thirty feet high and half a mile long, start a new one. Since this ore is somewhat sandy, tailings hold best when layered and stratified, so it doesn't crumble. The final tailings actually look like sandy white hills on the landscape (depending on your imagination and perspective) and can be reclaimed—overlaid with soil and grass, and dotted with cows, at a later time.

One word of caution: Sulfur oxides in the air can be dangerous. You've probably heard of acid rain. Also, keep in mind that ore is really just mineral-rich dirt, right out of the ground. It contains arsenic and asbestos, which when crushed make some pretty dangerous dust, so be careful where you eat your lunch.

By the way, the cancer rate is five times higher in these mining towns than in the general population.

My students are taking notes, asking questions.

It's all neat and clear and simple. Fantasy. But it makes for an interesting drive.

"NOWHERE TO Run, Nowhere to Hide." Martha Reeves and the Vandellas. Molly and Bilbo's first dance, at a frat party. He sauntered toward us, body loose and hard at the same time, a beer in hand.

He looked at me. Bright eyes gleaming or maybe just glazed.

I turned to Molly and snickered.—Here comes James Dean.

Her eyes never left him, her mouth slightly open, breath coming fast.

He gave her a slow grin, wiped his palm on his jeans, and held out his hand—Wanna dance?

And she was gone.

SENIOR YEAR I hardly saw her, and not much in the next three years. "House-Kept" Years, she called them.

Still she remained my friend, my anchor. Tried to advise me not to marry Loren.—He doesn't seem like your type.

How could I tell her—Without you, I lost the magic. I was raped on a date senior year. And my sociology professor grabbed me once in his office. I had no career plans. "High" was all I wanted to be. Without you, I lost the invulnerability. The protective sphere became a bubble of unreality. I wove a secret language, cryptic codes, conversations with myself. Wherever the party was, I was still there, drinking, dancing, dropping acid or whatever, but no one could touch me, none of it was real. I was out there on the edge alone. Nowhere to run, and too scared to leap. And this was Phoenix, not Berkeley. Barry Goldwater was the revolutionary here. I changed my major from sociology to education and slowly backed away from the void. Met Loren at a Get Out the Vote meeting a few years later. He rode a bike and had a beard. Nice guy, on firm ground with himself and Hewlett-Packard. So I fenced off that edge for good.

Next time I saw Molly and Bilbo, with my new haircut and husband, teaching contract, money in the bank, I said, Don't call me Mandy anymore. I'm sick of that taffy-colored puppy name. I'm Amanda now.

And they did call me Amanda, slipping only occasionally back to Mandy.

AFTER MY divorce, Molly hardly ever mentioned Loren and thumped Bilbo on the arm when he did. She remembered the names and occupations of each new boyfriend, kept up with my teaching news.

She was the kind of friend I could scribble a postcard to: *The ice-cream truck on my block plays "The Union Maid," I swear to God. That old Woody Guthrie song.*

A week later I'd get one back: *Ours plays "Don't Cry for Me, Argentina." It's some kind of plot.*

Sometimes we'd call each other just to hear—No, you're not crazy.

THEY NEVER visited me in California. Molly always promised she'd leave the kids with Bilbo for a weekend. We'd drink margaritas and go skinny-dipping in the ocean at midnight, but something always came up.

IN THE Claypool years, when I'd visit, the dynamics had a predictable sequence. I stayed two nights and three days. If I'd stayed only one day, we would have run the same course.

The first night was a blast. Great meal, drinking, laughing till tears came. Bilbo suspending judgment, glad to see Molly lively. Warm hugs. They'd put me in the den, I'd kiss them good night, knowing they'd make juicy love and I'd sleep like a baby.

The next day, hung over, we'd stumble about, reminding each other of last night, chuckling, time and space still opening before us, most things still possible. Bilbo off to play golf, Molly and I sharing deep thoughts and secrets, doing the laundry and dishes, dancing in the living room to old songs.

By evening she'd be more like the old Molly, bold and free, hair flying, making sharp comments to Bilbo—Get those boots out of here. They're filthy!

But Bilbo'd had enough. He'd look at me with flat eyes and flexing jaw, his body hunched and hard. I would not take my cue to reel her in, to back off. Molly and I were weaving the old magic. Bilbo could just sit there like a vulture sulking over his beers.

Finally, he'd say, I'm going up to bed, Molly.—It was still early.—Remember,

Bethany has softball tomorrow.

She'd nod and shrug.—You can take her.

And Trevor's got that Cub Scout thing. You coming to bed?

She'd roll her eyes, ever so slightly.—I'll be up *later*. Go a*head!*

We'd take an unopened bottle of wine and a corkscrew, drive to the 7-11, buy a couple packs of Marlboro Lights and some popcorn. Find a place to sit where we could see Sleeping Beauty but not the tailings. Drink out of the bottle, smoke like crazy, laugh, cry, and wonder how we got here. She'd want stories about the single life and I'd brag it up, for both our sakes. We'd look at the stars and tell each other how our lives were going to proceed, as if we could chart them.

We'd go back to the house rejuvenated, laughing from the belly, free and connected once again.

The next stage in the process, for me, was sweet dreams. For her, immersion in the marriage bed, with a strong solution of angry Bilbo. A lot of juice can get leached out on such nights.

The next morning the tension had settled in. Molly'd be banging pots around, whipping up pancakes, snapping at the kids. Not looking full-faced at me. Bilbo hiking up his pants, striding around, muscled arms clearing the table.

THERE WAS a variation on the second night in later years, when Molly's sexuality had eroded into that commonly comfortable denominator: proper married lady. I'd see books lying around about Driving Your Man Wild in Bed and Couples Communication.

Bilbo'd say, I'm going to bed, Molly. You coming up?

She'd lean toward him with a teasing, half smile.—Yes. I'm ready.—Glancing at me, the house guest, with a polite, unspoken dismissal: You understand.

IN EITHER case, the third day was just putting all the pieces back together. She'd hug Bilbo in the kitchen before he left for work, his arm cinched tight around her waist. He and I would hug, rough and jagged, having honored our detente, once again.

He'd say, Amanda, you need a man!

I'd say, Bilbo, get out of the pits.

EVERYTHING WITH Bilbo came through his body. You could know everything about him through his jaw, eyes, back, shoulders, leg jiggling under the table. When he spoke sometimes, the words came right through his stomach, moving in and out. His energy was almost tangible, visceral, commanding the space. At odd moments I'd feel his gaze sweep over my buttocks and hips, enveloping me. Sizing up the competition.

I know there was more to him. I'd seen him lift Molly's mother gently from her wheelchair. I'd seen him play softball with the kids. But whenever I've thought of him, it's his arms and broad back that I see, never his face.

Once I tried to joke with Bilbo about *The Hobbit*, but he was the only Bilbo he'd ever heard of. A universe unto himself.

ONCE AGAIN, I go over the details of that last time, six years ago. Was it a crystallizing moment or the end of a process? (Is it a wave or a particle, scientists ask. Latest word: It depends upon the observer.)

Maybe it was that damned story about my camping trip on Sleeping Beauty, those hills outside Globe that form the outline of a female lying on her back.

How does a mountain get a name? Someone goes, Look there! That's her face. And there's her hair, flowing down the mountain. And see? There's her breast, her stomach, her legs. And at the bottom, her feet. Amazing! Looks just like Sleeping Beauty. What if someone had seen Three Horses Passing. Would life in this valley be the same?

The last real conversation I had with Molly and Bilbo, I told them about how Sleeping Beauty came alive for me.

What were you on, Bilbo says.

Nothing. I don't do that stuff any more. It was a peak experience.

I got your peak experience.—He doesn't even have to reach for his crotch. It's an old joke with us.

Let Amanda tell the story, Bilbo.—Molly sweeps tortilla chip crumbs into her hand.

So anyway, we were hiking up the mountain.

We?—Bilbo's stomach puffs out.—Who'd you go with, that Fred, the pharmaceuticals man?

No, I went with Dante.

Dante! As in *The Inferno*?

He's just showing off, Amanda. Just listen, Bilbo.—She pushes the bowl of chips his way.—Did you sleep in a tent?

Yes, and I could somehow imagine Sleeping Beauty, this woman with coyotes roaming over her.

Jesus, you were on something.

And rattlesnake bracelets.

Oh my god.

Those pines and the streams, like a flowing dress. She was swaying . . .

Bilbo crunches a chip.—What does this Dante do?

He's a journalist.

Bet he was right at home out there.

TALKING WITH Bilbo is like being a nine-year-old girl on the playground, daring to play the boys' games. They always try to pull your pants down.

SO ANYWAY, it was getting dark. We got in the tent and, this is weird, but Dante had *laryngitis*.

You probably grilled him about his childhood and shit. He was faking it.

Molly turns her chair slightly away from him.—So you were in the tent.

It's dark and suddenly I'm hearing these coyotes howling far off. But then, they're coming closer and closer! I started getting nervous, feeling kind of scared.

Even with Dante there, huh?

Shut up, Bilbo.—Molly is getting tired.

I said to Dante, What should we do? He says, The coyotes just want to know everything's all right. We're in their territory. They want to know who we are.

Good thinking, Dante.

So I got the idea to howl at the coyotes. Dante couldn't howl, of course, so I unzipped the tent flap. And there I was on all fours.

Hmmm.—Bilbo rubs his chest and laughs.

The stars are out bright. I let out this howl.

Lemme hear you do it.

I can't do it now. So the coyotes are quiet. I howl again, and again. I'm trying to match their pitch, to find where that howl lives inside me.

Bilbo belches.

Excuse *you*.—Molly thumps his arm.—Ignore him, Amanda.

It was really strange. I felt connected to something . . . like an *animal* spirit inside me.

Yeah, Molly says. I feel that in my modern dance class.

Since when? he says.

I turn to her.—Have you ever wondered why coyotes howl?

Ah, now there's a good question!—Bilbo wants our eyes on him.

It's loss and longing.—Molly is quiet and sure, far away.

Everything stops. I notice her golden hair tinged with gray, falling to her shoulders. Her collar bones show through her shirt. Her face is sun-baked and lined. The old Molly is in there somewhere.

She shrugs, breaks the spell.—I love those hills. We go hiking up there with the kids sometimes, if *he* ever takes a day off.

Then it happens so quickly, cut in stone. Another time it might have been funny. Bilbo says, I'm going to bed.—Looks at his wife.—You comin' up, Mandy?

We don't exactly jump, it's more like we all *flinch*. Molly looks at me, eyes wide, shocked; I look at Bilbo, puzzled, pissed; he looks from one to the other of us, hands spread, seeming amazed and somewhat afraid.

But Bilbo recovers.—Damn! Honey! I keep *tryin'* to remember her *name!* A-man-da!—Scraping back his chair, he's up. Crooks an arm around Molly's neck.—Aw, shit, honey, it was just a slip. It was nuthin'.

Her face is doubtful, voice soft.—But Bilbo, you called me . . .

C'mon, baby, let's go to bed.

She looks at me sideways, suspicious, hurt, his arm like a boa constrictor around her neck.

Bilbo turns her away, heading out of the dining room, saying loudly, without looking back, good night, A-*man*-da!

So I am driving to the hospital in Tucson where they're keeping him hooked up on machines, cancer in his stomach, intestines, spreading. I heard about it from a mutual friend, several months ago. No one sees him in intensive care, she said, except Molly.

Over the years, I have pushed him out of my consciousness time and again, when the bitter rage roils up. When I heard about the cancer, I have to admit for a moment I felt a shameful flash of triumph. And then, I wanted to run and hide. Some things never change. So I can't think much about him yet. In a real human way. That will come, I suppose.

I wanted to call Molly, but I was afraid. For many reasons. One being that I'd say something about those damn copper mines and all that dust. Bilbo believes the cancer is hereditary, our friend says. His father died young of cancer. Maybe Molly thinks *I* caused it, planting some poisonous seed inside him.

In the end, I just decided I had to go there. Impending death has a way of leaching out fear, anger, shame, and most other trace emotions.

THEY WENT up to bed that last night, six years ago, and I didn't sleep much. In the den I watched TV with the sound off, going over every drunken time, every college party. Moving out to the patio, eating cold pizza, I wondered: Was it me? Subconscious wishes? But he'd never appealed to me, really. I never trusted him.

He'd told me once how he'd gotten the money for his and Molly's senior trip to Mazatlan, something he'd never told her. He and some frat brothers stripped a car, a '69 Mustang. Jacked it up, took the mag wheels, Slim-Jimmed the lock, pulled out the stereo, in fifteen minutes flat. He thought he might still have the fuzzy dice somewhere.

Watching the sky turn fuzzy pink that night, I thought maybe I was the only one who saw this "incident" as a rip in the fabric. How were they handling it? Fucking furiously, arguing, or just sleeping?

Bilbo had left the house the next morning before I got up. I slept late and Molly didn't wake me. I could hear the kids in the kitchen, asking when Amanda would get up so they could watch TV. The clatter of silverware and cereal bowls, drawers opening and closing, Molly's soft voice an undercurrent to it all.

With the brightness of morning, I believed maybe everything was all right.

I yelled.—I'm awake!

The air froze. The clatter and chatter stopped like a skipped heartbeat.

I went in the kitchen.—Molly, listen, I'm sorry.

Oh, forget it. It was nothing.

Which told me yes, it was *something*. And what was I apologizing for? What was she absolving me of?—You know there's never been anything between Bilbo and me, except you. I mean . . .

With her back toward me, at the sink.—Never mind. It was just a slip. No big deal. We drank too much.

I went upstairs to the bathroom, dread seeping through me. She was outside watering plants when I came down.

She yelled over her shoulder.—There's coffee and sweet rolls in the kitchen.

We avoided each other until it was time to leave for the airport. She let the kids carry on in the car while we cinched ourselves in heavy silence. I watched the landscape, thinking I'll be glad to get home. At the curb, a loose hug, hardly touching.

'Bye, see ya.

Thanks for everything.

That was it.

DESTRUCTIVE SUSTENANCE, I'll tell my students. What do you think that means? They'll scratch their heads, yawn, and smirk at each other.

Who wants to face the devastation of mining ore? Who wants to face a failed friendship?

But this is my story. Bilbo would tell a different one. And so would Molly.

MAYBE IT was not just a moment, but the tail end of a long process. Women's friendship being the overburden. The earth that supports the cactus, piñon pines, rattlesnakes, javelinas, lizards, and humans is discarded for the ore.

But the truth is, Molly and I could never revive who we had been in those early days. The last time we went to the 7-Eleven, buying licorice and Diet Cokes, she talked a lot about old boyfriends, stories I'd grown tired of, and lamented the loss of her college journalism dreams. My mind wandered. When she bragged about her kids, I got impatient. My teaching stories made her yawn. She lost track of my relationships. Our real selves were buried deep under a river of chatter.

The horizon was no longer wide open and sky blue. Not everything was possible. And I wasn't sure I cared who she was anymore.

THIS VISIT to the hospital is necessary, a duty, to honor the memory of once-upon-a-time closeness. But my heart is not in it.

When I get to the oncology ward waiting room on the seventh floor, people are clustered around the walls, shuffling, hands in pockets, talking softly. I know no one, but it doesn't matter. Death makes people easy with each other. No need for small talk. Or rather, small talk becomes smooth little gems that we examine with tender appreciation. But there's no one in the middle of the floor, as if the space is too bold, too frightening to occupy. As if there is a deep hole there. I stand by the door, seeing Molly right away, her back toward me, talking to some people by the window. Long hair, tense shoulders holding up a weary body. My heart opens a crack. Trevor sees me first. He's standing by his mother, tall and vigilant. Touches her arm, she turns, he nods toward me.

Her eyes are deep canyons of pain and sadness. We are middle-aged and facing death. A howl wants to escape my throat. She smiles and reaches out a hand. I step into the middle of the room.

Unnatural

CATHRYN ALPERT

CATHRYN ALPERT, 44, is the author of many widely published stories and the 1995 novel *Rocket City*, which is set in New Mexico. Formerly a director and professor of theater, she lives in Northern California with her husband, two sons, and the world's cutest dog. Her second novel (in progress) also takes place in the Southwest. "The desert Southwest is a landscape of interior—of our country and of the heart," Cathryn says. "When my characters need change, they journey there, to the land of red sky, rock, creek bed, and bone. Within emptiness, one finds replenishment; within harshness, a little humor and the will to be kind."

MARTA WOKE UP NAKED in a desert village. She felt warm, yet had the odd sense of not being entirely in her own body. Her tongue would not work to form language. The light hurt her eyes.

"What day is it?" she asked, and the fire answered, "It is no day."

Sounds, stranger than foreign language. A chanting and a crackle. They frightened her, and she made a noise. Warm skin and wet. A suck, then a sweetness. Tiredness thicker than river mud. From the earth, a gentle lowing.

SHE IS landing now, the plane a red-tailed hawk circling down off a thermal. The city lies before her, a spit mark on pavement. It is afternoon, August. The end of a millennium.

She has come to arrange for the donation of organs. Heart. Kidneys. Whatever they can use. Skin, too, if it hasn't all been burned. From this sea of misery, a small good rises.

The plane touches down in the northern end of town. Slot machines in the concourse and bars, cigar smoke lingering, coins clanking in plastic cups. Half-dressed women making conversation and change. Signs on the walls, on the doors of taxis: *Amber. Cherrie. Hot Hot Love.*

Her hotel is on the busiest section of the Strip. In the lobby, more slot machines; in the coffee shop, greyhound racing and keno. She deposits her bag, then heads to the hospital in a battered taxi. A little man with a brown cigarette. On his doors: *Girls! XXX Uncensored!* Like her son, before yesterday.

She stares through the cab's dirty windshield to the north. "Out there," she says, pointing. The cigarette dances in the rearview mirror. An eyebrow inquires.

In the hospital, the chiming of bells. 7 grapes 7— a game of chance. She is led down a hallway, up an elevator, then down another hallway to a tidy room where she is asked to wait. Bolstered by an understuffed sofa, she peers out the third-floor window over the ocean of desert below. The sun casts low-angle light on the mountains to the north. Canyons emerge. A jet roars silently westward.

There are papers to sign. Documents to complete. Gratitude to be accepted. When she asks to see him, she is led down a corridor, through an open door and into his room. It is much as she expected: tubes, life support, the beeping of a heart monitor. Still, she is not prepared for what she sees. The respirator, a white bird with wings, seems to siphon life, not give it. And she expected skin, not bandages, which makes no sense. On his ring finger (the one not burned), his scar from whittling. Yet this mummy thing is not her child.

He is still out in the desert. Caught driving where he shouldn't have been, with binoculars and maps and camouflage fatigues that melted to his chest when his car ignited. Area 51. Military. Off limits. A place that doesn't exist except in paranoids' imaginations.

Was he brought to this hospital by imaginary personnel?

NIGHT WELCOMES her back to the heart of the city. In her hotel's casino, coins slip down metal throats as ice melts in glasses and cigarettes dangle from thinning lips.

Bells ring, singing, the incessant dinging of bells. And the eye-searing smoke, silver clinking and jangling, lights flicking, tits flashing, chips falling, hopes waning in this soul-sucking, ass-hawking, chancre-invoking pit of America that is Las Vegas.

Rod Serling on acid.

Oliver North.

She doesn't sleep for thinking about her son. Sweet, big-hearted idealist named for a prophet, he wrote tracts and manifestos for underfunded journals that nobody reads or cares about. Expose this. Decry that. Born with a silver whistle in his mouth, he blew it once too often, and they came.

She stares out her window, north, toward Area 51.

When he was eight or nine, they drove from the city to the Sangre de Cristos. At night you could see the Milky Way. Gazing up at the stars, he asked, "What is all this?" Their terrier mix lay sleeping at their feet.

"No one knows," she said. She rolled onto her side and studied her son's profile. Their mutt whimpered in a dream. "You suppose dogs ask the same questions but just don't have the language to express it?"

"Dogs don't have to ask," said Elija. "Dogs know."

The memory brings a smile as she contemplates the desert night beyond the casinos. A flash on the horizon, a white strobe, fleeting. Perhaps the anomalous reflection of a half-expired sign. She looks for it again, presses hands tightly between forehead and pane; sees nothing but the faint outline of rock kissing sky, a deep kiss, unbroken.

At four-thirteen, the telephone rings. It is over, but she knew that.

AFTER DAWN, she goes outside again, unmercifully awake. The lights are always on in this city. People prowl the streets, not as many as before. Johns, prostitutes, pimps hawking their wares. Shoving pink and purple fliers at her, at anyone who passes by, male or female, young or old. Pictures of half-naked women. The sidewalks are littered with this chaff, a virtual carpet of buttocks and breasts and tongues licking lips. *Call Rhonda. Call Suzy.* Hot hot desperation.

"North," she says to the driver.

"Where north?"

"All the way north," she says.

Past the airport, past tract homes, past trailers peeling like scabs on the fingers of the city. Where gun-metal streets lick chapped desert the griseous color of abscess. When they can travel no farther, she asks the driver to pull over and stop.

The man looks worried. He argues with her, cites snakes and heat and lack of water. She snaps at him, parts easily with a twenty; climbs out of the backseat of the cab. The anger feels good. Hard. A bit into which she can bury her teeth.

Like it or not, he'll be back in an hour, people are crazy in this town, doing crazy-assed things, and he'll have no blood on his hands—no, not this man. The taxi heads south, almost cautiously. *Secret Pleasures. Call Raven.*

She sits on a rock until the receding taxi is no longer visible. When it returns, she will be just another gray spot on the desert, indistinguishable from the rocks and scrub.

The day grows hotter as she heads toward the mountains. She counts beer cans, animal bones; her feet begin to ache. An hour passes. Two. She thinks of coconuts, the Rue Saint-Honoré, the big toe of her ex-husband.

Twenty-nine beer cans, she loses track of time. The sun is at midheaven, but what does that mean? Noon? One? Is daylight saved in Nevada? Legs swollen, she trudges onward, her denim shorts chafing at her thighs. She removes them and drapes them over a tired bush. It has a name, this bush, but she doesn't know it.

She puts her shoes back on without her socks. The longer she walks, the more the sun seems suspended in the sky. Her mouth feels dry; her limbs, heavy. Blisters provoke her feet, yet the distant mountains grow no larger for her pain. Bones still, but no more beer cans. Thirty-three at last count, plus one sun-bleached bottle. Corona Light, a redundancy.

She lies down in sand, hotter than the air and far more punishing. A rest will do her good. She dozes, maybe, but when she awakes, the sun has not moved, and she wonders whether she has slept at all. Her tongue feels big, as if full of Novocain. Her legs sting red and prickly. The dust that covers her skin is the same dull gray she imagines fallout. Does time stop when the world does?

On her back, facing upward, she sees orange webbing through the canopy of her eyelids. The sun hovers. Hot. Hot. Her lids flutter; tears dry on her swollen cheeks. A strobe on the horizon, then a crow dancing. Top hat and tails and tiny cane.

The crow tells her a fable:

Years ago, there lived a young gray wolf. Like most wolf pups, he obeyed the laws of his elders. One such law held that no wolf was allowed to venture west into the Land of Red Sky. Only the sun was permitted to travel there, as it did at the end of each day.

Now, this wolf pup was a curious youngster, always sniffing at things and rooting beneath stones to see what bugs lay hidden underneath. Delighted when he found spiders, he tasted them, even the ones his elders had warned him never to disturb. Once, he lay sick for three days after swallowing a tarantula.

When he grew older, but before he had sired a litter of his own, the young wolf asked his grandfather where the sun went at the end of the day. Old Wolf's eyes grew hard as a thorn. "Some questions are better left unasked," he said. "There is a reason the Land of Red Sky is forbidden."

But the young wolf was not satisfied with this response. Early one morning, he stole away from the rest of the pack, following his nose for direction, for the setting sun smelled like a thousand fields of burning grass. For two nights and three days, the young wolf ran west. Each evening, the sun appeared larger on the horizon.

At the end of the third day, the young wolf arrived, exhausted, at the rim of the world. The precipice looked dangerously steep. Terrified, he peeked over the earth's horizon and saw what no wolf had ever seen before. His tail froze, and his fur stood on end.

"I must run back to my elders and tell them of this!" he cried. "But they will never believe me, for what I have seen is so unimaginable, so contrary to their teachings that they will surely think me mad. But they must believe me! They must! For I have seen what they have not, and I am now their teacher."

The terrified wolf spun quickly to return to his pack. But just then, the sun came down to kiss the earth good night. When the sun caught sight of the animal standing on the earth's rim, he shouted, "Run, wolf, run!" but it was too late. The sun brushed up next to the young wolf, igniting his fur so that he burned hot and white for all eternity.

Half a moon later, when Burning Wolf limped back to his pack spouting tales no elder had ever told before, his brothers and sisters all ran from him in fear. And so, Burning Wolf was left to roam the earth forever, a reeling ball of fire so hot and bright and crazy-headed that no earthly creature would let him draw near, not even the lowly centipede.

"This is Burning Wolf's punishment," says the crow. "This is the price of knowing."

The crow dances a jig, then turns into a raven. The sun moves backward in the sky. A taxi pulls up and a naked woman emerges from the backseat, cradling her breasts in her hands. "Call me," she whispers.

The woman does a bump and grind. She tongues her left nipple. "Do you know where your daughter is tonight?"

"I don't have a daughter," she hears herself reply. "I wanted one, but I only had a son. I don't have a sister, or a niece, even. Just a brother who's a shit. The chain is broken."

The naked woman cups her pudenda in her hand. She massages herself unkindly. "Want poontang?"

"What?"

"Beaver. Snatch. Pussy."

"No. No thank you."

"Honeypot. Hair pie. House of dong."

"House of schlong?"

The naked woman laughs a wild laugh as the cab driver thumbs through a boxing magazine. "Patpong. Ping pong, ting tang, wallawalla your thang."

"Urethane?" she asks. Her bottom lip splits painfully.

"You're a Thane," says the naked woman.

"Hamlet's a Thane. I'm common Irish."

"Polly, you're a Thane."

"My name's not Polly."

"Caw-dor! Caw-dor!"

She laughs now, herself, lying in the sand, the skin on her eyelids welting. She has wondered for years what this moment would be like; she never guessed it might be funny.

The naked woman does another bump and grind, then climbs into the front seat of the taxi. Her head disappears onto the driver's lap as the cab veers sharply toward the mountains. *Strictly Forbidden*, says the sign on the door. *Triple-X-Hot-Love Pleasures.*

A small, black beetle climbs up her palm, then falls back into the dirt, disoriented. When she curls her fingers, the insect freezes, thrusting its tail in the air, its head down low to the ground. A stench seeps from its protruding rear.

"Piñacate," says the beetle. "Or so the Spaniards named me. The presumptuous one is called that as an insult. The Spaniards did not realize that when I sense danger, I listen for guidance from the spirits of the earth."

She rolls onto her side and lays her ear to the scorching sand. From the ground, a gentle lowing. The sun grows larger as the beetle bows and supplicates. The wind sings her a lullaby.

SHE WAKES to the smell of grasshoppers roasting. She is hungry and the light hurts her eyes. When she cries, the liquid fills her mouth, more quickly than before. A suck, then a swallow. The breeze blows soft on what feels like skin. Warmth from the nearby crackle.

She asks the rocks what time it is.

"It is no time," say the rocks. "Listen to the fire. The fire knows."

RETURN

Days of Plenty, Days of Want

PATRICIA PRECIADO MARTIN

PATRICIA PRECIADO MARTIN, 56, is a native Arizonan raised and educated in Tucson. Two of her books, Images and Conversations *and* Songs My Mother Sang to Me, *are based on Mexican-American oral history; her prize-winning short stories have been published in two collections,* Days of Plenty, Days of Want *and* El Milagro and Other Stories, *and anthologized in such books as* Infinite Divisions *and* Latina. *Patricia helped to institute the Mexican Heritage Project at the Arizona Historical Society and serves as field consultant for projects dealing with Mexican-American heritage of Arizona. She lives with her husband of thirty-two years, Jim Martin, and has two adult children of whom she is inordinately fond.*

PART I
EN ESTE MUNDO NI SOBRA EL QUE VIENE
NI EL QUE VA

SUMMER WAS THE BEST season for Don Federico. The mornings were warm, and that meant he could start out before dawn with his horse, Benito, and his carreta, to buy fruit and vegetables from the Chinos at their truck farms by the river. It was convenient also, for at that early hour there was no traffic, and he could guide the carreta along a wide berth of the road without giving heed to the cars that were becoming more commonplace in the barrio since the war ended. The automobiles were noisy, meddlesome, created dust and fumes, and made his beloved and faithful Benito edgy.

Yes, the madrugada was the best time for the vegetable vendor. It was tranquil and he could concentrate on his thoughts without really watching the road—listening only to the melodious clink of his silver bridle and the steady rhythm of Benito's hooves until he reached the riverside milpas. The houses in the Barrio Anita were dark at that hour, except for the light in Doña Rosa's window. He knew she had already begun her morning devotions, lighting her candles on her home altar and moving her gnarled fingers rapidly along her clicking rosary beads.

"El hombre hace, y Dios deshace," she was fond of saying, and somehow it always consoled Don Federico to know that before sunrise Doña Rosa was attending to the spiritual emergencies at hand.

Sandía, melón, tomatillo, tomate, chile verde, cebolla, elote—the bounty of summer—these he would arrange in colorful mounds on his carreta after bargaining for the best prices with the Chinos. Then he would make his way down the shaded cottonwood lanes back to the barrios on the edge of town—El Hoyo, Membrillo, Barrio Libre, and his own Barrio Anita—calling out to the housewives with his now familiar whistle and song: "Aquí viene la carreta de Don Federico; no soy ladrón. Cómprenme algo y les doy pilón."

He always made sure to have a bag of saladitos or dulces to give to the children who skipped, descalzos, after his carreta, or hung from the silver bridle and clambered on the back of the long-suffering Benito, heedless of the scoldings of their mothers. If the morning was a good one, and the housewives in a buying mood, he would be home with an empty cart and a bolsillo full of coins before the scorching midday heat had set in. His afternoons he would devote to sharpening knives and scissors, to cutting firewood that was much in demand by the señoras for their estufas de leña, to cleaning the chicken coop, and to tending to his own small gardens at the back of the lot.

Don Federico himself was a tall and slender man, moreno. He sat straight on the board seat of his homemade carreta, immaculately groomed, thanks to the tireless efforts of his sainted wife, Guadalupe. His shirt starched and spotless, if somewhat frayed, his khaki work pants perfectly pressed, his botas polished, he cut an elegant figure in spite of his humble demeanor, as if it were his calling to give orders to men instead of only to an ancient and trusted steed. His wife insisted he wear a felt hat to ward off the summer heat instead of the wide-brimmed sombrero that he preferred. "El hábito no hace al monje," he would remind her. But she felt it undignified and beneath his station. Poor they were, it was true, but of pioneer stock, gente de razón, here before the Gadsden Purchase, she was fond of recounting to anyone in earshot. Why at one time the Sotomayores owned great ranchos with thousands of hectares from the Altar to the Avra Valley. But because of the great drought, the greed of the "Americanos" and legal skullduggery, she was sure, they had lost it all. "Papeles hablan; callen barbas"—and she had the pergamino to prove it, its faded proclamation scarcely legible, the yellowed parchment transparent with age and handling.

The pergamino and other memorabilia she zealously guarded in a wooden box that she kept under their bed: a linen cross-stitch sampler ("En tus apuros y afanes, acude a tus refranes," 1850), a lace handkerchief, a gold pocketwatch with missing hands and a cracked crystal, a leather-bound libro de oraciones, and dozens of faded photographs and tintypes of dour men in morning coats and prim women in yards of taffeta and lace. These she would take out on occasion, arrange on the kitchen table, and reminisce about their turn of fate to anyone—pariente or comadre—who would listen.

Don Federico would listen to his wife patiently when his turn befell him. She was hardworking, devout, and, most importantly, a loving madre y esposa, and he felt she merited the luxury of her nostalgia. But he himself was a practical man and there were more urgent asuntos at hand: five children still at home to feed and he not getting any younger. History interested him not as much as the weather, the crops, and the dispositions of the Chinos and the housewives.

Practical in all matters save one. There was one herencia Doña Guadalupe did not safekeep in the locked wooden box under their matrimonial bed. It was an herencia Don Federico kept for himself or, mejor dicho, for his horse, Benito, and it hung on a nail on the adobe wall of the sala when not in use: a silver bridle intricately worked by some forgotten craftsman, etched and embossed with a design of great beauty, leaves and flowers intertwined, inscribed with the initials J. A. S., its original owner and history vanished like the land.

It was Don Federico's only indulgence, and sometimes, he worried, an object of too much vanity. When the obligations of the day were done—the produce, the leña, the sharpening stone, the quarrelsome gallo, the gardens, the evening rosary—Don Federico would light a kerosene lamp and go out to the makeshift stable that housed Benito Juárez. There, seated on a stool made from a discarded kitchen chair, and bathed in the soft light of the lamp, he would groom Benito, unplaiting and brushing and replaiting his mane and tail, currying his hide until it shone, and rubbing the horse's aging muscles with salve. Then last, but not least, he would polish the wondrous silver bridle by lamplight, using a soft cotton cloth that he saved expressly for this purpose, shining it until the silver became warm in his hands and gleamed, its luster catching the light from the lantern like a thousand tiny stars. His wife would scold him if he stayed too late in the stable; it was foolish, she said, to lavish so much time on an old horse and bridle, and he was so weary, too, of late. The bad evening air would surely give him the evil humors and he would catch his death from a chill.

Perhaps she was right, he would think on occasion. It is likely a sin of vanity. But then again, Padre Eufrasio at the Sagrada Familia Church had assured him in his Easter confession that it is holy and proper to attend to and admire all of God's works. The innocent Benito is also much loved by El Señor; and as for the silver bridle, it is the product of a God-given talent and so manifests the Maker's greater glory. And so, with the whispered words of the kindly old priest and the daily intercessions of Doña Rosa, the conscience of Don Federico was put at ease . . .

The last morning was like all the other mornings. Don Federico arose in the darkness, being careful not to disturb his sleeping wife. He dressed in the clean clothes she had laid out for him the night before. He warmed his coffee, slipped the precious bridle from its nail hook, and, still sipping from the steaming cup, walked out to the stable to the waiting Benito. He slipped the bridle over Benito's head, adjusting it just so, all the while whispering to himself his morning prayers. He harnessed Benito to the carreta, opened the creaking gate, and began to make his way down the callejón to Otero Street and thence to the river, all the while listening to the musical sounds the bridle made, silver clinking upon silver, like miniature bells keeping time with the rhythm of the horse. He watched for the first rays of dawn to be reflected on the bridle's silver surface. Later he mused, the bridle would shine with a yellow light, almost like gold, the later morning sun the alchemist. Then the high noon sun would make the silver bridle flash with a blinding light that made him avert his eyes, a white and angular piercing light: like the pain between his ribs now that caught him so unaware that he let the reins drop from his hands with a sudden jerk. A flashing heart pain in his chest, silver almost, hot like a thousand suns, with tiny points of light fading into the distance and then going out one by one by one, like tiny candles in the wind.

PART II
LO QUE VIENE VOLANDO, VOLANDO SE VA

FEDERICO SOTOMAYER, "EL FREDDIE," "El Huilo," unstacked the produce boxes in the room at the rear of El Grande Supermarket. It was always dark in the storeroom behind the swinging wooden doors. It was damp, also, with small puddles of standing stagnant water all around, and it smelled of overripened fruit and vegetables and insect spray. Later in the morning, after prying open the wooden crates, Federico would place them on a metal cart and roll them out to the produce section in the front of the store. There, washing them with the fine spray from a nozzle and sorting the damaged ones as he went, Federico would arrange the fruit and vegetables in colorful pyramids in the cases. When El Chino Lee was very busy with the afternoon trade, El Freddie would help out at the second cash register, while El Chino kept an eye on him all the while, making sure that no pilón escaped his scrutiny, that no unwarranted coins left the till. El Freddie liked this part of his work day best; he liked answering the questions of the señoras who wanted to know if that or this was in season, if this or that was fresh, and why the prices kept going up. He liked waiting on the barefoot children who came in with their centavitos to buy soda and potato chips. He always managed to slip the buquis a saladito or dulces if El Chino was distracted and turned away his ever watchful eyes. Yes, El Freddie would think: I am good with vegetables and people.

El Freddie walked twelve blocks from his house at 800 North Anita to the Chinos. He would leave his carrucha at home to save on gas and to protect his prized possession from the elements, to say nothing of prospective vandals and joyriders. He would walk, mornings and evenings, at a leisurely pace, crossing the river that was dusty now and crisscrossed by an eight-lane freeway. The traffic drone never diminished in the barrios now. The hum of trucks and cars had become a part of everyone's consciousness, like a huge concrete insect buzzing in the ear day and night.

But he liked the walk anyway; there was always something going on in the barrio. People coming and going; toda la bola hanging out after hours around the Anita Street store. "¿Qué onda, Huilo?" A chula or two to eye. "Ay te watcho." Cooking smells wafting from the kitchens into the streets; buquis playing kick the can or softball in the dusty alleys and weed-strewn lots at all times of the day or night; the abuelas rocking on their porches exchanging remedies and milagros.

El Freddie's days were long—sunup to closing—Sundays too, with Saturdays off. But El Freddie did not mind working overtime. More work meant more feria and more feria meant helping out his old man and lady with what they needed to run the house. More overtime meant more left over for fixing his carruchita, which he parked in a makeshift garage he made from old boards he had found at the back of the lot.

El Freddie's mother, hardworking that she was, with five younger mouths to feed and never enough money to go around with the mines on strike again, fretted about her son's spending so much time working on his car. But she had faith and she kept her complaints to herself. He was a good son, wasn't he?, giving most of what he earned to make ends meet, and he was practical in all matters save one.

Late at night, after warming the leftover supper his mother had saved him, El Freddie would work on his '53 Chevy. He had strung an electric cord from the house to the garage and often worked well past midnight by the light of that one bare bulb. The car had been a junker-heap when he bought it from the gabacho's wrecking yard on South Twelfth Avenue. Anybody can buy a new car, man, you take out a loan. But to transform a ranfla was a matter of orgullo, respeto, and raza pride. You work hard and create something a little different from anyone else. It takes a little time, a little talent, plus lots of patience, bloody knuckles, and some greasy Levi's. But mostly work. The more you work, the nicer your ride becomes. The more you work, the less time you have to get in trouble.

He had rebuilt the engine, doing most of the work himself, scouring the junkyards for parts and accessories, looking for a bargain. He saved his extra feria to pay for what he could not do himself. In three years the car was a masterpiece: multi-color lacquer paint job, chain-link steering wheel, crushed velvet upholstery on swivel chairs, spotlights on the hood, metal spoke wheels. The back window was etched with Carnales Unidos. ¡Ay, ay, qué firme carrucha! And hanging from the rear view mirror along with some fuzzy dice were five sterling silver medallions attached to a worn leather strap, the largest of the medallions inscribed with the initials J. A. S. A gift from his old man, something handed down in the family, he said.

Late into the night he would work, tuning the engine, checking the batteries, polishing the chrome, and buffing the finish with a leather shammy, the luster catching the light from the bare bulb like a thousand tiny stars. He would be looking forward to Saturday . . .

That Saturday afternoon was like all the others: El Freddie all decked out in his khakis and plaid shirt and tapita, checking himself out in the bathroom mirror, shining his two-tone shoes on the back of his pants. Backing his carruchita out down the alley, slow, the buquis hanging on the bumpers, down to Otero Street and then to South Sixth to join the other vatos locos in the procession on the Avenue. Low and slow and mean and clean. Not a care in the world. The chulitas staring and the white guys too, with envy. Mi orgullo me levanta. His window was always rolled down to catch the breeze and to get a better look. The silver medallions on the rear-view mirror flashed with the last rays of the afternoon sun.

He didn't even see the chota running down the sidewalk, with gun drawn, after the hippie who had taken off out of the Ozark Bar. Then he felt the bullet in his shoulder, and the pressure in his neck that caught him so unaware that he let his hands drop from the steering wheel with a sudden jerk. A white and angular and piercing pain, silver almost, hot like a thousand suns, with tiny points of light fading into the distance and then going out one by one by one, like tiny candles in the wind.

DIOS DA Y DIOS QUITA, ESE.

Yolanda

KELLEY JACQUEZ

KELLEY JACQUEZ, 44, was adopted into the small New Mexican community of Blanco twenty years ago. "Even though I was twenty-four at the time," she says, "it's where I grew up. I learned that people are just people, and we're all doing the best we know how. I found that I was loved and accepted simply for being me—something I'd never had before." Kelley started writing at the age of forty and has had stories published in literary journals and read on the radio. Her collection of short stories about women living in New Mexico, entitled Nothing Ever Happens in a Small Town, *is looking for a publisher. Kelley currently lives in Fresno, California.*

THE WEDDING RECEPTION OF Yolanda Montes and Gary Montoya was held at the National Guard Armory mess hall. No one else was crazy enough to reserve the armory for the end of August so it had been easy to get. The end of September would have been a much better time for holding a reception at the armory since the outside temperature would have been a good twelve degrees cooler, but if they'd waited, Yolanda wouldn't have fit into her pale yellow wedding dress.

The women of Gary's family had unlocked the heavy gates of the compound and decorated them with yellow ribbons and white balloons. Inside the mess hall, the women had done all they could to disguise the ugly green walls by hanging home-painted banners with Gary and Yolanda's names entwined in hearts and singing birds. The birds looked more like beetles donning feathers, but no matter, the sentiment was the same. The sturdy metal tables were covered in yellow crepe paper and set with rosettes twisted out of Kleenex just like the ones pictured in the June issue of *Woman's Day* magazine.

Tables pushed against the wall supported roasters filled with pinto beans, green chile made with lean pork, and steaming tamales. Gary's mother and sisters, still in their wedding attire, were in the armory kitchen making tortillas and cutting tomatoes picked from their gardens for fresh salsa. The full flames under the tortilla flats drove the temperature in the mess hall up another eight degrees.

Jerry Alcon and his band played for free because he and Gary had been friends since childhood and had even managed to do time in Santa Fe State Prison together. They'd each served two years and walked out of one of the toughest prisons in the country vowing never to return. After three years of parole and no violations, the state of New Mexico had pronounced them successfully rehabilitated. Gary and Jerry believed the state of New Mexico had successfully scared the shit out of them and decided that stealing tires wasn't their line of work. Actually, Jerry and his band played a lot of gigs for free because everybody had known everybody since childhood and the band wasn't good enough to get paying jobs anyway. They'd start a song and you'd hear Jerry say, "Coyotes stupidos, la cancion es DE COLORES. Bueno, start again. This time, together."

My first glimpse of Yolanda had been at the church, loosely holding the arm of Gary's father as he stolidly escorted her down the aisle. She was smiling as she walked, but her head was down so the smile seemed to be for no one, as if she'd been reminded to smile just before encountering the congregation. Her teeth were white but set widely apart, like she'd been allotted only so many and the hand of genetics had placed them where they would do the most good. The placement made her smile resemble a friendly jack-o'-lantern. Her long black hair had been piled high, each roll looking like it supported a Budweiser can beneath it, and two Shirley Temple curls hung at either side of her face. One of Gary's sisters was a beautician and no doubt responsible for Yolanda's hair.

A lot of people were getting their first glimpse of Yolanda. We'd all heard how Gary had gone to Mexico to find a bride because he wanted a woman who knew who was the boss and "how to keep her mouth shut." I don't remember which cousin had a cousin by marriage who knew a family who had a neighbor who had an unmarried daughter of tolerable appearance who had a male child out of wedlock and was properly shamed so that she would have to accept any offer of legitimacy, but that's pretty much how it happened. The truth is, Yolanda really fell in love with Gary, and she would have married him without the promise of going to the United States to live the good life. Gary didn't mind that the woman already had a son; in his mind, it only meant she could have more.

At the reception I studied Yolanda's profile, listened to her laugh as she held her hand in front of her mouth, watched her eyes move from face to face with timid curiosity, watched the abiding smile turned sweetly on her husband.

YOLY'S HOME was a shack five miles outside of Aztec. Only the most tenacious shrub brush survived in the alkali soil, but she had managed to bring color into the scenery by planting petunias in little broken pots and setting them under windows and along both sides of the front door. She and her small son had hauled conglomerate rocks from the nearby arroyo and made a welcoming walkway leading to the house.

I went to Yoly's house a month after the wedding to invite her and Gary to an end-of-the-summer barbecue. Between my hesitant and perpetually present-tense Spanish and her nonexistent English we talked for three hours. We often had to use our hands to draw pictures in the air, or pick up objects to demonstrate nouns, and body language to act out verbs, but somehow we managed to make each other understand. We also made each other laugh.

I played the part of Gary's mother, first sticking out my rump, then running into Yoly's bathroom and stuffing towels down the back of my jeans and front of my shirt to resemble Mrs. Montoya's corpulent protrusions. I raised my nose and clucked my tongue while delivering biting commentary about every family residing in San Juan County until Yoly was holding her stomach and begging me to stop. "Alto, alto," she implored, her jack-o'-lantern smile somehow beautiful.

It was Yoly's turn next. She stuffed a washcloth down her jeans rolled up like a giant penis, puffed out her chest, and barked orders in Spanish. "Traeme una cerveza . . . Ayudame con mis botas . . . Haz las tamales." I tried to make my laughter sound genuine, but the truth is I was afraid her pantomime of Gary was as accurate as mine of Mrs. Montoya.

"Es mi Gary," Yoly said, afraid I wasn't understanding.

"Si," I said, and I laughed very hard.

AT THE barbecue, Gary strutted and passed out cheap cigars imprinted with "It's a Boy" on the cellophane although Yoly still had five months of pregnancy to go. No tests had been done to support Gary's boast; it all rested on his confidence that Yoly was a producer of males. Yoly told me later that she had not seen a doctor yet but was content that everything was fine because it felt just like the first time.

The child was a girl.

Baby showers weren't unheard of in our little area, but poor women seemed to have a hard time putting one together. Women worked different shifts, got paid at different times, had husbands who objected, small children who demanded too much time, lives that took too much from them to have any energy left over. It was more common that, in the months following a birth, women just sort of showed up with little gifts or a box of diapers and stayed for coffee, often stayed to help scrub the kitchen floor or hang laundry. Doing chores was considered a present too.

I came to Yoly's house with two pink T-shirts rolled inside the comic section of the newspaper and tied with used Christmas ribbon. Yoly said she loved my wrapping paper; it would help her learn more English, particularly English humor. I told her not to count on the funny papers for a real understanding. She learned English quickly. In a matter of months she was putting together complete sentences, although she had the same problem moving through the tenses in English as I did in Spanish.

I held the baby while Yoly made coffee and Wonder Bread toast. I asked her how she was feeling and she answered that she was feeling fine, just a little tired. Then she began to cry.

"Mi Gary estas enojado conmigo." The baby let out a whimper and that was all it took for Yoly to take her gently from me.

"Why is Gary mad at you?" I asked. She held her daughter close.

"Porque the baby es una girl." I looked at Yoly and realized that Gary's anger was more than the typical male disappointment that usually wanes after a few weeks succeeding the birth of a female. She was frightened of Gary and convinced that she had let him down.

"This won't be your last child, Yoly," I said feebly, then feeling a surge of madness myself. "Besides, it's not your fault it's a girl. What? Did Gary sleep through biology in high school?"

"Biologia?" said Yoly, her face wrinkled into a network of confusion.

"Biology, Xs and Ys, Yoly. The man's sperm decides the sex of the child."

"The esperma makes the baby girl or boy?"

I should have never said it. The next time I saw Yoly she was in the hospital with, as they say, multiple contusions and a hairline fracture of the skull. She had told Gary about the Xs and Ys thinking he would forgive her. She told me I couldn't talk about biology anymore. She told the doctor she'd fallen down some stairs. The doctor told her to be more careful, especially since she was pregnant. It was a girl.

When Yoly had her fourth female child, I was doing much better financially. I came to the house with a brand new car seat, presents for the other children, and an Estee Lauder collection of makeup for Yoly. I had been banned from the Montoya household since the biology lesson, but Yoly kept me aware of Gary's working hours and I always made sure I was gone long before he came home. She called me a different name in front of her children. Gary never knew that the woman his children called "Chela" and gave his wife gifts was me.

Yoly was very pleased with the makeup and asked me to show her how to put on the eye shadow.

"Does Gary like you with makeup?" I asked. She couldn't answer right away because I had her stretching her lips wide while I applied red lip liner to her mouth. I pulled away, poising the lip pencil in the air and assessing my work.

"Si, he like it," said Yoly, "pero, I don't have so much time for the makeup."

I looked around Yoly's house, clean but cluttered with children's toys, fresh laundry yet unfolded, and wondered how she kept any order at all in the small house holding a family of seven. I picked up a tube of lipstick and began filling in the lines drawn on her lips. She obediently stretched her mouth taut again.

"Do you ever think about not having any more babies?" I asked as nonchalantly as I could. It was none of my business, but sweet Yoly answered me anyway.

"Oh si, I think about it a lot. I wish about it a lot."

"Hold still," I said, fastening a pair of fashion earrings through her pierced ears.

"Is it the money, Yoly? I could loan you the money for one of those tubal things."

"I can no do it, amiga." Yoly picked up a hand mirror and looked at herself, pleased but unsmiling.

"Of course you can. We could make up some lie for Gary. Men were meant to be lied to, they bring it on themselves, and you could take ages to pay me back. You could make tortillas for the food business. I need the help, really I do. I've got more orders than I can handle."

Yoly had begun shaking her head before I ever finished. "You no understand, amiga, Gary will no let me."

"Jesus, Yoly, this is America, the twentieth century, does he expect you to keep having babies until you run out of eggs?"

"No mi amiga, just until I have a boy."

YOLY MANAGED to not get pregnant again for three years. By that time she was thirty-four years old and even the doctors in Farmington had begun demanding certain tests for any woman over the age of thirty. The tests revealed that not only was her sixth baby not going to be born with Down's Syndrome but she was to have a boy. Gary bought a fresh stock of cheap cigars.

A celebration was planned to take place at the little Montoya house. Gary was so filled with good humor at the thought of his forthcoming son that he lifted my banishment and allowed me to attend. Again the Montoya women descended into Yoly's life, decorating the little house with blue streamers, setting up picnic tables bulging with platters of food. A young goat, gutted and stuffed with garlic, had been buried in the ground and covered with wet leaves and hot coals and left there to roast for thirty hours. When it was exhumed, the meat was so tender it fell from the bones with barely the prick of a fork. Jerry Alcon and the band played well into the night, sounding better and better with each pass of the tequila. The revelers stayed late and drove away fat from the food, half drunk from the tequila, and filthy from dancing in the barren dirt outside Yoly's house. Gary had fallen asleep beside the bonfire, clutching a bottle, cigars spilling out of his shirt pocket.

Yoly and I sat in folding chairs in front of the dying fire holding sleeping children and laughing once again at the jokes told at the party.

"The sleep of children is sweet," I said, looking down at Yoly's youngest child.

"And so are the dreams of a fool," she answered. It was a New Mexico expression. If someone called you a fool, the retort was always, "Then you must envy me, for a fool's dreams are untroubled." I'll never know if Yoly was thinking the same thing I was at that moment, but we both looked over at Gary.

SOME MONTHS later Yoly woke Gary, telling him that the child would soon be born and they'd better start the twenty-five-minute trip to the hospital. Gary roused himself, complaining that she had never given birth during daylight. While he attempted to stuff his foot into the wrong shoe, Yoly found a flashlight, slipped on a coat, and held her stomach while she walked to the neighbor's. The neighbor had promised to watch the children when the time came, and she and Yoly walked back into the house whispering agreement on what the children should eat for breakfast.

It was March, and the Aztec Highway was slick with frozen dew so Gary drove slowly. Yoly sat next to him, resting her head on his shoulder; she squeezed his leg and whispered, "You will soon have your boy, mi corazon." A small sound like the intake of breath punctuated by a hiccup escaped her throat, and Yoly was still for the rest of the trip. Her hand remained on Gary's leg, but more relaxed. Gary reached across her belly and pinched a handful of her outer thigh and returned his hand to the steering wheel. Yoly didn't seem to notice and they drove on in silence.

The lights over the emergency entrance illuminated an empty driveway and Gary thought that perhaps Yoly's timing wasn't so bad after all. He pulled the car up to the entrance, bobbing his shoulder up and down a few times to make Yoly wake up. "Mira, Yolanda, estamos en el hospital." Her head only bobbed up and down with the shoulder, and Gary wondered out loud how it was that a woman could sleep through labor "after all that bitching about how much it hurt."

Two nurses slothed toward the sliding glass doors to see what kind of trouble had pulled into the driveway. Gary pushed Yolanda's head away, leaving it to rest on the back of the seat while he opened the car door. He smiled at the nurses over the top of the car and said, "She's in labor, but she's asleep."

The nurses looked at Gary like he'd just delivered a message in Gaelic, looked at each other, and lunged for the passenger side door.

"Get a gurney!" screamed the one who'd made it inside the car first. She grabbed at Yoly's wrist, then put two fingers to her throat.

"How long?" shouted the nurse at Gary who was bent over looking back into the car.

"How long?" Gary repeated.

"How long has she been like this?"

"You mean asleep?" said Gary as he watched the nurse punch Yolanda in the chest.

"How long, you fucking idiot?" screamed the nurse and punched Yoly again. Yoly's body simply recoiled against the car seat. Her head bounced off the upholstery and came to rest at a twisted angle, making her neck look broken. The red lights spelling out "Emergency Entrance" neutralized the blue tint of her skin.

"Twenty minutes," said Gary through clenched teeth.

The gurney arrived with the other nurse and a man, and they pulled Yoly out of the car. The nurse from the car began blowing air into Yoly's mouth while the man pushed on her chest, all of them steering the gurney through the doors and leaving Gary standing alone in the glow of the emergency lights.

"Is the baby gonna be all right?" Gary hollered. "Is *she* gonna be all right?" he shouted to the backs of the nurses, now almost too far away to hear. The words echoed off the glass doors and floated into the night like balloons set loose by a careless child.

IT WAS the policy of the *Farmington Daily Times* to announce births and deaths at no charge to the families; a family member need only call to have a funeral announced. Births were even simpler. The information was gleaned over the phone from the hospital receptionist every early morning and printed the following day. And so it was written and appeared in the newspaper on the same day that Yolanda Maria Esteban Montes Montoya had died, and that a healthy son had been born to her.

Magenta Molly's

MARILYN TAYLOR

Marilyn Taylor, 47, spent her childhood in southern Arizona where her family lived as ranchers and miners. Eight years ago her sister moved to Tonopah, Nevada, and Marilyn found herself traveling a different desert. It was during those long drives across sand, sagebrush, and alkali lake beds that "Magenta Molly's" first filled her inner landscape. A winner of the 1992 Syndicated Fiction Project, Marilyn has had fiction and poetry published in the Flagstaff Women's Newsletter *and the first* Walking the Twilight. *She has been a court reporter in Flagstaff, Arizona, since 1974.*

IT'S THE ONLY REST area within 250 miles that has bathrooms, jade Porta-Potties sprouting from the black cinders to the white Nevada sky. The sign at the turnout reads DEATH VALLEY. The road cuts west across the desert and disappears into another country, the faraway California mountains an uneven lavender blur. A few hundred yards down the road is the Hi-Way Trailer Court, a strand of silver mobile homes separated by redwood picnic tables and faded Detroit pickups.

In between the place where travelers pause and locals sleep away their days is Magenta Molly's, a tall skinny building painted candy pink. A carved sign swings from the second floor balcony. The door below is boarded shut. In crude printing are the words ARTIST AT WORK, and a yellow stripe that starts at the right edge of the building ends around the back corner in an arrow. There, a series of archways once part of a Reno wedding chapel surround a tiny, emerald green yard. Plastic chairs line the back porch, and inside is the studio and gallery. That's downstairs. Upstairs is the large open room that serves as home to Michael and Fred.

My one-time stepdad, Michael, is the resident artist and half-owner of Molly's. His old friend, Fred, is the other half. Fred takes care of just about everything. He picks up cigarette butts and sweeps the floors, mows the yard and burns the trash. He works the early kitchen shift at the Stagecoach Inn across the highway. Some weeks he is the only one to put any money in the gray lockbox hidden upstairs.

A few years back I had helped them when they decided to buy the building. They were both tired of working at the test site up north and desperate to live someplace more private than the mancamp.

We headed south until we saw the sign pointing to Death Valley. I would have driven by except for Michael yelling, "This is it! Stop the truck!"

We got out. Fred walked the property line, staring at the dust that settled on the toes of his boots. Michael trotted backwards ahead of Fred, twirling, pointing, all the time talking. He had learned to dance when he had tried to teach me in junior high. I never mastered even the most basic steps. He discovered that dancing was part of his soul. I loved to watch him dance. He was the only person I knew who lived inside every bit of his body. There was so much energy left over it leaked out in glorious ways, bones, skin, hair, each cell shimmering.

Fred squinted at the casino on the other side of the highway. "Is that a Help Wanted sign in that window?" he asked.

"It is," I said.

"I suspect this place is as good as any," he said. "But it looks to me like it's gonna take an awful lot of work to turn it into what you think you see."

Fred was right. It did. We caulked the holes to stop the wind whistling through and bought gallons of paint. We coated the outside with enough pink to make the place sizzle in the noonday sun and throw a rosy shadow into the Nevada night.

Fred came up with the name. He whittled the letters into the sign. I painted them chartreuse against a background of plum garden. Michael added dark green vines and rosettes.

The night we hung that sign, we dragged the lawn chairs around front. We sat in a row up near the road and drank cheap champagne that smelled like Easter egg dye. We watched the neon outline of the Stagecoach Inn flash on the front of our gallery. We watched the lights of cars bounce hard and fast off our sign and disappear.

We watched stars cut through the sky to touch the desert that surrounded our new home. We agreed we needed our own special lights.

Fred dug in the Christmas box and pulled out a tangle of bulbs. Michael draped them over our balcony and around our sign. I plugged them in. We walked back to the road to see if we had it right.

I sat between the two men and watched the soft, steady glow of red and blue and green and white draw in and hold all the light that touched us. I saw the light of Magenta Molly's around my body and I saw that same light around Michael and Fred. Nobody moved. We just sat there, quiet, in the middle of all that magic.

I THINK of that beginning as I close in on the last few miles. It has been four years now since we first stopped, two years since I've been back. By that last trip Michael had filled the gallery with paintings of Nevada sunsets slashed across canvases and Fred had settled into the canary jumpsuits he wore at the Stagecoach.

Michael had seemed younger. He wore Levi's and T-shirts splattered with his left-over sunsets, his hair longer, still dark and curly, tied back with an old shoelace. Fred looked older, his skin burned red and tight, tiny lines accenting his clear blue eyes, copper hair turned silver, the ends still burnished.

They were both happy, I could tell. They had friends, kids from the trailer park, miners who came to town for supplies and the all-you-can-eat, prostitutes on a day off. It had been good to sit on that cool grass in the evening and feel like I belonged right in the middle of as much family as I had ever known.

NOW I drive up to an empty building. There are no cars out front, no tourists inside. I stand in the doorway and call for Michael and Fred. There is no answer.

I step into the dry heat of the studio. As my eyes adjust to the afternoon light, ribbons curl around my heart, knotting, unraveling, freezing, melting, beat after beat. I feel the red rhythm inside . . . and outside. I can't separate myself from what I see in the gallery: huge paintings, all of the same subject, a back view of a young nude woman sitting on crumpled sheets in a darkened room. The sunsets have disappeared. The only color in the room is red. All the women have red hair.

As I walk among the canvases, one woman leans forward, ribs curving away, each knob of bony spine pushing through her translucent skin, ginger hair sweeping the floor. I hear husky laughter and turn to see another toss her head, auburn curls sliding down the slender length of her back. A few feet away a woman weaves a russet braid with her long scarlet nails.

My head fills with the musky scent of sex, and its sounds, growls choked deep in the throat, wordless murmurings, tiny cries broken by the whispered demands of lust . . . yes . . . no, not there . . . yes, there . . . do you like . . . yes . . . now, yes . . . you are so . . . now . . . no, wait, not yet . . . yes . . . you feel so good . . .

"So what do you think?" he asks, his voice soft behind me. "What do you think of her?"

I turn and look into the face of my stepdad. The eyes that have always been bright with my reflection are filled instead with the women that live in the room.

"I can't quite get her right," he says, brushing past me. "I'm so close. But she's not exactly right."

Fred follows Michael into the room. Next to him an old woman with a yellow curtain of skin and a ponytail that pulls her hennaed hair thin and tight steps carefully. Her eyes are circled with kohl, cheeks rouged, lips slicked with orange. She smiles and I see two rows of perfect plastic teeth.

"So you are Sarah," she says, her voice deepened with a lifetime of cigarettes and whiskey.

I watch her eyes move over my body, measuring me in a way I have known before but have never thought to name.

"I've heard so much about you." Sarcasm stretches her words. They fall, bent, onto the sheets of the red-headed women. "I think Fred is right. You just might be the one we need to help us with our little problem."

She coughs, a rasp that scrapes her throat dry before it stabs the gray tar, forever trapped in her lungs.

I turn to watch Michael. He moves from painting to painting with his palette, adding a curly wisp to one, deepening the sheen on another, lengthening waves with long strokes.

Fred puts a hand on my shoulder and leads me outside. The woman follows. We sit in the shade of the back porch, our chairs pulled in a tight circle.

I have not yet spoken. I can't think of where to begin.

The old lady takes one of my hands in hers and speaks to Fred. "Ah, this dear child," she says. Her words mock me. "I think we'd better tell her," she continues, "before the poor thing comes to the wrong conclusion."

She laughs then, a shrill sound that breaks across the edges of my own hysteria. It cuts through my confusion. The terror that has been sitting in my stomach crawls up my spine and soaks my back.

I look at Fred.

"Sarah," he says, "I want you to meet Molly. She's our mother."

"Whose mother?" I hear myself asking.

"Our mother," he says. "Michael's mother. My mother." His voice drifts.

"Your mother," I state, willing my words to lay flat in the air. A statement. Not a question. "You and Michael are brothers."

Fred nods.

I watch my stepdad inside his studio, still moving, rearranging his paintings, talking to someone who cannot be seen.

All at once I can't bear to think of who he thinks he is talking to. "What is wrong with him?" I cry, rocking now. I no longer hear my voice outside my head, only inside, where each word is a separate scream:

WHAT . . . HAS . . . HAPPENED . . . TO . . . MY . . . MICHAEL?

I look at the hand that the old woman holds. It is crushed between nicotined fingers with chipped nails the color of ground-ripened citrus. I remember it is my hand, but it is strange, this hand. It lives its own life. The hand jerks, small spasms rippling the skin, pulling it up to touch Fred's cheek, a restless stroking that threatens to claw.

"You tell me," I demand, leaning close to Fred's face and the hand that skitters across it. "You tell me why he's painting all those awful women."

"That's me, honey." Her voice surprises me. "Not me now," she drawls, "not me in a truckload of years, but that's me when they was my little boys. That's what my Michael remembers. He just don't know why."

"Stop it, Ma," Fred snaps. "What she's trying to say is Michael doesn't know how to let her be alive . . . and old." Fred pauses. His eyes search the face of his mother.

When he finally speaks, his voice is higher somehow, younger, and his words are those of a child. "It wasn't her fault. She did what she had to do. Nevada is a hard state, Sarah," he says, as much to himself as to me, "a place where a woman can survive only if she sells everything."

He stands and looks someplace beyond Molly.

"But it ain't no place for a mother," he says.

"Michael was too little to remember Ma very good when she left us with family in Tonopah. He knew better, but he just made her dead to explain why we lived with Uncle Ted. And I think after making her dead for a while, he started believing it." He shakes his head. "We've never talked about it."

"Even when you chose the name of this place?" I ask.

Fred turns. He watches as Michael stacks paintings in a corner and moves others onto easels. We hear him humming under his breath.

"Never," Fred says, "not once did we talk."

"How long has he been like this?" I ask.

"About a week," he says. "He's done all that in a week. Ma stepped off the bus last Saturday and he started painting and hasn't stopped."

Molly stands then and begins to walk away. I watch the slow roll of her shoulder and the sway of her hips, and she almost disappears as the space between us fills with the bodies of the hundreds of men who have followed her down hallways and up stairs and behind doors, and I know why Michael can't stop painting that young woman.

I stand and face her.

"Why did you do this?" I whisper. "If you ever loved him, why did you come here?"

I bite my lip and nurse the blood. Not my blood. Hers. Blood that colors the desert as canvas, that spurts around snapped bones and drips from chunks of wrinkled flesh. Blood that brings the big black birds.

She turns then and faces me, suddenly whole again, an old woman who walked away from her kids, leaving them with an uncle.

A real uncle, I wonder, this Uncle Ted?

I try to remember what my father looks like, my real father, the man who has lived most of my life as a snapshot in my wallet. I remember my own succession of uncles, Uncle Denny from long ago, Uncle Bart, and Michael, who hung around long enough to be my stepdad, Uncle Ernie, whose kisses scared me, and Uncle Lander who didn't want me to use his first name, all men I had watched follow my own mother down hallways and up stairs and behind doors.

My own mother with her strong blond beauty, I try to remember what she looks like. I blink her features onto the face of the woman standing before me and watch them fade.

The sun drops low in the sky and disappears behind Molly. She is surrounded by a fierce white light. On her face is the gaze that judges me. Her words float to me on golden waves of heat: *You are not one of us; you'll never know about the fire.*

"She has no place else to go," Fred says.

I look at him and try to understand why he would say such a thing.

"You asked why," he reminds me. He looks at Molly. "And, she's dying."

I see his eyes bright with tears. I hear Michael in the studio, singing now, and dancing, as he dabs more paint on a canvas.

"And so is he," I say.

As evening cools sky and sand, I turn to Molly. She stands in shadow. Inside my body I feel the smoldering, the flicker of tiny flames. I breathe and let the heat spread. You are wrong, I tell the shadow, I know about fire. But this fire is mine.

I walk inside and select one of his paintings. "This is the one, Michael," I say, softly, so I won't scare him. "I think this lady is the most beautiful woman I've ever seen. You had to love her to paint her like this."

He reaches to brush in yet another strand of hair. I stop him.

"Dance with me, Daddy," I beg. "Dance with me now."

I take his paintbrush and try to pull him close. He jerks back, his eyes flashing hard and angry. I stand on tiptoes to look past this moment. I see my reflection in those dark eyes and I see he sees me, me, his daughter from a long time ago.

"Teach me to dance," I whisper. I drape my arms over his shoulders, press palette and paint between us.

And we dance.

Two Deserts

VALERIE MATSUMOTO

VALERIE MATSUMOTO has a Ph.D. in history from Stanford University. Her dissertation was a study of three generations in a Japanese-American farming community in central California. She has worked on incorporating the history of the World War II Japanese internment camps into UCLA's Asian-American studies center curriculum, and has taught at the University of Arizona in Tucson.

EMIKO OYAMA THOUGHT THE Imperial Valley of California was the loneliest place she had ever seen. It was just like the Topaz Relocation Camp, she told her husband Kiyo, but without the barbed-wire fence and crowded barracks. Miles of bleached desert punctuated sparsely by creosote bush and abandoned debris faced her from almost every window in their small house. Only the living room had a view of the dirt road that ended in front of their home, and across it, a row of squat faded houses where other farmers' families lived. They waved to her and Kiyo in passing, and Jenny played with the Garcia children, but Emiko's Spanish and their English were too limited for more than casual greetings.

Emiko felt a tug of anticipation on the day the moving van pulled up at the Ishikawas' place across the road—the house that in her mind had become inextricably linked with friendship. She had felt its emptiness as her own when Sats, Yuki, and their three children gave up farming and departed for a life that came to her in delicious fragments in Yuki's hastily scrawled letters. Yuki, who made the best sushi rice in the world and had given her the recipe, who could draw shy Kiyo into happy banter. Yuki, whose loud warm laugh made the desert seem less drab, less engulfing.

She had been thinking about Yuki that morning as she weeded the yard and vegetable plot in preparation for planting. Sats and Yuki had advised her to plant marigolds around the vegetables to draw away nematodes, and she liked the idea of a bold orange border. Emiko liked bright colors, especially the flaming scarlet of the bougainvillea that rose above the front door, where Kiki their cat lay sunning himself. There was a proud look in the amber eyes, for Kiki the hunter had slain three scorpions and laid them in a row on the porch, their backs crushed and deadly stingers limp, winning extravagant praise from Jenny and Emiko. The scorpions still lay there, at Jenny's insistence, awaiting Kiyo's return that evening. Emiko shuddered every time she entered the house, glancing at the curved stingers and thinking of Jenny's sandaled feet.

Emiko had finished weeding the front border and was about to go inside to escape the heat when she saw the new neighbor woman plodding across the sand toward her. A cotton shift could not conceal her thinness, nor a straw hat her tousled gray curls. Her eyes were fragile lilac glass above the wide smile.

"Hello, I'm Mattie Barnes. I just thought I'd come over and introduce myself while Roy is finishing up with the movers. Your bougainvillea caught my eye first thing and I thought, Those are some folks who know what will grow in the desert. I hope you'll give me some advice about what to plant in my yard once we get settled in."

They talked about adjusting to desert life and Emiko learned that Mattie's husband, Roy, had recently retired. "We decided to move here because the doctor said it would be better for my lungs," Mattie explained, wiping her brow.

"Would you like a glass of lemonade?" Emiko offered. "Or maybe later, after you've finished moving—"

"Oh, I'd love something cold," Mattie said, adding vaguely, "Roy will take care of everything—he's more particular about those things than I am."

Emiko preceded Mattie into the house, hoping that Jenny was not lying on the cool linoleum, stripped to her underwear. As she crossed the threshold Mattie gave a shriek and stopped abruptly, eyeing the scorpions lined up neatly on the porch.

"What on earth are those things doing here?"

"Our cat killed them," Emiko said, feeling too foolish to admit her pride in Kiki's prowess. "Jenny wants me to leave them to show her father when he comes home from the field."

"Awful creatures," Mattie shuddered. "Roy can't stand them, but then, he can't abide insects. He said to me this morning, 'Of all the places we could have moved to, we had to choose the buggiest.'"

There was no buggier place than the Imperial Valley, Emiko agreed, especially in the summer. In the evening the air was thick with mosquitoes, gnats, and moths. The cicadas buzzed in deafening chorus from every tree. They danced in frenzied legions around the porch light and did kamikaze dives into the bath water. All of them came in dusty gray hordes, as though the desert had sapped the color from them but not their energy. Late at night, long after Kiyo had fallen into exhausted sleep, Emiko would lie awake, perspiring, listening to the tinny scrabble of insects trapped between the window glass and screen.

". . . but I like the desert," Mattie was saying, dreamily clinking the ice cubes in her glass. "It's so open and peaceful. As long as I can have a garden, I'll be happy."

Within a few weeks after their arrival, the Barneses had settled into a routine: Roy making daily trips to the local store and the Roadside Cafe; Mattie tending her garden and walking to church once a week with Emiko and Jenny. By the end of June Mattie had been enlisted with Emiko to make crepe paper flowers for a church bazaar.

"My, your flowers turned out beautifully," Mattie exclaimed one morning, looking wistfully at the cardboard box filled with pink, yellow, scarlet, and lavender blossoms set on wire stems. "They'll make lovely corsages." She sighed. "I seem to be all thumbs—my flowers hardly look like flowers. I don't know how you do it. You Japanese are just very artistic people."

Emiko smiled and shook her head with a polite disclaimer, but the bright blur of flowers suddenly dissolved into another mass of paper blooms, carrying her more than a decade into the past. She was a teenager in a flannel shirt and denim pants with rolled cuffs, seated on a cot in a cramped barrack room helping her mother fashion flowers from paper. Her own hands had been clumsy at first, striving to imitate her mother's precise fingers that gave each fragile petal lifelike curves, the look of artless grace. The only flowers in Topaz when elderly Mr. Wakasa was shot by a guard were those that bloomed from the fingertips of Issei and Nisei women, working late into the night to complete the exquisite wreaths for his funeral. Each flower a silent voice crying with color; each flower a tear.

"I did a little flower-making as a teenager," Emiko said.

"Will you come over and show me how?" Mattie asked. "I'm too embarrassed to take these awful things, and I've still got lots of crepe paper spread all over the kitchen."

"Sure," Emiko nodded. "I'll help you get started and you'll be a whiz in no time. It isn't too hard; it just takes patience."

Mattie smiled, a slight wheeze in her voice when she said, "I've got plenty of that, too."

They were seated at the Barneses' small table surrounded by bright masses of petals like fallen butterflies, their fingers sticky with florist's tape, when Roy returned from shopping. When he saw Emiko, he straightened and pulled his belt up over his paunch.

"A sight for sore eyes!" he boomed, giving her a broad wink. "What mischief are you ladies up to?"

"Emi's teaching me how to make flowers," Mattie explained, holding up a wobbly rose.

"Always flowers! I tell you," he leaned over Emiko's chair and said in a mock conspiratorial voice, "all my wife thinks about is flowers. I keep telling her there are other things in life. Gardening is for old folks."

"And what's wrong with that?" Mattie protested, waving her flower at him. "We *are* old folks."

"Speak for yourself," he winked at Emiko again. "What's so great about gardens, anyway?"

"I hold with the poem that says you're closest to God's heart in a garden," said Mattie.

"Well, I'm not ready to get that close to God's heart yet." There was defiance in Roy's voice. "What do you think about that, Emi?"

"I like working in the yard before it gets too hot," she said carefully. Her words felt tight and deliberate, like the unfurled petals on the yellow rose in her hands. "I don't have Mattie's talent with real flowers, though—aside from the bougainvillea and Jenny's petunias, nothing ever seems to bloom. The soil is too dry and saline for the things I used to grow. Now I've got my hopes pinned on the vegetable garden."

"Vegetables—hmph!" Roy snorted, stomping off to read the paper.

"Oh, that Roy is just like a boy sometimes," Mattie said. "I tell you, don't ever let your husband retire or you'll find him underfoot all day long."

"Doesn't Roy have any hobbies?" Emiko thought of her father and his books, his Japanese brush painting, his meetings.

"He used to play golf," Mattie said, "but there's no golf course here. He says this town is one giant sand trap."

"There have been times when I felt that way, too," Emiko admitted lightly.

"Well, don't let Roy hear you say that or you'll never get him off the topic," Mattie chuckled. "The fact is, Roy doesn't much know how to be by himself. I've had forty years to learn, and I've gotten to like it. And I suppose maybe he will too."

Her voice trailed off, and Emiko suddenly realized that Mattie didn't much care whether he did or not.

One day while Emiko was engrossed in pinning a dress pattern for Jenny she suddenly heard a tapping on the screen, like the scrabbling of a large beetle. She half-turned and felt a jolt of alarm at the sight of a grinning gargoyle hunched before the glass, hands splayed open on either side of his face, the caricature of a boy peering covetously into a toy store.

"Hey there! I caught you day dreaming!" he chortled. "Looks to me like you need some company to wake you up."

"I'm not day dreaming; I'm trying to figure out how to make a two-and-a-half-yard dress out of two yards," she said. "Jenny is growing so fast, I can hardly keep up with her."

Roy walked into the house unbidden, confident of a welcome, and drew a chair up to the table. He fingered the bright cotton print spread over the table and gazed at Emiko, his head cocked to one side.

"You must get pretty lonesome here by yourself all day. No wonder you're sitting here dreaming."

"No," she said, her fingers moving the pattern pieces. "There's so much to do I don't have time to be lonesome. Besides, Jenny is here, and Kiyo comes home for lunch."

"But still—cooped up with a kiddie all day. . . ." Roy shook his head. He chose to disregard Kiyo, who had no place in his imagined scenarios and was hard at work miles away.

Emiko delicately edged the cotton fabric away from Roy's damp, restless fingers. I'll be darned if I offer him something to drink, she thought as he mopped his brow and cast an impatient glance at the kitchen. "I haven't seen Mattie outside this week. How is she feeling?"

"Oh, 'bout the same, 'bout the same," he said, his irritation subsiding into brave resignation. "She has her good days and her bad days. The doctor told her to stay in bed for a while and take it easy."

"It must be hard on Mattie, having to stay indoors," Emiko said, thinking of her peering out through the pale curtains at the wilting zinnias and new weeds in the back yard.

"I suppose so—usually you can't tear Mattie away from her garden." Roy shook his head. "Mattie and me are real different. Now, I like people—I've always been the sociable type—but Mattie! All she cares about are plants."

"Well, Kiyo and I have different interests," Emiko said, "but it works out well that way. Maybe you could learn a few things from Mattie about plants."

Even as the suggestion passed her lips, she regretted it. Roy viewed the garden as the site of onerous labor. To Mattie, it was the true world of the heart, with no room for ungentle or impatient hands. It was a place of deeply sown hopes, lovingly nurtured, and its colors were the colors of unspoken dreams.

"Plants!" Roy threw up his hands. "Give me people any time. I always liked people and had a knack for working with them—that's how I moved up in the business."

"Why don't you look into some of the clubs here?" Emiko tried again. "The Elks always need people with experience and time . . ."

"Sweetheart, I'm going to spend my time the way I want. I'm finished with work—it's time to enjoy life! Besides, how much fun can I have with a bunch of old geezers? That's not for me, Emily, my dear." She stiffened as he repeated the name, savoring the syllables. "Emily . . . Emily . . . Yes, I like the sound of that—Emily."

"My name is Emiko," she said quietly, her eyes as hard as agate. "I was named after my grandmother." That unfaltering voice had spoken the same words in first, second, third, fourth, fifth, and sixth grades. All the grammar school teachers had sought to change her name, to make her into an Emily: "Emily is so much easier to pronounce, dear, and it's a nice American name." She was such a well-mannered child, the teachers were always amazed at her stubbornness on this one point. Sometimes she was tempted to relent, to give in, but something inside her resisted. "My name is Emiko," she would insist politely. I am an American named Emiko. I was named for my grandmother, who was beautiful and loved to swim. When she emerged from the sea, her long black hair would glitter white with salt. I never met her, but she was beautiful, and she would laugh when she rose from the waves. "My name is Emiko, Emi for short."

"But Emily is such a pretty name," Roy protested. "It fits you."

"It's not my name," she said, swallowing a hard knot of anger. "I don't like to be called Emily!"

"Temper, temper!" He shook his finger at her, gleeful at having provoked her.

"Well, I guess I'll be in a better temper when I can get some work done," she said, folding up the cloth with tense, deliberate hands. She raised her voice. "Jenny! Let's go out and water the vegetable garden now."

If Jenny thought this a strange task in the heat of the afternoon, it did not show in her face when she skipped out of her room, swinging her straw hat. It still sported a flimsy, rainbow-hued scarf that had been the subject of much pleading in an El Centro dime store. At that moment, Emiko found it an oddly reassuring sight. She smiled and felt her composure return.

"Tell Mattie to let me know if there's anything I can do to help," she told Roy, as he unwillingly followed them out of the house and trudged away across the sand. After they went back inside, Emiko locked the door behind them for the first time. When Kiyo returned home, his face taut with fatigue, she told him it was because of the hoboes who came around.

Emiko went to see Mattie less and less frequently, preferring instead to call her on the phone, even though they lived so close. Roy, however, continued to drop by despite Emiko's aloofness. His unseemly yearning tugged at her with undignified hands, but what he craved most was beyond her power to give. She took to darning and mending in the bedroom with the curtains drawn, ignoring his insistent knock; she tried to do her gardening in the evening after dinner when her husband was home, though it was hard to weed in the dusk. She was beginning to feel caged, pent up, restless. Jenny and Kiyo trod quietly, puzzled by her edginess, but their solicitude only made her feel worse.

Finally, one morning Emiko decided to weed the vegetables, sprouting new and tender. Surely the mid-morning heat would discourage any interference. Although the perspiration soon trickled down her face, she began to enjoy the weeding, pulled into the satisfying rhythm of the work. She was so engrossed that she did not notice when Roy Barnes unlatched the gate and stepped into the yard, a determined twinkle in his faded eye.

"Howdy, Emi! I saw you working away out here by your lonesome and thought maybe you could use some help."

"Thanks, but I'm doing all right," she said, wrenching a clump of puncture vine from the soil and laying it in the weed box carefully to avoid scattering the sharp stickers. Jenny was close by, digging at her petunias and marigolds, ignoring Mr. Barnes, who had no place in the colorful jungle she was imagining.

"If I had a pretty little wife, I sure wouldn't let her burn up out here, no sir," his voice nudged at her as she squatted on the border of the vegetable plot. If Mattie looked out of the window she would see only a pleasant tableau: Roy nodding in neighborly fashion as Emiko pointed out young rows of zucchini and yellow squash, watermelon, cantaloupe, eggplant, and tomatoes. Mattie would not see the strain on Emiko's face, turned away from Roy when he leaned over and mumbled, "Say, you know what I like best in this garden?"

Emiko grabbed the handle of the shovel and stood up before he could tell her, moving away from him to pluck a weed. "I know Mattie likes cantaloupe," she said. "So do I. Kiyo prefers Crenshaws, but I couldn't find any seeds this year. What do you and Mattie have in your garden?"

"Just grass," he said, undeterred. "Mattie's always fussing over her flowers—you know what she's like," he chuckled indulgently, "but I'd rather spend my time doing other things than slaving in the yard."

Emiko hacked away at the stubborn clumps of grass roots and the persistent run-ners with myriad finer roots, thread-thin but tough as wire. She worked with desper-ate energy, flustered, her gloved hands sweating on the shovel handle, forehead damp. She was groping for the language to make him understand, to make him leave her in peace, but he was bent on not understanding, not seeing, not leaving until he got what he wanted.

"You know what, Emi?" He moistened his dry lips, beginning to grin reminiscently. "You remind me of somebody I met in Tokyo. Have you ever been to Tokyo?"

"No," she said, digging hard. "Never."

"You'd like it, it's a wonderful place, so clean and neat, and the people so friendly. When I was in Tokyo, I met up with the cutest geisha girl you ever saw—just like a little doll. She'd never seen anybody with blue eyes before and couldn't get over it." He chuckled. "I couldn't think who you reminded me of at first, and then it just hit me that you are the spitting image of her."

"Did Mattie like Tokyo too?" Emiko said, continuing to spade vigorously as his eyes slid over her, imagining a doll in exotic robes.

"She didn't go—it was a business trip," he said impatiently. Then his voice relaxed into a drawl, heavy with insinuation. "After all, I like to do some things on my own." He was moving closer again.

Then she saw it. Emiko had just turned over a rock, and as she raised the shovel, it darted from its refuge, pincers up, the deadly tail curved menacingly over the carapaced back. It moved a little to the left and then the right, beginning the poison dance. Emiko glanced to see where Jenny was and saw Roy jump back hastily; the scorpion, startled by his movement, scuttled sideways toward Jenny, lying on her stomach, still dreaming of her jungle.

The blood pounded in Emiko's head. She brought down the shovel hard with one quick breath, all her rage shooting down the thick handle into the heavy crushing iron. She wielded the shovel like a samurai in battle, swinging it down with all her force, battering her enemy to dust. Once had been enough, but she struck again and again, until her anger was spent and she leaned on the rough handle, breathing hard.

"Mommy! What did you do?" Jenny had scrambled to Emiko's side, fear in her eyes, gazing at the unrecognizable fragments in the dirt.

"I killed a scorpion," Emiko said. She scornfully tossed the remains into the weed box, and wiped her brow on her arm, like a farmer, or a warrior. "I don't like to kill anything," she said aloud, "but sometimes you have to."

Roy Barnes recoiled from the pitiless knowledge in her eyes. He saw her clearly now, but it was too late. His mouth opened and closed, but the gush of words had gone dry. He seemed to age before her eyes, like Urashima-taro, who opened the precious box of youth and was instantly wrinkled and broken by the unleashed tides of years.

"You'll have to leave now, Mr. Barnes. I'm going in to fix lunch." Emiko's smile was as quiet as unsheathed steel. "Tell Mattie I hope she's feeling better."

She watched him pick his way across the dirt, avoiding the puncture vine and rusted tin cans, looking as gray as the rags that bleached beneath the fierce sun. Jenny stared past him and the small houses of their neighborhood to the desert sand beyond, glittering like an ocean with shards of glass and mica.

"Do you think we might ever find gold?" she asked.

They gazed together over the desert, full of unknown perils and ancient secrets, the dust of dreams and battles.

"Maybe." Emiko stood tall, shading her eyes from the deceptive shimmer. "Maybe."

Bear House

MARY SOJOURNER

MARY SOJOURNER, 56, has written a novel, Sisters of the Dream, *two journals,* Sister Raven, Brother Hare *and* DreamWeaving, *and numerous award-winning short stories and essays. "Passion lives in these holy places: anger, emptiness, shame, sorrow, pain, fear, and joy," Mary says. "If you sit in these places—if you don't run—passion will emerge. In country where light burns deep in fleshy rock, glitters maniac in rapids of high desert rivers, bounces fierce and dangerous off the back window of a pickup screaming north on a dead-hot Mojave highway, here, too, passion lives. Stories lie in the Southwest like canyon garnets, waiting for the light." Mary lives in Flagstaff, Arizona, with her many cats.*

I'M LIKE A TEENAGER when the phone rings. Generation Duh, ever hopeful, stomach lurching, heart racing, all of which would make sense under other circumstances. For instance, if I truly was fifteen and there was a potential boyfriend, or if I was actually writing enough to engender massive public approval. Neither of those circumstances is true, so when the phone rings and I jump, having not had the self-discipline to turn off the tone so I can get in some hard time at the computer, I feel guilty. Worse yet, I feel reprieved.

"Sheila," this husky voice says, "Sheila?"

There are no more words, just sobs, and the sound of somebody choking and coming up for air.

"Who is this?" I ask.

There is silence.

"It's me," somebody whispers, and I know it's Rae.

"God," I say, "what is it?"

"Just a second," she says. "I have to get some tissues. I didn't think I'd lose it like this."

"It's your dime," I say. "You want to call me back?"

There's no reply. I hear her snuffling and cussing in the other room. I can picture her, big and fierce and truly blond; I can see the room, lush plants and perfect hand-thrown pots shining like agate and anywhere from five to seven cats lounging in the late morning sun. I imagine her big, splayed fingers, the nails never quite free from clay, and I see her gaze, intent as a hawk's, if a hawk had ice-blue eyes. She picks up the phone. I put the computer to sleep.

"I'm positive," she says.

"You've never been positive a day in your life," I say.

She is the most cynical woman I know. Something else occurs to me.

"What do you mean? You're fifty-seven. You had a hysterectomy when you were forty. No way you're pregnant."

"No," she says. "The other." She's off again, in a flash-flood of hard wet noises.

"Wait," I say. "No."

"Yes."

We are both quiet.

"Come on," I say, "you can't be. You've had the sex life of a marble."

"No," she says. "I am. One charming old guy. And me going, 'Oh well, that doesn't happen to grandmothers.' That's all it took."

I am furious. Death always makes me furious. And in my book, what Rae is telling me is she's dying.

"Okay," I say. "Just positive, or Kaposi's, or that lung crap, or what?"

"*Just positive*," she says. "Oh yeah, no big deal, just positive."

I cry. I go from icily furious to head down on the computer keyboard, phone clutched to my ear, what I can't shape in words howling into the keys.

"Oh great," Rae says. "My friend, the mental health professional."

"Shut up," I say. "Just shut up."

We eat a couple bucks' worth of long-distance silence, her hiccuping, me trying to make myself breathe. The only other time I cried like this was when Daniel, my one true love, took off, and it was Rae walked me through that one.

"Okay," I say, "what do you need?"

We are both part of the great sisterhood of single aging women. Most of us have learned to rely A. on ourselves, and Z. on one another, and A–Z, on combinations of those options depending on the severity of the crisis. Crises for single aging women range from the fuzzy spot on the mammogram, to five years since the last time you slept with another human being, to one MBA or one electronic gadget being hired to replace you and two other employees, the difference between the MBA and the gadget being negligible.

"What I need," Rae says, "is to hear the lab tech was drunk and made a mistake."

"Well?"

"No luck, got a second opinion. This is it."

"So."

"So. I need sun. I need you. I need to see places I've never seen, eat a ton of good Mexican food, see light that makes me want to fool around with shapes and glazes when I get home. I need to dance around those See-dough-now woo-woo circles, try anything anybody tells me will hold this thing off."

This last is a shock. She visited me four years ago. We wandered around the little New Age town south of here. She named it See-dough-now, as in: the nouvelle California ladies with perfect nails and power pyramids in their shops see you, see dough, and want it now. Rae's final word on it all had been, "The Town That T-Shirts Made."

"Are you nuts?" I ask.

"Maybe," she says. "I do not want to die. I most especially do not want to die with my brain turning to blue jello. If anything can stop that, I'll try it."

"Come out," I say. "Tomorrow."

"No," she says, "I've got Charlevoix this summer and that big show in Maryland. I won't be free till September. I'll come then."

"Rae," I say patiently, "what are you going to need money for?"

"I don't," she says. "I just need to keep doing what I do."

She's a potter, not artsy-fartsy but steady, centered as the bowls and cups and lamps she turns out on her wheel, winter after winter, spring after spring, when it's cool enough up north to fire the kiln without succumbing to heat stroke, when it's cold enough that the lady lawyers and people with terminally great hair won't come out to a craft show, no matter how much they need the perfect piece for the summer place.

"I know," I say. "I understand."

Single aging women earn their own livings. Most of us have for years. We know just enough about vehicles to bully garage guys. We can make minor electrical repairs. We, very likely, raised our kids by ourselves and, in addition to being gourmet cooks, make the best love you ever went cross-eyed over. We are good at many things and great at a few. What we hate is the glitch, the moment when everything stops, when the house is abruptly quiet and nobody needs us and what we've got is what we see, our beautiful solitude, our lives alone.

"Sheila," Rae says.

"Yeah?"

"This is between you and me. Get it?"

"I don't know," I say. "I can't do this alone."

"You're not," she says, "I am."

"Fine."

"Hey," she says, "when it's all over, you can write about it. But, not till then."

"Lovely," I say.

"I'll sign a release form," she says. "In September. On your back porch."

RAE TAKES the train. "I want to see the glorious width and breadth of this great country of ours," she says.

I've taken the train. I know that what she really wants to do is sit down in the club car and flirt. She tells me that the diagnosis has removed her from the front lines, but that in no way is she going to give up being an operative. Her one and only husband served a half tour in Nam, got sent back with one of those million dollar leg wounds, and got sympathy-laid for the next twenty-five years. When he's lonely, which is usually about six months after he marries the next wonderful woman, he heads out to a little Thai restaurant and makes quiet references to the Tunnels. It's never failed him. Did *he* get this nasty, creepy, fatal disease?

Tell me God isn't a man.

Rae picked up that Nam lingo from him, which he still uses as abundantly as any other wannabe Platoonik, except for the term Rear Echelon Mother, which he was, his million dollar wound caused by his own gun. Though he, that marriage, and that war are twenty-five years cold, she still talks like an army wife.

"I guess he's still my skinny grunt with the perpetual hard-on," she'll say. Most of her friends are no longer kind enough to not point out that he *is* still just that, and that his gun is aimed in other than her direction.

I drive into town to pick her up. Our sixteen square blocks of neon shimmer against the dark mountains. The moon is in Venus, a frail crescent riding above the northernmost peak. I've rolled down the window and the rosemary scent of ponderosa pine forest rushes past me. I feel brutally healthy, grateful, and guilty. Why her? Why not me who had the sex life of a mink and the dating skills of an amoeba? Bump me, I'm yours.

The train is miraculously on time. I stand on the platform, three green chile enchiladas in a take-out bag in my right hand, nothing in my left but the hug I wrap around her as soon as she is within range. She looks great. She's wearing the big lady uniform, dark tights, a bulky sweater, suede high-heeled boots. She's taller than me by a couple of inches. In the boots she can rest her chin on my head. Which she does.

"I love it here," she says. "There were two young cowboys who got off in Winslow. They told me the West was made for women like me."

I pull away and grin at her.

"You've never looked better," I say. "When did you start wearing makeup?"

"Around Raton," she says, "when those sweet boys got on. Bartender loaned me hers."

We wrap our arms around each other. I bump her with the enchilada box.

"Food," I say, "real Mexizona food."

"What I want to do," she says, "is pick up a couple bottles of Dos Equis, a lime, a pint of mocha ice cream, and I want to have a picnic in that little park in front of City Hall."

"You *want*?" I say. "The Great Earth Mother *wants*?"

"This diagnosis is an awful miracle," she says. "A late-for-it, stupid, terrifying miracle."

"It's clear," I say, "that the epiphanies have started early."

"Easy," she says. "I'm not in pain. I can think. I am not exhausted by the effort to take a breath. I've been reading. I've been going to the weekly Positive Opportunities support group. And, for once in my life, I've been listening."

"So?"

"I figure I better do the good part now."

She begins to cry.

"Oh shit," I say. "God damn it."

I take her big hand in mine.

"I know," she says between sniffles, "you don't know how to do this."

"I don't."

"Keep it simple," she says. "Ice cream. Cerveza."

"There's a brewery-pub-espresso-over-priced-deli on the corner of the next street."

"This is wonderful," she says. "I had killer sales at Charlevoix and Gaithersburg. I will be able to afford the simple charms of this unspoiled western town."

THE PARK is pure emerald under the new Victorian street lights. The moon hangs fat and glorious in the southeast. Couples are everywhere, sitting on the new antique benches, lying beneath the pines, huddled together on the hillock that rises to the war memorial pylon.

"Boocoo boom-boom tonight," Rae says pensively.

"Rae," I say, and hand her the enchiladas, "eat. The war is over."

"Yeah," she says, "just tell me the part again about how numb-nuts and Nam are long ago and far away."

"Nam is the place to be seen this vacation season," I say. "Besides, are you sure he was there?"

"I am," she says. "There's a gay guy, Eddie, in my group. He was over there. He keeps talking about how it is to walk with death. They dragged him over there in '69, up near Lang Vei, him and a bunch of other Friggin' New Guys. He says this is like that. Death all-the-time on your ass, not knowing where it's coming from, can't tell a cold from the Big One, just like they couldn't tell a nice old lady with melons in her basket from VC."

"Plus," I say, "you just might make it through for a while and then what?"

"Thanks," she says, and takes a bite of enchilada. "Listen. I think we've got to be careful that we don't spend this whole trip talking about nothing but what I've got."

"Right," I say. For the life of me I can't, at that moment, figure how we're going to talk about anything else. "You bet."

She opens a Dos Eq, rubs the lip of the bottle with lime.

"Yes," she says. "This is perfect."

"So," I say, "tell me about the kids."

"Jerree is pregnant again." Rae looks at me over the top of the bottle.

"Nifty," I say. She snorts.

"J. Ellen made seventy-six thousand eight hundred and fifty-three dollars last year. Jen is regularly attending Love Your Child Within meetings and thinks I need to confront my eating disorder. Judy fell in love with a guy ten years younger than she is who is a professional skateboard designer." She takes a big bite of enchilada. "And yours?"

"Steve is working sixty-five hours a week in corporate headquarters in Bangkok. Max is in Nepal teaching Tibetan refugees English. Ceily is raising Mollie twenty-two hundred miles east of here. Cal is too far east, making music I hear in my head whether he's playing it or not." I shrug. "Well, I told them I needed space."

We look at each other. In the green light, Rae looks like a hologram of her probable future. I know I'm not supposed to be thinking that way.

"So," I say, and I can't think of one appropriate thing to follow. I am sitting on a historically accurate park bench with pale globe lights like perfect little moons in the heart of the most wonderful place I've ever lived. It is my second-favorite month of the year and I am with one of my best friends in my whole life and I can only pick up an enchilada, which I do not want, and take a bite out of it.

"They are very busy," Rae says, "my four. In some ways, they might as well be in Bangkok."

This information is a shock. Rae and her tribe have performed *Mother Courage* for years, going forward, husbandless, fatherless, through want and weird clothes, into a future of matriarchal solidarity. Christmases together, Easters, Fourth of July, Friday nights in front of the fire with Rolling Rock beer and pizza and a rating system for the girls' suitors. When Jerree got married, Mom and Les Girls held a bachelorette party that drew two town cop cars and the discovery of Rae's private basement mushroom plot next to the pickled peaches.

"What are you telling me?" I ask.

"Things change," she says.

"Why?"

"I'm not sure."

"Is it because . . ." I stop. How do you say it? In those circles where it is common, how do people talk about it? It occurs to me that I'll have to go to the town's alternative bookstore and read up on this.

"You're thinking you better read about this, aren't you?" Rae says. "Sheila, this isn't quite like being a woman who loves too much or a fudge-junkie or whatever is currently the national diagnosis."

". . . you told them you're positive?" I finish.

"No," she says. "I didn't tell them."

"So," I say, "you're going to just soldier on till something shows up and let them have their young womanhoods, right?"

"Right," she says.

"Hey," I say, "it's exactly what I would do."

"Besides," Rae mumbles.

We say it in unison. "I don't want anybody to feel sorry for me."

SHE WON'T stay with me. I live in a cabin with an outhouse and she is of Germanic origins.

"I need a shower," she says, "and a bathroom where nobody sees me hike up to it in my baby dolls."

She rents a room in an old turquoise adobe motel in the heart of town. The flamingo neon of the Indian restaurant next door lights up her evenings, she tells me, and at dawn she can sit on the stoop, drink her coffee, and know that she's had one more day. I begin to realize that she is here not only to see me but to see what she sees when she is out on that stoop, watching early morning traffic, studying how the light moves on the mountains in new patterns. The aspen begin to go pure yellow. Most mornings, a wreath of vapor circles the tallest peaks. Snow dusts the blue-black rock and is gone. She tells me all of this and she says that glazes and bowls and goblets are taking form in her mind.

She borrows my truck, takes off for hours. When she returns, we sit in the sun on my back porch. We drink coffee. She is quieter than I have known her. She doesn't tell me where she goes, but she brings me dried seed-pods, tiny geodes, feathers, a couple of perfect black-on-white pottery sherds that we agree neither of us will remember that she picked up. One fine afternoon, she brings home a grease-spotted paper bag and pulls out two slabs of Navajo fry bread.

"I'm getting used to you being here," I say.

We are sitting on my back porch, eating fry bread and honey. Rae is perched on the top porch step. We face south where we can watch the bird feeder stuck in the two-trunked pine. My cat, Vicious, chitters at the Steller's jays. They scream and dive-bomb the food and drop peanut shells on her head. She is furious, her tail switching back and forth. I think of Bette Davis playing Queen Elizabeth I.

"Has it ever occurred to you," Rae says, "that there is something faintly peculiar about loving birds and setting up this avian claymore?"

"Claymore?"

"Land mine," she says. "Directional."

"Cats eat birds," I say. "And, in Vicious's case, play Ping-Pong with them. She does it whether I feed them or not."

"In all honesty," Rae says, "it reminds me of your youthful dating style."

"In all honesty," I say, "youthful appears to have been my *only* dating style."

We both sigh.

"Daniel," I say, "loved my dating style. Fabulous meals and then mutual pouncing. He can play Ping-Pong with me whenever he wants."

"That was fifteen years ago," Rae says.

I dip my fry bread in my coffee. Nothing dies quicker than fry bread and nothing brings it back to life like coffee.

"Christ, this is great," I say. We're both quiet for a minute.

"So how is Daniel?" I ask. One of us has to get this obligatory Q & A over with.

"He's happy. I see him maybe twice a year. He's got rentals and a cellular phone and he still looks like a pirate."

"What else?" I look down into my coffee. I remember to breathe.

"She's older than he is. Three kids, nearly grown. They're all living in that old place on Barkin Street."

"Thank you," I say. "That's enough." Rae tears off a corner of fry bread, scatters the crumbs into my fire pit. The Steller's jays begin a long, involved analysis of her gesture.

"You haven't ever let go," she says. "Our Positive Opportunities facilitator says we can't move on till we let go. She says that at every meeting and somebody always reminds her that, in our situations, we don't exactly want to move on."

"There it is," I say.

"What happened to Wiley?" she asks. "The last time we talked, you said he'd moved into town."

"Well," I said, "the ol' wildcat himself is marrying my former dear friend, Rolynne. He, who believed it was suffocating to a man's free spirit to own property, bought a nice house up on the hill, and, when last seen, was following Rolynne into the local Santa Fe–tasteful furniture store. I suspect that if I ever have the heart to drive by their place, there will be a polymer-resin coyote in the front yard next to their Greenpeace banner."

"Letting go," Rae says. "Never your strong suit."

"I'm over it," I say. "It's weird. I didn't feel much about this one. Almost three years together, me and Wiley, a personal best for me since Daniel, and the most I feel is irritated."

"Well," she says. "Well."

THE LIGHT begins to cool. My neighbor Jake pokes his head around the corner of the cabin.

"You guys want company?" he asks. "It's beautiful out here and I can't read another page."

Jake is a wiry little guy who rows the Big Colorado in the summer and hates college the rest of the year. He's thirty-nine, and a sophomore. He's never been married and he rides a stripped-down Kawasaki. I love his hair. It's black and shining as the raven feathers that drift down from the pines. He's pulled it back in a ponytail and on him, that's not a cliché. When he wears tank tops, which he does till mid-October, you can see what appear to be skinny claws emerging from his shoulder-blade. It's a tattoo. He got it when he had ninety days without cocaine.

"The monkey on my back is me," he tells anybody who asks. "All I have to do is look in the mirror to scare myself shitless. Scared shitless is the only way I won't do it again."

"Sit down," I say. "Rae brought fry bread. You want coffee?"

"Oh no," he says, "not me."

We laugh. He drinks maybe fifteen cups of coffee a day. His P. O. tells him he's lucky it's legal. He tells her he knows it. I fix him up a cup with brown sugar and half-and-half. He pulls off a piece of fry bread and dunks it. Rae watches him. She is grinning. This evening, the tank top is fuchsia and against it, in this soft, moonstone light, Jake's dark skin looks better than the coffee he's drinking.

"Rae," he says, "you can't go back."

"I know," she says. "But, I've got to."

"Why?"

"My work," she says. "You can't just disappear from the craft circuit. You're gone one year, you're dead."

"Same with the riv," Jake says. "All those young hunks are lined up waiting for an old geezer like me to falter."

"You come live with me," Rae says. "We'll split the rent." We all grin at each other.

"You and your friends," Jake says to me, "are the kind of women men ought to sell their souls for."

"And you," I say, "should set up basic training for guys over fifty."

Jake stands up, kisses the top of my head.

"Thanks, Sheila," he says. "I gotta get back to Piaget and those Swiss babies. You never know when it's going to come in handy."

Jake met a bunch of Rez kids in rehab. They all snuck out to share a joint. They told him how much they hated school. Nothin' but bilagaana history. No old Navajo stories. No decent thrasher tunes. Nothin' for a bro to do. Jake, being the kind of guy who ran Class 10 Crystal Rapid on shrooms, got fire in his eye and told them he'd get his fuckin' degree and come up there to teach. They could count on it. Cause he'd show.

"Whoa," he spins on his heel, "I forgot to ask you. My Archeo prof is taking us down to Honanki next weekend. Do some clean-up. Some touron sprayed the petroglyphs. He asked us to bring volunteers." He grins and he is five years old. "I spaced it. Could you guys help me out?"

"What's Honanki?" Rae asks. "What's a touron?"

"Touron. Tourist-moron. Honanki. House of the Bear. Beautiful. In a cliff. You look out over a valley. This time of year it's like pure gold."

"A ruin?" Rae asks. She is hot for ruins.

"Sinagua," Jake says. "Eleventh century. So beautiful." He looks at me. "Right?"

I nod. I remember an April full-moon night, Wiley and me and Rolynne and her husband, Mark. Mark had put Copland's *Appalachian Spring* on the truck stereo and opened both doors. The sun was going molten in the west, the moon already flooding Honanki's red walls with silver. Wiley and Rolynne and Mark had been pounding beers all day. I can't anymore, so I fled up into the rocks following the clear call of an owl. The sunset was behind me and then, the sound of a man crying. When I finally turned, the sky was the color of ripe cantaloupe. Wiley was patting Mark on the shoulder. Mark waved me down.

When I reached the two of them, the light had begun to cool and Mark said to Wiley, "Do you know the words to this?"

He waved hugely at the music drifting around us. I remember thinking that it was as if we were held in a great scarlet bowl, the four of us and the music . . . sweet evening pouring in, filling the moment to overflowing.

"Ohmygod," Mark said, "you guys are my best friends ever in my whole life. You gotta know the words."

He put his arm around my shoulders and pulled Wiley and me into a three-way hug. Wiley looked over Mark's shoulder. His eyes were focused on something I couldn't see. I leaned my head on his big chest.

"'Tis a gift to be simple," Mark sang and, drunk as he was, his voice was beautiful, "'tis a gift to be free."

What overflowed in my heart was soft and blue as the light around us.

"Mark," I said. "Wiley." And then, I could not stay there in that beery embrace. My breath twisted. I wanted to feel what they were feeling and I knew I couldn't. I stepped back. Mark looked at me.

"Damn it, Sheila," he said, "where are you? I want you here."

I remember tapping the side of his beer can.

"Not here," I said, "not anymore," and when I looked up, Wiley was walking away. Moonlight poured over the perfect walls of Honanki. The world was silver. And, I was all alone.

Jake touches my arm. "You okay?"

"Yes," I say. "I got lost for a minute. Honanki is perfect. Not Sinagua though. Early Hopi. Parrot clan, maybe."

Jake puts his hands together in front of him and bows.

"So sorry," he says.

He knows how I feel about anthro-archeo-academics. Figuring out history, making up names when all they have to do is ask the Hopi, shut up, and listen.

"Sheila," Rae says, "you can be such a pain in the ass. Once a Catholic, always a Catholic."

"There's wrong," I say, "and there's right. Making up stories about people who know the truth is wrong."

Rae looks at me. I shiver. If anybody makes up stories, it's Modern Romance me.

"You'll go," Jake says. "How could you not?"

"There it is," I say.

He kisses us both on the cheek and walks away through the mint growing at the side of the cabin. The scent floods the air, wild and green.

"Do you really want to go?" Rae asks.

"Sure," I say. "Why?"

"You looked funny," she says, and looks up into my face.

"I need to go," I say. "I haven't been there since . . . I mean . . . I think they had already started up. I think Wiley was staring off to where he thought Rolynne was."

"Excuse me," Rae says gently, "maybe you could tell me the whole story."

So I do.

RAE SPENDS the night. Jake tells us we have to be ready to leave at five A.M. because as the light shifts, the petroglyphs change. The desert bighorn that leaps out at dawn disappears at noon. The Snake priests striding across the redrock at three P.M. are nowhere in sight by early morning. Masau'u, He Who Watches, the silent Lord of Life and Death, is gone through the day. Only at twilight, when the aqua light falls cool and fading, does he stare out at you, his mouth a great O, his eyes staring at you and seeing that which feeds him.

"Masau'u," Rae says sleepily. She's lying on my therma-pad on my floor. I've thrown a quilt over her, and with her sun-burnt cheeks and half-closed eyes she could be a kid on a camping trip. "You said he eats people?"

"No," I say. "That's just what I say when I pray." I stop. I'm embarrassed. The last thing Rae and I would have ever discussed was prayer.

"When you pray you say something to Masau'u about eating people?" she whispers, and giggles.

"No." I can't believe I'm going to tell her this. "I turn to the west . . . actually, I turn to the west, after I face east and south. I'm outdoors, usually." I stop.

She is quiet. I wonder if she is asleep.

"Are you asleep?" I whisper.

"No," she says, "keep going."

"Well, I face east and I say some kind of prayer, and then south, and then in the west I talk to whatever eats that which is no longer necessary." I pause. "And then I face north, which if I'm here is toward the mountains, and I ask for help getting older."

"What a good idea," Rae says.

I wait for her to say more. She is silent. I realize she is asleep.

THE ALARM buzzes at four A.M. I whack it. It falls on the floor.

"Sheila?"

"It's time to get up."

"I'm freezing."

I pull on my sweatshirt and socks and stumble into the dark living room. I light the morning candle.

"Where are the lights?" Rae asks.

"I light a candle first," I say. She fumbles under her pillow, pulls out her flashlight and shines it on my face.

"Why?"

"I told you," I say. "It makes me feel good."

"Shei-la?" she says. "Hon-ey? This isn't like you."

"I know," I say. "I can't talk about it now. Let me get some coffee. It's no big deal."

"It's okay," Rae says. "Just promise me one thing?"

"What?" I step out of the flashlight's beam. I know Rae's mind. I know she's going to say something like "Warn me if you're going to start speaking in tongues."

"If you know anything that can help me," she says, "you'll tell me."

She huddles down deeper into the quilt.

"Rank," she says. "Mornings."

"What I do with the candle," I say, "is I light it and then I feel slightly encouraged and I agree that I'll consider what appears before me during the day."

Rae sits up.

"I can do that much," she says. She wraps the quilt around her and stands in front of the candle.

"Would you go in the kitchen?" she says.

I know how she feels. I have known for a while, and I suspect it's why the Hopi have closed their dances to outsiders. I go into the kitchen. I feed the cats which, on this particular morning, requires a lot of noise. I slam cans and doors. I talk to Vicious and Bad and Jaco. They don't look up. When Rae comes into the kitchen, they are head down in their bowls. She could probably drop dead right there and they'd go on eating.

"Well," she says, "I did it."

I nod. I realize I am going about this as delicately as I once would have listened to a woman talk about sex.

"I held the candle and I couldn't figure out the directions, so I just talked to all of it at once. I told the guy in the west that I am not ready to be eaten." She snorts. "And that is the first time in my life I ever said that to any man."

I grin.

"Apparently you're still necessary," I say. "Here's your coffee. Kona. The real thing. Here's to the simple life."

She lifts the cup to her wide, beautiful mouth.

"I don't want to die alone," she says. We stare at each other.

"If you need me . . ."

She doesn't let me finish.

"No," she says, "not you, because I want to die at home and you can't just take off for as long as it might take."

"That's true," I say. I almost wish I was married to a nice, safe, rich man so I could do just that. "But I'll figure out how to be there . . . whenever."

"I know," she says. "Let's sit in the living room, drink this here cowgirl cawfee, look at the holy candle, and talk trash."

JAKE PULLS up in the Department's navy blue van. We are the last people to be collected. I look around. Judgment rises in me as though I had the right. Thirteen charming, middle-aged people in Patagonia and REI and Gramicci hiking gear, the requisite November-May couple, eight single women, two gay guys, and Dr. Chuck Collum.

Rae catches my scan, catches the stifled disappointment in my eyes.

"We never stop hoping, do we?" she whispers in my ear.

"Never," I say.

"Who's the guy with all the pockets and flaps on his jacket?"

"Dr. Collum."

"Chuck," Jake says, "you want me to go Route 17 or down the canyon?"

"Chuck?" Rae whispers.

"Not to you," I say. "Jake is the only one who calls him that. To you, he's Dr. Collum."

"It's 1994," Rae says. "That went out with Nehru suits."

"This is Arizona," I say. She nods.

"Route 17," Collum says.

May, of the November-May couple, raises her hand. She is slender, almost ferret-faced. She's outfitted herself at the local hip earth-wear shop, black tights, lilac ragg socks, purple and gray hiking boots. She's pulled her slightly altered blonde hair back in a ponytail and she's wearing the requisite cool baseball cap. The logo says *Earth First!* I doubt it.

"Dr. Collum," she says, "I read an article in *Archeology Today* that suggested we could do more harm than good if we try to clean off the graffiti."

She sounds just like Rolynne. I hate her immediately. November, a fat guy with a beard and about a thousand bucks' worth of L.L. Bean boots, vest, shirt, shorts, pack, sunglasses, and Tilley hat, stares out the window. You can't tell if he is uneasy with her amateur archeologyitis or just hung over. He reminds me of Wiley. I figure either the morning prayers didn't work or I am a little nuts.

"Yes," Collum says, "I read that piece. We're trying something different here. A different approach. No solution, just water. But thank you for the input."

She smiles primly. November keeps looking out the window. She flushes. I see her pick something off his fleece sleeve. He grunts. Wiley, for sure.

"Ya know," Rae says, "there are those moments when my solitude shimmers before my eyes like a Mo-nay waterlily."

"Yes," I say. I am briefly grateful.

Collum smiles at us. "Are there any other questions?" he asks.

"Who on earth bought you that jacket?" Rae hisses in my ear.

"Excuse me?" he says.

"My friend was asking me," I say, "do we need a special outfit for this? You know. Decontaminated or something?"

Collum considers this. "Oh no," he says, "all we're going to do is take plain water and cotton rags and gently, gently wash away what we can."

"Oh good," Rae says, "I don't do windows."

Collum looks puzzled. "No," he says, "there are no windows at Bear House."

May pipes up. "These were built," she says authoritatively, "in the *early 1100s*. Anasazi. Before windows as we know them."

"Now, Anasazi," Rae says, and she has suddenly acquired a vague but brightly curious look, "that's like Hopi, right?"

Jake's neck goes red. Collum rears back a little on his heels. May leans forward in her seat.

"Anasazi is a period," Collum says. He looks hard at Rae. "I'll be briefing all of you once we're at the site." He turns and sits down.

May leans over and taps Rae's arm.

"Technically," she says, "Anasazi represents a period in pre-history. The people were here, then gone. Poof, like that. Nobody knows what happened."

Rae wrinkles her brow. "Didn't they disappear about 1100? I think I read that in a *National Geographic*."

The truth is we spent one intensely caffeinated night arguing this with Jake while he broiled us steaks and told us how much he loved arguing with smart women.

"Yes," May says. November has fallen asleep. He is snoring.

"Well," Rae says, "since that one village up at Hopi was settled sometime in 1100, don't you think they might have just headed up there?" She smiles.

"Oh no," May says, "I took a docents' course at the museum and they told us emphatically that the ruins and carbon dating show that we just don't know where they went." I hear Rolynne, knowing the last word on everything, good girl getting it right. I want to go home.

"Hmmmmm," Rae says. I've heard her say the same thing when some couple tells her that the glaze on the big pot doesn't quite go with the paint in the front hall.

"You know," Rae says, "I have so often felt that way myself."

May looks blank.

"Just didn't know where I went."

"Oh?" May says. "I'm afraid I don't follow you." She smiles sweetly, flips down her dark glasses, and snuggles in against November's thick side.

"Don't you just love it," Rae whispers to me, "when these nice older men take their young friends out on excursions. I bet he's a professor and she's a little student."

Dr. Collum stands up again. He starts to tell us interesting facts about the settling of the valley. He says "these simple but wise people" a lot. I count the flaps on his L.L. Bean jacket. There are ten. I wonder if I could sleep till we get where it is we're going.

"THIS IS a little tricky," I say.

"What?" Rae asks.

"Being here. I didn't think I would feel anything. But I do."

Jake has parked us in the same place Wiley and I parked the day of the night of the beginning of the end. I look around at juniper and agave and the dull green blades of yucca. I remember staring at a blooming cactus trying to clear my mind for what I was going to say. I remember telling Wiley that Rolynne had told me I was too good to him. I remember the strange way he looked at me. The silence. And then, how he had pointed to the cactus flowers and said, this guy whose conversational themes were limited to beer, beer, boats, duct tape, and beer, "Look, honey, aren't those . . . I mean I don't mean to change the subject, but aren't those flowers pretty." I remember looking at him and knowing. Not knowing anything specific, but feeling that skipped beat in the air.

Rae and I are sitting in the van alone. Everyone else has cheerfully soldiered on, Jansport daypacks and calibrated water bottles and purple fanny-packs bouncing behind them. I watch them climb the trail to the ledge. May has charged ahead and is chatting brightly with Jake. November is sitting on a boulder at the foot of the slope. He is smoking a cigarette and is sweating hard. Collum walks up to him and points to the cigarette. I can't hear anything, but I see November stub the smoke out on his heel and field-strip it. He waits till Collum is climbing the trail, flips him the bird, and lights another cigarette.

"I don't think November is a professor," Rae says mildly.

"You can't tell anymore," I say. "There's a bunch of them at the college who ride Harleys. I find it personally embarrassing . . . you know how if you see somebody our age acting all girlie?"

"I do," she says. She looks at me. I'm wearing plaid flannel shorts, black high-tops, and a hooded flannel shirt.

"Hey," I say, "I've always dressed this way."

She pats my hand. "It's true. I figured that was why Daniel loved you. You were the only other human being who dressed so he looked good."

I burst into tears. They are the first romantic ones I've cried since Wiley sat up in bed at 1:21 on April Fool's Day, 1993, and said, "I have to leave. I feel trapped. I'm not romantically involved with you anymore." And I said, "Is there someone else?" And he said, "No, I swear it."

"I hate this," I say. Rae puts her arm around me. I bury my face in her warm neck and I let loose.

"Hang on," I say. "This is supposed to be the other way around."

"I don't think so," she says. "Not right now."

"Duh," I say. I am crying so hard I'm scared I'll have a stroke.

"Is it Daniel?" she says. "Still? After fourteen years?"

"Yes," I say, "and no. It's all of it. From Daniel to Wiley and everyone in between. And I'm fifty-four and I'm scared to death there won't be anymore. Ever."

Rae holds me. I keep thinking I'm supposed to be the one comforting her. This trip is for her. She's supposed to be out there looking at those nine-hundred-year-old desert bighorns and priests and killer Gods of Life and she's supposed to be learning something, something that will grant her the grace to stay truly alive long enough to die.

"Sheila," I hear her say. She sounds a little stern.

"What," I say. No question, just flat, just *what do you want from me*, I admit I'm a mess, I admit I have the friendship capabilities of a liver fluke. *What.*

"We don't have to get out of this bus," she says. "We can stay here if you want."

"I love you," I say. "Rae, I really love you."

"Thanks," she says. We sit quietly. I look out. Collum and his drones are moving up over the rocks. May has stripped off her jacket. She's wearing a tank top. Her skin is skim milk pale against the burgundy rock face. She moves well. I see Rolynne. I remember her grace. I wish *she* was the one dying. I don't care if that is precisely the kind of thought that will cause the God of my childhood to strike me dead.

"Rae," I say. "Why you?"

She shakes her head. "I thought maybe when I came here I'd answer that. I've been to every power spot on the fifteen dollar See-Dough-Now Power Web map. I've lain face down in the holy vortex, drunk spring water that's probably going to kill me before this frigging virus does. I've had crystals laid on my chakras, drunk fermented Siberian mushroom tea . . ."

She starts to laugh. She's laughing and I'm crying and then, she says the thing that I will think of every day from then on.

"Sheila," she says, "I was careless. There it is. But I've got to say this. This romance shit is what's going to kill *you*. It's as bad as what I've got."

My tears stop dead.

"When's the last time you wrote?" she says fiercely. "Anything more than some card to some guy?"

"Before you got here. A little. Not much, but steady."

"Don't stop," Rae says. I nod.

"That woman," I say, "she isn't Rolynne."

Rae looks puzzled.

"That woman that was telling you about the Anasazi? May? She's not Rolynne."

"Oh yeah," Rae says. "Did you think she was?" She looks worried.

"I'm okay," I say. "I'm not nuts."

"But?"

"But every time I see a guy about Wiley's age and a younger woman I want to puke."

"I know," Rae says.

Collum sticks his head in the door. "Ladies," he says, "we need you. We've got two empty spots left on the grid."

THE STORY in my head is that Rae will be assigned to clean Masau'u and I will work next to May, who will turn out to actually be November's daughter. We will find sisterhood in our honor for the early people. Rae, by virtue of cleaning *Dean 'n' Kristy 4-ever* from Masau'u's great brow, will be instantly cured. Dr. Collum will have to admit the old Hopi grandmas and grandpas are right, and Jake and I, despite the great barrier of our ages and the fact that I outweigh him by forty pounds, will find the ancient priestess-consort connection together.

None of that happens. Rae works on a two-foot-by-two-foot block of wall that holds half a spiral and the tip of a bighorn's tail. May and November work side by side. I overhear them. He is helping her correct her errors in cleaning away what appears to be a charcoal drawing of a crystal. She has to bend over to do it. He spends most of his volunteer time studying her butt.

Collum crouches at my side and tells me the details of a grant proposal he's writing. He's heard I'm a part-time writer and he's wondering if I'd like to line-edit his seminal paper as part of my contribution to the cause. I don't say anything. What I love about male professors is that you don't really *ever* have to say anything.

JAKE WILL tell me later that he fell in love that day. A little after four, when the light was going amethyst, he came around the corner of the room where Masau'u lives. He heard someone talking. He stopped. He slowed his breath. He could hear his heart pounding in his ears. The wind changed. The sharp, medicine scent of juniper drifted up around him. He looked down at his hands and he saw that for the first time in months, they were not shaking.

Rae crawled through the little doorway. She sat next to Jake. He says she touched the claws on his shoulder.

"Where should I put mine?" she said.

He watched her tears fall into the red dust. She touched the spots with her fingers. "Like stars," she said. "In a red sky. What happens," she whispered, "when I really don't make sense anymore?"

He says he took her hand in his and told her he loved her. "No more jokes," he said. "You are truly beautiful to me."

"And," she said, "if I wasn't dying?"

"The same."

He told her to come back next summer. He said that he would take her places filled with blue shadows and garnet rock and seeps dripping with columbine. He to⸢

her to come back, year after year. He would be here and if it got so she couldn't carry much, he would sherpa for her.

"I understand," she said. He kissed her on the lips.

"It wasn't romantic," he tells me. "But it was personal."

And then, he made her promise something. He made her promise that she would tell her kids the truth as soon as she got home.

HE DOESN'T tell me that last part. She does. It's the day before she leaves. Bear House is ours. And Montezuma's Well. The perfect one-room tower at Mesa Verde and the ancient juniper that rises by its broken wall. The October wind hissing in the ancient ball-court at Wupatki, persistent, inescapable, so you think of what was played there and what the winners lost. We have stood in all those places and in each of them, we have lit a candle. We have turned north, then east, then south, then west. We have heard each other pray. We have sometimes said the words together.

"Why us?" we have said.

Then, with the candle flame near-invisible in the bright southwestern sun, my friend Rae and I have said, "Thank you." Those moments, I know, will someday burn in my memory, the after-image of light so terrible and beautiful it cannot be held for longer than a breath.

Buffalo Wallow Woman

ANNA LEE WALTERS

ANNA LEE WALTERS, 49, was born in Pawnee, Oklahoma, a child of two tribes, Pawnee and Otoe, "whose literature is oral"; her early life was shaped by words rather than by possessions. In her most recent book, Talking Indian: Reflections on Survival and Writing, *she reflects on the significance of this as she melds fiction with autobiography, history with storytelling. She has also authored a novel,* Ghost Singer, *and a collection of short stories,* The Sun Is Not Merciful; *co-authored a textbook,* The Sacred; *and edited an anthology,* Neon Powwow: New Native America Voices of the Southwest. *She works at Navajo Community College on the Navajo Reservation in Arizona, where she lives.*

My NAME IS BUFFALO Wallow Woman. This is my real name. I live on the sixth floor of the whiteman hospital, in the mental ward. This is not the first time I have been in a mental ward; I know these places well. I wander through this one like a ghost in my wrinkled gown. My feet barely brush over the white tile floor. The long windows reflect the ghost that I have become: I am all bones and long coarse white hair. Nevertheless, there are slender black iron bars on the windows to prevent my shadow from leaving here. Bars on sixth-story windows puzzle me. On the other side of the bars, the city lies safely beyond my reach, the wrath of the ghost of Buffalo Wallow Woman.

Bars or not, I plan to leave this ward tonight. I've already been here too long. This place makes me ill, makes my heart pause and flutter. Sometimes it makes me really crazy. I told that to those in white, but they refused to listen, with the exception of one. I said, "Hospitals make me sick! Here my strong heart is weak." In response, one of them shrugged, another frowned suspiciously. A nurse replied, "Now, Mrs. Smith, you don't want to hurt our feelings, do you?"

Well, that made me grab her arm and dig my long fingernails into it. I wanted to scream but I controlled this urge and said calmly, "What's that you called me? My name is Buffalo Wallow Woman." She and I stared each other in the eyes for five minutes before we separated: she to her mindless patients, and me to my room to locate the clothes I ought to wear to escape from here.

My clothes are missing. Why would someone take a ghost's clothing? My possessions are so old. My moccasin soles consist only of patches by now, but I don't care. They take me where I want to go. I look at my feet stuffed into polyfoam and I hunger for beautiful things that are no more.

The closet is empty. Perhaps my clothes were never there. Perhaps I really am a ghost now. Perhaps I did not live at all. I look in the window to reassure myself—my spirit shimmers and fades, shimmers and fades. Am I deceased or alive? At this moment I really don't know.

I float down the hall, going from room to room. I search each one. Because I am a ghost, I go where I please. No one takes me seriously. Those who see me stare for a minute and decide to ignore the bag of bones and wild white hair that I have become. They underestimate me. They do not believe that I am really here. Down the hall and back again I haunt the ward. My clothes are not anywhere on this floor. I return to my room, climb up on the bed like a large clumsy child. I am waiting for nightfall, hours away, to make my departure. After all I've been through, this brief wait is nothing to Buffalo Wallow Woman.

Through the barred window, clouds fly rapidly to the north. They call to me. By name they know me. *Buffalo Wallow Woman*, they whisper through the glass and the bars to remind me who the old bag of bones is and why I am here. I lift my head and square my sagging shoulders.

Far away, I hear a melody flow toward me. It is from my people's golden age and it has found me in this insane place where I am now held without respect or honor. A thousand years ago, or yesterday, in the seasons of my youth, my people danced and sang to the cloud beings in spectacular ceremony as the cloud beings gathered to shoot arrows of zigzag lightning and fiery thunderbolts across the sky. The cloud beings darkened to spirals of purple and dark red. They all twisted and turned in space like the mighty and powerful beings they truly were. And in the torrents of rain to fall later, slapping down upon the earth, filling the dry beds there to overflowing, my people lifted their heads and drank the rain thirstily. Afterward, with that taste still in their mouths, they sang in unison. "O you! That mystery in the sky!"

Miraculously, the words return to me in this alien room. I feel the wind of those clouds blow across my face, the raindrops splash the crown of my head one at a time. My face and hair feel soaked with rain. I lift my face and open my mouth. I sing, *"Hey yah hah O!"*

My voice is as small as a red ant. It is swept away in the noises coming from the vents, crushed under the hospital sounds of announcements and rolling carts and beds going back and forth in the hallway. My room is suddenly quiet and dry. The clouds are disappearing in the sky, too. Bah! There is no magic in man-made places like this. This is why Buffalo Wallow Woman always brings it with her.

I look at my wrinkled hands. They are wide and large boned. My nails are faded yellow and longer than they need to be. I wish I could hold a birchbark rattle with painted streaks of blue lightning on it in my idle fingers. I would shake it this way and that, in the manner of my people. They lifted their rattles to the cloud beings and shook them softly in that direction. To show the departing cloud beings that I remember who they are, their magnificent splendor and power, and also who I am, I stand on the step to my bed and face them. I lift the imaginary rattle and shake it just so. A soft hiss emanates from it.

Behind me, someone says, "Mrs. Smith."

I see part of him in the window. He is the doctor who arrives each day to study me, but now I am tired of him and I think he is tired of me as well. Nothing has been exchanged between us, and he always arrives at times like this. I look at the bars before I look at him.

I think of the animals my men have taken in communal hunts before there were grocery and convenience stores. The beautiful glassy eyes of a dozen soft-brown deer people stare at me from the walls of this room. They look me right in the eye, but I do not flinch. They say, *Buffalo Wallow Woman, here we are.* I see the trail of their last misty breaths arc up into the sky-rainbows they are. I hear a shaggy buffalo bull as he turns his great frame to face me. I see the dust rise in smoky spirals under his trotting hooves as he charges toward me. His breath is hot steam on my face.

Then come the human sounds, the footsteps, a pumping heart, blood rushing to the face, and the promised words of appeasement to the animals as they silently fall with a shattering thud, offering themselves to us. For this ultimate gift, we offered everything in return, our very lives were traded on the spot, and those animal people taught us thousands of prayers and songs to honor their spirits and souls from then on. In that way they permitted us to live, and they too lived with us. That is how we mutually survived all those years. The man behind me, the man who is here to help, doesn't know this.

He occupies the chair near the door.

"Do you come with prayers?" I ask. I turn to face him. The eyes of the deer and buffalo people surround us. They wait for his answer.

He is tall and angular with dark hair standing straight up. His eyes are foreign to me, colorless and jumpy, as if they must run somewhere. He glances behind him, over his shoulder. I am the one suspended here, but he acts trapped too. "If you come with prayers, I'll talk to you," I say, trying to figure out this odd creature whose habitat I do not know. Each day his behavior and appearance have become more unsettled. His presence disturbs the room.

He decides to speak. His voice booms at me. "Mrs. Smith, do you know how long you've been here? Do you understand that you have made no progress at all?" He is angry at me for being here.

I refuse to answer for this. I zip my lips together but I face him head-on. I have time, lots of time. I can outwait him. I become the ghost again. I start to disintegrate before him.

"Now don't do that!" he orders. He rubs his eyes and runs a hand through his wiry hair. His eyes dart everywhere. His breathing is rapid. He manages to hold his eyes in one place for a few seconds and he forcibly calms himself. He moves closer to me.

"All right, Buffalo Wallow Woman, if that's who you say you are, how did you get here? Do you know where you are?" He is still brusque and impatient, but he has called me by my real name and I must reply. My body becomes more solid and earthly again. I lean toward him.

"Do you come with prayers?" I venture again in my small voice.

"What kind of prayers?" he asks.

"Prayers to the spirits of those whose fate is in your hands." My voice is like the red ant again, crawling quietly across the room.

"What do you mean? I don't understand," he says while his eyes jump all over.

"You have no prayers then?" I persist.

"No!" he says.

"It is as I feared," I answer, turning away from him. "That is why I must leave here. Ghosts and spirits long for them. The hearts of human beings cannot beat steadily without them for long either. I know my own can't." I stand on the stepstool to move down to the floor.

"You aren't going anywhere. You don't know where you are, let alone who you are!"

We are almost the same height now. I stand before him, and he observes me from his throne.

"Where are my clothes?" I ask in my most rational voice. "I am going to leave here tonight."

He ignores me.

"You're very ill," he says with a frown. "You have no family, no one to take care of you. With your bad heart, you may not last long outside of here."

This time there is something in his voice I haven't heard before, but I want him to go. I seal my lips, and he sees immediately what I have done. He stands and goes. The room settles again.

FOR SEVERAL weeks, there has been one in white here who is unlike this doctor and the others. Today she will appear when the sun reaches the third bar in the window. It will be soon now. In the meantime, I decide to haunt the hallway once more. I've covered its distance at least a dozen times each day for the last three months. It is the only exercise the patients have. I think of wolves in zoos, running in circles inside their cages, as I leave my room.

Today I look carefully at the occupants of each room and those people in the hallway. There are thin walls separating the two, skinny lines that distinguish the patients from the staff. I can't tell them apart except by their clothing. If truth be known, the doctors and staff may be more quirky than the others. We patients just show our quirkiness.

In Room 612 sits a skeleton with frozen eyes. I am drawn to it, magnetized by its forceful pull. "I am a ghost," I confess to it. The skeleton does not move at all.

Something whispers to me that its spirit is gone. I look around the room for it but I am the only ghost here. I leave 612 and go across the hall.

The man there is waiting for me. He embraces me tenderly and strokes my wild white hair. He calls me Grandmama and weeps on my gown. I sit down beside him, we stare into each other's souls while he holds my hand. He babbles at me, I nod. He weeps until his eyes are bright red. Then, exhausted, he lies down on his high bed. Asleep, he relaxes his grip on me and I move on.

Two nights ago, a hysterical young woman was brought into the next room. There she sits now, sullen and old before her time. Her wrists are wrapped in white bandages. I pause at the door. She raises a hand and a finger at me. "I am a ghost," I say. "That means nothing to me."

My words anger her. She rises abruptly to rush at me but hesitates after a step or two to clutch her belly and groan. It is then I notice the rise of it under her gown. I go to her rescue and she leans on me, breathing hard. Her eyes are scared.

"You would kill your child?" I ask as she bends into me. The moment passes, and she is able to stand on her own.

"Not my child," she says, "me!" Then she looks at me and adds, "I thought you were a ghost."

"I am," I repeat. This is our introduction to one another.

There is a loud disturbance in the hall, scuffling and a shouting exchange of words. One of the hospital staff is wrestling a middle-aged man. I and the young woman go to the door to watch. All the way down the hall, different colored faces appear in the doorways of each room like wooden masks. The faces are expression-less and blank, like those on the street.

The patient is overpowered and wrestled to the floor before our eyes. A silver needle punctures his arm. After the initial outburst of anger, the whole scene takes place in silence. The patient is lifted up, whisked away. The staff quickly tidies the area as if nothing happened, and the hall clears. Seconds later, no one remembers what just occurred.

Only the young woman and I remain. She asks if the incident really took place. I say, "That's what will happen to all of us if we don't do what they say." The girl frowns at the bars on the windows. She has just discovered them.

"When you leave here, you must live," I say. "If you don't see to your child, it could end up here."

The girl is confused. She looks at her bandaged wrists and again at the bars. She rubs her belly. I leave her there, alone and troubled. I make my way down the hall, looking in on each person in each room along the way.

Most everyone, patients and staff alike, look right through me. My presence is not acknowledged at all. Quite unexpectedly, from deep within me, I feel the wrath of Buffalo Wallow Woman for this indignity. My blood begins to boil. It is hot and dangerously close to making me explode! My heart flaps against my chest, voices caution me.

I pause and reflect on this feeling. That old fire still burns? Rage, this overpowering, is still a part of Buffalo Wallow Woman? How very strange. I thought that I had given up this human feeling years ago, the very first time I went into a mental hospital. I mutter my thoughts aloud and head toward my room.

Back there, Tina awaits. She is nervous, frantic, because of what I am about to do. Her soft voice is usually a coo. Now it is high and squeaky.

"Where were you?" she asks tensely. "For a minute I thought maybe you had already gone." She rushes toward me and embraces me.

I pat her tiny hand. "It's not time yet." I go to my bed, climb up on it and say, "My clothes are gone, but where I am going, clothes don't matter, I guess."

The first day Tina walked into my room I knew who she was. It was evident in her dark hair and high cheekbones, though her skin was more fair than mine. But where it really showed was in her behavior and her usually carefully chosen words. She was such a tiny thing. She carried bed pans past my door all day before she finally came in.

She read my name on the door and over the bed. "Mrs. Smith," she said, "I'm Tina. I'll be your evening nurse until you leave here, or until the shifts change in a few weeks, whichever comes first."

I stood at the door and watched her adjust my bed.

"It's Buffalo Wallow Woman, Tina, not Mrs. Smith," I responded, "and I am a ghost."

"I know," she replied seriously. "I've heard."

She gave me a red lollipop from a pocket and asked, "Why are you here Buffalo Wallow Woman, if you don't mind me being so direct?"

I tore the shiny wrapper off the lollipop and stuck it in my mouth. I didn't answer. I sucked on the candy and counted the bars on the window, the way I did with the doctor when I wanted him to leave.

"Why are you here Buffalo Wallow Woman?" she asked again.

I sucked the candy hard and motioned that my lips were sealed. I climbed on the bed, sure that she would leave.

Instead, she pulled out a wire hairbrush from the nightstand and answered with a mischievous smile, "If I ask you four times, and if you really are Buffalo Wallow Woman, then you will have to tell me, won't you?"

She began to comb my hair, pulling my head here and there. "Ghost hair is hard to comb," I said, as if this was our secret.

She replied, "You are not a ghost, Buffalo Wallow Woman. Do ghosts like lollipops?"

"Ghosts like a lot of earthly things," I said. "That's what often keeps us here."

"Why are you here Buffalo Wallow Woman?" she asked a third time, and I knew then that I wanted someone like her, someone important, to know.

She braided my hair tightly around my head. Her fingers flew.

"I'm lost, Tina," I said. "I'm caught between two worlds, a living one and a dead one. This is the dead one," I motioned out in the hall, "right here. And this is the root of my illness. I have to return to the living one in order to be whole and well."

Tina's fingers stopped a second. She chuckled, "This is the dead one? How do you figure that?"

"Look around," I answered. "There is no magic here because everything is dead. I think that only ghosts are capable of surviving here."

Before I realized it, she asked me the fourth time. "Why are you here Buffalo Wallow Woman?" She pulled a chair close to me as if she really planned to listen.

I decided to tell. I composed my thoughts for a moment and then began. "I am the ghost of Buffalo Wallow Woman. Do you know what a Buffalo Wallow is, my child?"

Tina nodded. "A watering hole, or something like that?" She reached over and held my hand as I spoke. Her hand was half the size of mine.

I asked, "Do you want to know about my name?" She nodded again.

"The name was taken about a hundred winters ago most recently, but I suppose it is older than that. It came out of a time when the animal people still had possession of the world. Then, they were the keepers of all sacred things.

"Wallows are shallow depressions in the earth that were made by most animals when they rolled around there and lay down. Several large ones are still visible today. They usually surround water holes or later become them because of the shallow bowls they eventually form. Today most of them, of course, are gone. They have either blown away, or towns or other things sit on top of them.

"The marshy areas that the wallows were, or became, often dried up as the summer days grew hot and long. Each, in turn, disappeared. Some time ago, there was one large wallow with water, a buffalo wallow, left. All the others had turned to dust. It was a precious thing to all life then, especially to a stranded or lost human being. One day, there appeared on the horizon of that sacred place a lost woman, on foot and traveling alone. The buffalo people stood up one by one when they saw her approach. They saw her stumble and fall from either weakness or illness, and the searing heat of the sun. Near the wallow, she collapsed and failed to rise again. One of the old buffalo bulls told two younger ones to go to her aid. The young bulls trotted through the evaporating marsh to the ailing woman. Behind them, where their hooves sunk into the marsh, pools of water began to gurgle and bubble up. They trotted around the stranger in circles until she lay in a dirty pool of water, but she was cooled and revived. Afterward, she received more help from the buffalo people and then was able to travel on. She took the name Buffalo Wallow Woman out of humility to the buffalo people, out of gratitude for her life. She understood that it was the buffalo people and the spirit of the wallow who gave her humility and gratitude, as well as her life. These were the lessons she had learned in the hands of the buffalo people."

Tina expected more. I promised, "Tomorrow I'll finish if you still want to know."

The next day she arrived in the afternoon and brought with her a dark green leaf of Indian tobacco and a small red tin ashtray. She lit the tobacco and burned it in the tray. The odor of that one small curled leaf filled the mental ward, but it was not enough to take away all the pain and fears contained on this floor. She hid the tray in the drawer just before another nurse popped in the room to ask what was burning.

Tina shrugged her shoulders and winked at me. "Would you mind if I called you something other than Mrs. Smith or Buffalo Wallow Woman? Where I come from we don't call each other by such names. One seems too formal and the other too sacred. Would I offend you if I called you Grandmother?" she asked politely.

I gazed at her with admiration and answered, "That would not offend me, my child. That would honor me. And if this is your plan and decision, then I must call you Grandchild, if that's the way it is to be."

Tina offered her hand to me and I took it. This is the way we joined forces. When her schedule permitted, I resumed my story.

"Buffalo Wallow Woman died in the year of the great smallpox epidemic, near the very place she had been saved as a younger woman. This time, she and others who were sick isolated themselves from the remainder of the people and, therefore, did not receive formal burials.

"As a young girl of perhaps eleven or twelve winters, I visited this place unexpectedly. At the time I didn't know who Buffalo Wallow Woman was or her story. I had been traveling by wagon with my family through an unfamiliar stretch of open plains country that was partly frozen but was beginning to thaw in a sudden burst of sunshine. When the wagon became bogged down in deep gray clay, the men got off to dig out the back wheels. I, too, climbed off and noticed a place to the side of the wagon trail that tugged at me. It was a very large shallow pool covered with ice. Its size was perhaps half a city block. Birds were soaring overhead and chirping at me. I watched them dip toward the frozen pool and fly away in flocks. Soon my family had dug out the wagon and were ready to leave. By evening we had reached our destination, and I thought that I had already put the shallow pool out of my mind.

"But that night I dreamed of it. I saw it in all the four seasons. There were buffalo at the pool's edges, and their reflections were in the water with the clouds and sky. Other animals were also there, such as bears, deer, and all species of birds.

"Every night I dreamed of the pool, and it seemed to be speaking to me. Then one night, Buffalo Wallow Woman visited me in my dreams and in a mysterious way told me who she was and what had happened there. She said that she had not died after all, and that in another world she had learned that she never would. She said this was all true and because it was, our people had never lied to us. They understood everything all along.

"She told me that it was an old spirit who had called me to the watering hole, the same spirit that had guided her there each time she was close to death, and for this reason, she and I were tied together by it. The same spirit had called the buffalo people, the bird people, and all the others who came to drink, because that spirit made no distinction between the life of a buffalo, a cloud, a mountain, a stone, or a human being. It was the same indescribable force, no matter what form it took.

"At my tender age, it was truly remarkable that I actually understood what Buffalo Wallow Woman said. It was wonderful that I understood she had claimed some invisible part of me, and I claimed some part of her, and I accepted our relationship without question. I could not understand with my head, though. I grasped it at the level of and at the center of my heart. I understood that I had been thirsty but didn't know it myself, and I had gone to the wallow so that my soul might drink. The spirit of the wallow knew me better than I knew myself."

Tina didn't press for more right then. She was quiet, staring outside at the evening sky. The room was quiet. We didn't speak about me again for several days. Then she came into the room and sat down without a word. She waited for me to continue.

"All my life, I have been told by the whiteman that I am crazy, my child," I picked up where I left off, "because I see things that other people do not. I hear voices that no one else does. But the craziest thing I do, they tell me, is take these visions and voices seriously. This is the way of all Buffalo Wallow Women, I suppose. I structure my life around the visions and voices because it pleases me to honor them this way. I am never alone because of this. It is my inheritance from Buffalo Wallow Woman, from my own flesh and blood, from the visions I have received, and from my identity as this kind of person.

"But each day the doctor asks me if I know who I am, and I have to bear this outrage. He also asks me if I know where I am. He talks about 'reality.' He tells me to face it, that this is, after all, a new time that has no room for Buffalo Wallow Women. His questions, pretensions, and arrogance are ludicrous to me. I feel that he is more ill than I am. I am Buffalo Wallow Woman! Wherever I go, the spirits go with me.

"I am suspect and feared because I admit that I am a ghost. This is dangerous, I am told. It is the one thing the doctors have said that I know to be true. I *am* dangerous. I am dangerous because my craziness may spread from me to another and on and on. I am dangerous because I still have some rage left about what's happened to me over the years. It's not entirely squelched yet, although I've tried to empty it out of me. This surprises even me at the moment. And I am dangerous because I have great destructive powers within me that I haven't used yet.

"For instance, I can kill with my eyes if I so desire. I can shoot out poison and make my victims squirm with agony. There's all kinds of poison for this, but most come from pure hate. I can use words in incantations that will steal the soul, the spirit, the will, and mind away."

Tina looked at me mischievously. Before she could speak, I said, "Now don't say a word until you walk through this ward, look closely at every patient, and are able to explain how they became that way!"

We ended here, and Tina left. That night, lying in the dark, I decided to ask Tina to help me escape this unbearable indignity of forced confinement. A few days passed before I voiced my question.

I said, "Tina, my child, I am going to escape from here, I am going to fly away. When the time comes, I would like you to be there, to help me at the very last."

Tina replied, "If you're a ghost, why can't you just go?"

"It's not that easy. Some earthly person has to release me, you see."

She stood at the window staring at the iron bars. She turned around and asked, "You can really do it?"

I nodded.

She took a deep breath and crossed her heart like a small child. "Okay," was all she said.

NOW THAT the time is here, Tina seems reluctant to have me leave. She's had weeks to prepare, but her eyes are actually moist and red.

"Tell me I am doing the right thing," she says. "I mean, you're my patient, what am I doing?"

She is panicky. She flutters all around.

"You and I, my child, are more than patient and nurse, much more than that. Don't make our kinship so small, so insignificant. This is the stuff that links the whole chain of life together, old to young, grandchild to grandmother, and on and on."

It is dark outside. Not even the bars on the window can be seen. I climb off the bed. My nightgown floats loosely around me.

Tina is watching me. She has a large brown sack with her. When she speaks, her voice is calm. "I brought everything you asked of me, and something that I thought of myself." She takes out a thin red flannel blanket from her package, folds it in half, and puts it at the foot of the bed. "This is for you," she says.

"Thank you, my child," I answer, touched by her thoughtfulness. I pick up the blanket and hold it to my heart.

"What do you want me to do?" she asks. I see her hesitate before she moves.

I lift the blanket and ask her to lay it on the floor.

"Sit here." I point to one end of the blanket. She takes her sack with her. I sit down at the other end.

"Now," I say, "I want to speak to you before I leave. Please, child, put those things between us."

Tina lays out a pouch of green tobacco and cigarette papers, and the red ashtray. She puts a beaded butane lighter inside the tray.

I ask her to turn out the fluorescent lights over us. Only a soft light comes from the bathroom. The door to it is half closed. Then I ask her to take my hair down and pull off my shoes.

We sit together in silence for a long time, gathering our thoughts together for the last thing we are about to do for one another.

Finally, I am ready. I say, "My child, you are the answer to a prayer, the prayer of Buffalo Wallow Woman. To find you in a place like this is very sweet to someone like me. I feel a stab of victory for Buffalo Wallow Woman, for though she is a ghost, you are alive and are as strong and thoughtful as she has ever been.

"You came to me with open arms and received a ghost in them, and you did not flinch at anything I said. All of it you took in, in your strong, gentle way. You have been taught well. I have told you everything—good things, ugly things, sacred things, and unholy things. We have even sung together. You have given me honor and respect in a way that only kin can. In exchange for that, kin to kin, grandmother to grandchild, I want to include you in my prayer tonight.

"Everything I have told you these last few weeks is the truth, you know. Sometimes we ghosts are full of rage and anger, such as I have been at certain times, but the ghost of Buffalo Wallow Woman can only speak the truth, even when it hurts, as it sometimes does.

"Anyway, I thank you, child, for the honor you have brought me, by listening to me, by singing with me, by calling me your grandmother, by praying for me tonight, and by setting me free.

"I have spent a lifetime in and out of this insane place that the doctors call reality, or the real world. I have spent a lifetime waiting to be set free, because no one else but you could do it for me. This is what we mean to each other. This is what life means.

"These are my parting words to you, my child. Do you wish to say anything?"

Tina nods her head. I can almost hear the movements. The spirit people have come into the room. They surround us.

"You don't understand," she says. "I am not what you want me to be. I have flaws. I went to school. I can't speak my language because of this. I don't want to live in poverty the way my family does. I'm weak, and worst of all, I'm not very spiritual."

She pauses, threatening to break into tears.

"And I agreed to this because I thought you would change your mind. I didn't think you would really go through with it. I never thought I would actually be here right now."

"But you are here," I answer. "You are here with the ghost of Buffalo Wallow Woman. Most of us never know what we will do at a certain moment until that moment arrives. Then we know. Do you have doubts now?"

"Not doubts," she says, "but lots of sadness."

"This is not a bad thing, Tina," I say. "Soon you will feel like singing out, *Hey yah bah O!*" I say. "I promise you that you will feel it in you."

I pick up a cigarette paper and the Indian tobacco and begin to roll a smoke. I give it to Tina. I say, "When I have gone, you must light the smoke, then blow a puff to the earth and sky and then to the Four Directions. Then you must say in a clear voice, 'I offer this smoke for the spirit of my grandmother, Buffalo Wallow Woman. May she be forever at peace and may she forever live in nature all around me.' You must say this, Tina, not only think it."

The spirit people make noises all around me. Some of them are in the darkness, others are in the light.

Tina is flustered, but she acknowledges my directions.

I close my eyes and begin my prayer. "O Mystery of Life! The time has come for

Buffalo Wallow Woman to depart," I say to the spirits in the room, the spirits that follow me everywhere. They agree with my words. Their voices answer *Yes* in chorus. I continue. "I want to leave this world without anger or hate, for in this final moment, I want none of that to remain. I leave this world to my grandchild sitting here. May she love it and care for it as much as her elders did. My final requests are that you spirits accept me and take me home, and that in my departure, you watch over my grandchild here."

My heart flaps against my breastbone. I feel it pause, flutter, and thump my breastbone again. I open my eyes. The room is cold. The spirits are everywhere. There are deer people, buffalo people, and cloud beings—so much life in one little room! They chant and sing.

I am strangely weightless and transparent. I feel myself break up into a fine, wet mist. Then I am looking down from the ceiling. Tina sits alone. I see my body lying across the floor, a bag of old bones and long wild white hair.

Tina is holding the smoke. Her hand shakes violently. She looks up at the ceiling, takes a deep breath, and steadies herself. She picks up the beaded butane lighter and lights the sacred smoke. She tries to speak. Her words are timid and frightened. She clears her throat and starts again.

She says it all perfectly, word for word. The spirits answer joyfully, *Yes! Yes!* They turn to me and say, *Buffalo Wallow Woman, now you are free. No bars shall ever hold you again.*

The spirits guide me to the window, but now it is my turn to hesitate. I look back at Tina, my grandchild. She is sitting there all alone. She looks troubled and sad.

We'll always be here, the spirits say, and I nod. Then, as we begin to slip through the bars, I hear little Tina sing, *"Hey yah hah O!"*

Permissions